THE MOVIES IN THE AGE OF INNOCENCE

THE MOVIES
IN THE AGE OF
INNOCENCE

By Edward Wagenknecht

UNIVERSITY OF OKLAHOMA PRESS : NORMAN

OTHER BOOKS BY EDWARD WAGENKNECHT

BIOGRAPHICAL: *The Man Charles Dickens* (1929); *Geraldine Farrar, An Authorized Record of Her Career* (1929); *Jenny Lind* (1931); *Mark Twain: The Man and His Work* (1935, 1961); *Longfellow, A Full-Length Portrait* (1955); *Mrs. Longfellow: Selected Letters and Journals* (1956); *The Seven Worlds of Theodore Roosevelt* (1958); *Nathaniel Hawthorne, Man and Writer* (1961); *Washington Irving: Moderation Displayed* (1962).

CRITICAL: *Lillian Gish, An Interpretation* (1927); *Values in Literature* (1928); *A Guide to Bernard Shaw* (1929); *Utopia Americana* (1929); *Cavalcade of the English Novel* (1943); *Cavalcade of the American Novel* (1952); *A Preface to Literature* (1954).

ANTHOLOGICAL: *The College Survey of English Literature*, with others (1942); *Six Novels of the Supernatural* (1944); *The Fireside Book of Christmas Stories* (1945); *The Story of Jesus in the World's Literature* (1946); *When I Was a Child* (1946); *The Fireside Book of Ghost Stories* (1947); *Abraham Lincoln: His Life, Work, and Character* (1947); *The Fireside Book of Romance* (1948); *Joan of Arc, An Anthology of History and Literature* (1948); *A Fireside Book of Yuletide Tales* (1948); *Murder by Gaslight* (1949); *The Collected Tales of Walter de la Mare* (1950); *An Introduction to Dickens* (1952); *Chaucer: Modern Essays in Criticism* (1959).

INTRODUCTORY: *The Chimes*, by Charles Dickens (Limited Editions Club, 1931); *Life on the Mississippi*, by Mark Twain (Limited Editions Club, 1944); *A Tale of Two Cities*, by Charles Dickens (Modern Library, 1950); *Great Expectations*, by Charles Dickens (Pocket Books, 1956); *The Wizard of Oz*, by L. Frank Baum (Reilly & Lee edition, 1956); *The Art, Humor, and Humanity of Mark Twain*, edited by Minnie M. Brashear and Robert M. Rodney (1959); *The Innocents Abroad*, by Mark Twain (Limited Editions Club, 1962).

LIBRARY OF CONGRESS CATALOG CARD NUMBER: 62–16473

Copyright 1962 by the University of Oklahoma Press, Publishing Division of the University. Composed and printed at Norman, Oklahoma, U.S.A., by the University of Oklahoma Press. First edition, October, 1962; second printing by offset, April, 1963.

For Lillian and Dorothy Gish

Acknowledgments

B ECAUSE of this book I am heavily indebted. Miss Lillian Gish has been urging me to write it for many years, and Miss Dorothy Gish provided hospitality for my family and myself when I went to New York City to work on it. Both the George Eastman House and the Museum of Modern Art may be said in a manner to have subsidized it, for both invested much time, trouble, and money in screening innumerable films for me in the summer of 1961; the Museum also sent films to my house in West Newton, Massachusetts, where a theater was improvised in the basement, and my son Walter Wagenknecht acted as operator. To Mr. Richard Griffith and his staff in New York, and to Mr. James Card and Mr. George Pratt in Rochester, I express my warmest gratitude for many kindnesses far beyond the line of duty, not least among them being a careful reading of my manuscript; this last service was also performed by Miss Lillian Gish. Mr. William K. Everson showed me some important films in his own collection which I had not been able to find elsewhere, and my fellow Bay Stater, Mrs. Zena Keefe Brownell, spent an evening talking with me about her own career and particularly her associations with the Vitagraph. The Boston University Graduate School made a small research grant toward my expenses while away from home. Finally, I wish to thank my publishers, without whose faith in me and interest in motion pictures and willingness to spend the money needed to make a proper kind of motion-picture book nobody else's kindness would much have availed.

Edward Wagenknecht

Contents

Pictures

Pictures

Sources of Illustrations: Pictures 1, 2, 3, 4, 10, 13, 16, 20, 51, 52, 55, 71, 72, and 79 are courtesy of George Eastman House; Pictures 12 and 70, Harvard Theatre Collection; Picture 54, Miss Geraldine Farrar; all others are from the author's collection.

THE MOVIES IN THE AGE OF INNOCENCE

The best in this kind are but shadows;
and the worst are no worse, if imagination
amend them.

A Midsummer-Night's Dream

Of Film and I, and How This Book Unwittingly Got Itself Started

I REMEMBER once seeing a book described as the work of a good scholar on holiday. Whether I am a good scholar or not must be left for others to judge, but I have certainly written what are generally called scholarly books, and I have surely enjoyed a delightful holiday working on this one, especially during the period which I devoted to reviewing old films and coming about as close as possible to living my life over again. I do not of course mean that I have wrought carelessly. This book will appear in my literary chronology between a study of Washington Irving and a study of Edgar Allan Poe, and I think the confrontations involved quite delightful. Many of the same techniques which I applied in writing my histories of the English and American novel are used again here. Yet there is a difference between reading manuscripts at the Houghton and Morgan libraries and watching films at George Eastman House and the Museum of Modern Art Film Library, and somehow one turns over the files of *Photoplay Magazine* and *The Moving Picture World* in a different spirit from that in which one searches out articles in *PMLA* and *Modern Philology*.

This volume is not a definitive history of the silent film. I once cherished the hope of writing such a history, and this book was conceived as a preliminary study for it. Now I do not quite see

3

how anybody could ever produce such a history. Most of the requisite material is unavailable, and if it were here it would be quite too overwhelming to get through. By 1913, American producers alone were turning out two hundred reels of film a week. From the critical-aesthetic point of view, most of these films were of course not worth seeing. Yet fine things have a way of cropping up in unexpected places, and how can you judge that which you have not seen? Furthermore, a film which is quite contemptible aesthetically may still have great human interest, and great value too as an indicator of public taste. Far too many writers on the film give the impression of regarding it as only an exercise in technique. Surely Ernest Lindgren was right when he declared that "the art of the film, like all representational art, is to be valued primarily as the expression of an attitude to life. Technique is only a means to this end. . . . It is the human values which ultimately count, not the use of an original camera angle or a piece of clever cutting."[1]

I wished to write this book most of all because I thought it high time that some American should attempt to record what the first motion pictures looked like to the generation for which they were created—not the older people upon whom they intruded in a sometimes troublesome way, but the children and young people who grew up with them and made them a vital part of their lives. Most of those who have written about the movies know very little about this; they see early films only in retrospect, as we all see, say, the Elizabethan drama, and one cannot get the whole picture that way. Yet, now that I come to consider the matter more carefully, it occurs to me that nobody, not even I, will ever be in a position to know whether or not I have really succeeded. Those who remember the old films will draw upon their own memories as they turn my pages; how can they be expected to differentiate between what I have given them and what they have merely recalled? And even though younger readers may finish my book

[1] *The Art of the Film* (London, George Allen and Unwin, 1948), ix.

4

with a very clear impression, who can determine the degree of correspondence which exists between the image in their minds and that which I have sought to communicate?

I am a little uneasy too—I even feel a little guilty—over the special privileges and exemptions which the principle of selectivity which I have invoked has conferred upon me. Simply because I am not writing an all-inclusive study, I have chosen my materials upon a more or less personal basis; the films, the stars, the directors over which I linger longest are those that were important to me, and in many cases I have set down what I had to say about them in the manner of an essayist rather than a historian. I do not belong to any of the currently popular "schools" of motion-picture writing; neither do I feel the urge to join any of them. Here, for once, in these pages, an old-time movie fan has won the right to speak his piece about the things he cared for, and those who do not like it will simply have to lump it.

When I began to write a good many years ago, I was terribly concerned about "expressing my individuality"; as I grew older I became progressively less interested in myself and more interested in my subjects; this book is, in a sense, an unwilling reversion to type. If I am to tell you how the film impinged upon the consciousness of an America that had never seen films before, I must tell you how it impinged upon mine—not because I think my consciousness more important than other people's, but simply because it is the only consciousness I know well enough to be able to write about it. I was, I think, in this aspect, fairly typical of my generation, enough so at any rate so that reasonable generalizations can be set up and reasonable inferences will hold; but of course I was not a carbon copy of any other movie fan, nor was any other a carbon copy of me. I often get the impression that some movie fans enjoyed all films and loved everybody who appeared in them; I did not. I disliked some pictures as much as I enjoyed others; some personalities aroused as much antagonism in me as others did admiration; and there were still others whom I accepted more or less passively for what they had to give but toward whom I was quite indifferent so far as any marked personal reaction was concerned.

I must confess too that I am quite unable to understand what anybody means by speaking of the "passive absorption" which is supposed to have been encouraged by the silent films. Silent films seem to me to have required far more active and uninterrupted concentration than sound films do. We had to put a great many two-and-two's together which the author and the actor and the director put together for the audiences of today; we collected materials from a rapid-fire hail of images, made in our own minds combinations which left considerable room open for individuality of interpretation, and drew our own conclusions in correspondence with our own personalities and scales of value. I have never known what it means, in any form of art, to "identify" myself, as many people say they do, with the hero or the heroine, and I very much doubt that those who claim that this happens to them are accurately reporting their own experiences. In many cases, I am sure, they do not mean that they experience anything more than a very close and intense sympathy, or that they have learned how to look out upon the world, for the moment, through another person's eyes. This experience it is one of art's most important functions to give us, but when we pass beyond sympathy to identification, we also leave the sane world of art for a private world of self-delusion. I myself, at any rate, am always aware of the character's individuality and of my own, and of the reaction of the one to the other, and in the case of all forms of dramatic art, I am conscious further of the distinction which must be made between the character and the human being who embodies him.

I have confined myself in this book to the silent film, partly because this is enough for one volume, and partly because I loved silent films as I have never loved their successors. If the reader does not share this feeling, he should not allow himself to become too greatly agitated at this point; since the film as it came to me *was* silent, I had very little choice in the matter, and in this particular

6

study I should still have had to do substantially what I have done even if my "views" had been quite different. I may add that unless you belong to the older generation of movie-goers, you probably do not know enough about the silent film to have an intelligent opinion about it; you have seen few examples, and chances are that these were not projected at the proper speed.[2] I do not wish to be either dogmatist or extremist, however. Everybody now admits that the early talking films—*The Doctor's Secret,* George Arliss' *Disraeli,* etc.—were not motion pictures but photographed plays, and that since that day directors have learned how to recover and preserve and adapt to the sound technique many cinematic devices. Personally, however, I do not believe that they have ever come all the way home, and I am not alone in this. "There is no doubt that silent movies had plasticity that is not always apparent in films today," says King Vidor, "and this obviously accounts for much of their magic," and Ernest Lindgren adds that "in its silent days, in the hands of D. W. Griffith and Pudovkin and Eisenstein, the film came nearer to being an art form, in its own right, than it has ever been since."

Nobody admires such great sound films as Carl Dreyer's *Day of Wrath* and *The Seventh Seal* of Ingmar Bergman more than I do, yet I believe that even such masterpieces would have been better cinema if they had been done without sound. "The film is the language of images," cried Pirandello, "and images do not speak." In 1922, Charles Chaplin told St. John Ervine that sound would ruin pictures "as much as painting statuary. I would as soon rouge marble cheeks. . . . There would be nothing left to the imagination." What people overlook in considering the limitations of the

---

[2] Sound film runs at a uniform speed of twenty-four frames per second, and most theaters are not equipped to show films at any other speed. It is, however, an unwarranted simplification to say that silent films were shown, and should always be shown, at sixteen frames per second. See James Card, "Silent Film Speed," *Image* (published by George Eastman House), Vol. IV (1955), 55–56.

silent screen is that, as Ernest Betts has emphasized, silence is a positive as well as a negative thing; in pictures it accentuated "the other means—gesture, timing, facial expression, and grouping— by which an actor's intentions are expressed." Because its silence set it apart from the real world, the film was a created thing, integral and self-sufficient. The addition of sound disturbed this but other aspects of apartness incongruously remained: "Our sense of unreality in the motion-picture hall," wrote Agnes Repplier, "has been enhanced by the conversational film, by the drollery of hearing sounds emanate from the lips of a photograph." The film world was still flat, and the color which it sometimes now added was certainly not realistic color. It had, therefore, sacrificed its individuality without achieving realism. "Miss Greta Garbo was a most gifted actress after the introduction of sound," wrote Clifford Leach; "before that, she was not so much an actress, an interpreter, as a being created for our wondering contemplation, a part of that other world of the cinema which had the excitement, the separateness, the hinted fearfulness, the authority, of our dreams." This too must have been what Hugo von Hofmannsthal had in mind in what is perhaps the grandest tribute ever paid to the silent film, and it comes with special force from an artist who, in collaboration with Richard Strauss, himself created, in as different a medium as possible, some of the greatest art of our time. "What people seek in the motion pictures . . . what the masses of working people demand of them," said the great poet, "is a substitute for dreams. They would fill their imaginations with pictures, powerful presentiments charged with the very essence of life itself." He went further yet, for it was his view that "the motion picture is the only medium through which the men of our day . . . are able to come together for the purpose of enjoying a wonderful—nay, a spiritual —heritage and of making their own lives a part of the common life of humanity." Speaking for myself, I must say that no matter how long it has been since I have seen a silent film, when I do see one again, it always seems to me exactly as if I had never seen a sound film. I may even add that although I agree with the many film aestheticians who find the film more closely allied aesthetically with music than with any other art—except with a picture like *The Birth of a Nation,* which had a fine and memorable musical score which I still remember—I do not even miss the music when silent films are projected privately.[3]

It may be objected that the subtitle was as uncinematic an intrusion as sound has ever been, and in a sense this is true, but the subtitle did not become a serious problem until World War I; early films contained few subtitles (sometimes, it must be admitted, fewer than they needed for clarity). When the French pioneer Ferdinand Zecca issued *The Little Story of a Crime* (1900), which he regarded as the first film drama, there were three subtitles in it, and some exhibitors returned their prints, insisting that they were buying motion pictures, not literature. In Douglas Fairbanks' early films, on the other hand, Anita Loos's wisecracking subtitles were designed as an attraction secondary only to the acrobatics of the star, and when producers came to realize that this kind of thing was throwing their films off balance, they did not, as one might have expected, attempt to cut down on subtitles; instead they employed people like Ferdinand Pinney Earle to decorate them and lend them pictorial values often quite unrelated to those of the films themselves. I may add that the subtitle problem was greatly accentuated by the apparent determination of all producers to leave every subtitle on the screen long enough so that every intelligent cat in the theater had an opportunity to read it through exactly seventeen times.

[3] I may be a heretic at this point, for everybody except Vachel Lindsay seems to agree that silent films need musical accompaniment. Even Lillian Gish has lamented that "the movies married words instead of music"; see her "In Behalf of the Silent Film," in Oliver Saylor, ed., *Revolt in the Arts* (Brentano's, 1930). Lindsay, however, preferred the buzz of conversation in the audience to musical accompaniment, comparing the latter to "a man with a violin playing the catalogue" at an exhibition of paintings; see *The Art of the Moving Picture* (Macmillan, 1915).

Now obviously, if you are going to work in a silent medium—
or in any medium, in any art—you must choose materials which
can be adequately embraced by your medium. Even great directors
often erred in this. Griffith filmed *Pippa Passes* for Biograph, and
later he made a feature-length film, *Home Sweet Home,* in which
influence comparable to that which Browning ascribed to Pippa's
song was attributed, in three different crises, to another composition. Obviously such subjects must have been much more effective
in sound films, where the song could actually have been heard. In
Griffith's *Isn't Life Wonderful* we lost much because we could not
hear but only imagine the villain's diabolical laughter sounding
through the forest and terrifying the hero and heroine. Now that
we have become accustomed to superimposed titles in foreign-lan-
guage films, it seems strange that producers did not at least experiment with this device for conversational titles, as distinguished
from those used for expository purposes or to mark transitions.[4]
Among full-length silent films, F. W. Murnau's *The Last Laugh*
(and a number of other German films not shown in this country),
The Old Swimmin' Hole with Charles Ray, and many of Chaplin's
have come closest to presenting their material wholly in visual
form and without subtitles. This is clearly the cinematic ideal, al-

[4] For the actual methods used in cutting in conversational titles, see
William C. deMille, *Hollywood Saga* (Dutton, 1939), 108–109; cf. his discussion of how directors learned to substitute visual symbols for words (pp.
117–18). A. R. Fulton, *Motion Pictures: The Development of an Art from
Silent Films to the Age of Television* (University of Oklahoma Press, 1960),
131, contrasts a title in *What Price Glory?* to Erich von Stroheim's skillful
transformation of audio symbols into visual symbols in *Greed*. In Nestor's
old *Mutt and Jeff* series, in which the cartoon characters were played by living actors (I believe this antedated any attempt to animate the Bud Fisher
cartoons themselves), all the dialogue was given in a space by itself (white
letters on a black background) at the bottom of the screen, never interrupt-
ing the pictures and never intruding upon them. This suggested Carl Emil
Schultze ("Bunny"), creator of Foxy Grandpa, the only comic-strip artist
I know who treated dialogue in the same way, never permitting "balloons"
to intrude into his pictures.

though I am frank to admit that many stories could not be told in this way. With a little more intelligence and respect for the medium, however, a great deal more could have been done in pictorial terms, though it should always be remembered that even essentially cinematic language may be used stupidly and unimaginatively. Once the flashback had been invented, directors took to it like a duck to water, using it when it was necessary, and also when it was quite unnecessary, as if to suggest that nobody in the audience could be supposed capable of remembering anything.

One of the finest imaginative uses of the flashback I recall was that made by King Vidor when Mimi was dying in *La Boheme,* starring Lillian Gish and John Gilbert; Vidor took us into Rodolphe's mind by carrying us back to that wonderful day in the country, early in the film, when Mimi, radiantly beautiful and bursting with health and happiness, had first told Rodolphe that she loved him, and certainly this was a thousand times more effective than any subtitle or "Do-you-remember?" dialogue could have been. In *Amarilly of Clothes-Line Alley,* Marshall Neilan wished to suggest that three women at an afternoon tea were, in the slang sense, "cats." Instead of having somebody call them cats, he dissolved the three women into three beautiful Persians and then dissolved the cats back into the women. This was the cinematic way of doing the thing, which was right, as contrasted with the literary way, which would have been wrong. After the scenes showing the Battle of Poltava in the German film *Peter the Great,* starring Emil Jannings, the director Dimitri Buchowetzki found himself wishing to make a comment. But he did not permit himself even anything corresponding to Griffith's terse and eloquent "War's peace" in *The Birth of a Nation*: instead he flashed a pyramid of skulls upon the screen and after a few frames removed it. I will permit myself one final illustration to show that even though this kind of thing may be more difficult in sound films, it is not impossible. In George Sidney's production of *Young Bess,* starring Jean Simmons, we see the Princess Elizabeth living at the court when she is in favor with her father King Henry VIII and at Hatfield House when she is not, each transition being marked by a long shot of her caravan traveling up the hill toward the palace or down the hill toward Hatfield. In one scene we see (and hear) the princess storming that she *will not* return to Hatfield House. Nobody replies to her, but the next shot shows the familiar caravan traveling *down* the hill. This is an excellent example of how a shot may owe its meaning in a film entirely to the position it occupies.

I saw my first motion picture, somewhere along about 1905 or 1906, in a little barn-like theater at "The Chutes," a small amusement park, at Kedzie Avenue and Van Buren Street, Chicago, where the West Side carbarns now stand. It was all about the adventures of the devil and a beautiful girl whom he had lured to his picturesque domains. From its general resemblance to the French Pathé films which I was soon to see at my first neighborhood theater, I judge it to have been of French manufacture. The devil was a prominent character in many of these early films. He was essentially the *Faust* operatic devil—with horns and a very realistic tail—and he usually appeared and disappeared in a puff of smoke, which, to us who were new to the movies, was in itself a very wonderful photographic effect. Indeed I have often said that the devil was the first movie star and that if we had known some of the things that the future had in store for us, we might have appreciated him more than we did.[5]

Hell, as it appeared in this old French film, was a very beautiful place, full of couches and bowers and drapes and hangings. Indeed it might be described as a kind of Frenchified version of the notion Bernard Shaw was almost contemporaneously presenting in *Man and Superman*. I remember very well that I, who had been

[5] Much as I should like to trace this film, I have been unable to do so. I have hopefully investigated *The Devil's Son Makes a Night of It in Paris* (Pathé) and *Merry Frolics of Satan* (Méliès). Both were the light that failed.

taught to fear hell, and was doing my best—intermittently at least—to keep out of it, at once began to wonder if it was not possible that the place might have been maligned. I can personally testify, therefore, that the very first time I approached the movies, they proved themselves the insidiously corrupting influence which their critics have always declared them to be.

I think this film was in color; if it was not, other films which I saw very early certainly were. Since color processes were not yet in use, this meant that each copy had to be colored by hand; and with motion-picture film running sixteen exposures to the foot, it must have been an amazingly tedious and eye-destroying task. Distributors offered some subjects plain or colored, depending upon the price the exhibitor wished to pay. I once owned a scrap of a French Pathé *Abraham's Sacrifice,* thus colored by hand.

At the St. Louis Exposition of 1904, George C. Hale, former chief of the Kansas City fire department, first exhibited "Hale's Tours and Scenes of the World." He may have got the idea from the "Phantom Rides" which were being exhibited in England or from the more ambitious plans R. W. Paul was trying to work out in connection with a film based on H. G. Wells's *The Time Machine.*[6] I was too young to travel "Hale's Tours" in St. Louis, but they soon established themselves in downtown districts in all large American cities; Adolph Zukor, in his early days, was a "Hale's Tours" exhibitor in association with William A. Brady. They were travel films, shown in tiny theaters built to resemble railway coaches. The "conductor" stood on the back platform to receive your ticket, and when you went inside and took your seat you really seemed to be settling down for a journey. Presently the lights were extinguished, the car rumbled and swayed, and on a small

[6] See Leslie Wood, *The Miracle of the Movies* (London, Burke Publishing Co., Limited, 1947), 124–25; Cecil M. Hepworth, *Came the Dawn: Memories of a Film Pioneer* (London, Phoenix House, Limited, 1951), 44–45.

screen in the front of the coach you saw Yellowstone Park or the Yosemite or whatever locality might be on exhibition that day. Since the films had been taken from the platform of a moving train the illusion was complete.

As I remember it, "Hale's Tours" in Chicago were located on the west side of State Street, between Adams and Monroe, where the Bijou Dream Theater was afterward erected. Apparently nearly every city had a Bijou Dream in the early days of the movies, all constructed upon approximately the same pattern. The motion-picture theater was on the second floor, with the screen in the front of the building. To reach it you climbed a glass staircase, with a waterfall running under it, illuminated by colored electric lights. (And that, too, in a day when electric light was still relatively new, was both spectacular and romantic.) The thing was ingeniously planned so that when you left the theater after the show, you went down the back stairs and passed through the penny arcade on the ground floor before reaching the street. If you had any children with you, you very likely dropped a few coins on the way.

Most motion-picture theaters of the period were much less elaborate than that. Many of the neighborhood theaters were merely converted stores. Sometimes they did not even trouble to remove the plate-glass windows (after all, the building might be used for another purpose six months hence) but merely pasted the posters up against them on the inside. Such was the little theater on West Twenty-second Street, just east of California Avenue, where, one never-to-be-forgotten night, I first saw *A Trip to the Moon*. As late as 1925, when I moved away from the Chicago area, the Oak Theater, on West Twelfth Street, near Oak Park Avenue, though fairly spacious inside, had this kind of a front. Sometimes the ceiling was so low that the top of the picture escaped the screen; this was true at the little Kedzie, on Twelfth Street, just west of Kedzie Avenue, where the great Balaban and Katz theater empire began. Later, as the industry expanded, specially designed theaters were constructed. The Victoria, also on Twenty-second Street, but just west of California, where I saw so many films in my youth, had a marble-lined exterior and caryatid-like figures holding up the ceiling interiorly, with little cupids perched on top of the building; but the whole edifice was still only the width of an ordinary Chicago city lot.

My own first neighborhood theater was larger than this, however. The Family Electric Theater occupied a former dance hall with boarded windows (the premises house a restaurant today) in a large building on the southeast corner of Ogden and California avenues, just across the street from Douglas Park. There was no box office. The proprietor, a man named Brown, stationed himself at the end of a long, dingy corridor, and you passed in, handed him your nickel, and took your seat. If it happened to be Saturday afternoon, he would hand you a five-cent package of chewing gum by way of encouragement. How he ever managed to make both ends meet I have no idea, for so far as I could see, I was his only steady customer.

The Family Electric Theater was a rather dismal place, and indeed the fact that films had to be shown in darkness handicapped them greatly with many Americans of the time. Darkness was evil, or if not it might easily become a cloak for evil. This feeling was so strong that there were places where customers were allowed to sit in the light and watch the pictures through holes in a curtain.

The rule at the Family Electric Theater was three reels of film and an "illustrated song" for a nickel. The illustrated song would be one of the popular ballads of the period—"Clover Blossoms" or "In the Good Old Summertime" or maybe "Come Away with Me, Lucille"—sung by the girl Sophie who played the piano (her cousin Helen was in my room at school) to the accompaniment of colored slides on the screen. Incidentally the making of song slides became, for a time, a comparatively thriving industry, with increasing care being taken in the matter of modeling and background; Norma Talmadge posed for song slides before getting into the movies.[7] I think Sophie, who sang a good deal better than she played, was Mr. Brown's only employee, with the exception, of course, of the projectionist, who seemed to me a very mighty man; I think perhaps I was under the impression that he made the pictures himself. The boarded windows were all decorated with posters with somebody's picture on them—Edison's, I fancy—but at the time I am sure I thought it was the projectionist's.

These were the only printed posters Mr. Brown used. Apparently posters were not yet issued with individual film subjects; at least Brown's posters were all hand-painted on canvas, with fancy lettering and fascinating scrolls and, in the early days, small pictures; the world began to grow cold to me when these pictures no longer appeared. In *A Small Boy and Others,* Henry James describes how, as a child, he would "dawdle and gape" before the billboards of his youth; I am sure he never did it better than I at the Family Electric Theater.

As I remember it, all the films shown at this theater were French Pathé,[8] and if I loved the posters I loved the titles and subtitles even more. They were always tinted red, with enormous lettering, and there were two of the famous Pathé roosters at the bottom of each title, one at the right and the other at the left. The rooster's feet were brought smartly together under his body and

---

[7] See Charles K. Harris, "Song Slide the Little Father of Photodrama," *The Moving Picture World,* Vol. XXXI (1917), 1520–21; John W. Ripley, "All Join in the Chorus," *American Heritage,* Vol. X, No. 4 (June, 1959), 50–59.

[8] The dominance of the French film in the early days can hardly be exaggerated. Charles Pathé himself declared that "only the armaments industry made profits like ours." See Georges Sadoul, "Napoleon of the Cinema," *Sight and Sound,* Vol. XXVII (1958), 183; and cf. his *French Film* (London, The Falcon Press, 1953), 7–9, 15. It is said that by 1914, Germany had more than repaid the Franco-Prussian War indemnity in rental fees for French films.

fastened to a bar on which the words "Trade Mark" were printed. I shall never forget how disappointed I was when the design of the rooster was afterward changed. The trade-mark, of course, was ubiquitous in all early films, as an intended precaution against duping prints. Not only did it appear on all the subtitles; it might be seen in the pictures themselves, nailed to the walls of the sets. In Vitagraph's 1908 production of *Romeo and Juliet* it served as a decoration on the canopy of Juliet's bed.

The Family Electric Theater had, I fear, a rather melancholy end. In a desperate effort to keep things going, the proprietor finally opened a saloon in the front of the building whose rear was occupied by the theater, and the back door of the saloon opened into the corridor through which one entered the theater. I thought he looked pretty sheepish about it the night we were there, but we could not have studied his reactions very carefully even if we had wished to do so, for the little film trade he had at once deserted him, and the theater closed.[9]

I do not recall the titles of many of the films I saw at Brown's. I think the earliest I can remember is *Bobby and His Balloon* (1907), an early fantasy about the adventures of a small boy who was carried off to realms beyond the clouds by a toy balloon. The continuity of motion-picture themes and interests was strikingly illustrated for me when France sent us *The Red Balloon* in 1956, but fine as that film was, it was much less imaginative than the earlier work. Much more primitive was *Travels of a Flea,* which was merely a variety of people scratching themselves with exaggerated French pantomime. Anyone who has seen the Zecca, Cohl, and Durand reel circulated by the Museum of Modern Art Film Library knows how fascinating these early French films can be. The gem of the Museum collection is Cohl's utterly delightful *The Pumpkin Race* (1907), which also has affinities with *The Red*

[9] For a delightful account of an early English film theater, see Wood, *The Miracle of the Movies,* Chap. X.

Balloon, and whose wonderful chase scenes are more imaginative, though less tense or suspenseful, than anything Griffith or Sennett were to achieve in kind.

George Eastman House has an original exhibition print of Pathé's utterly charming *The Fairy of the Spring* (1904). A fairy, disguised as an old woman, enters a poor peasant's hut in winter. The snow is falling heavily, and falling, incidentally, right *through* the window. When the peasants treat her kindly, she throws off her cloak and proceeds to work magical transformations for their benefit. The film as a whole is in black and white, but the fairy's clothes and the gifts she brings are in color, all of which is logical enough. The picture ends in the snow-covered garden, where various trees and shrubs are made to bear gorgeous bloom. Finally two little naked babies come out of the flowers; this presumably is the fairy's crowning gift to her kind hosts—a somewhat doubtful blessing, one would think, unless an endowment was provided.

Of all the films I saw at the Family Electric Theater the one which impressed me most was a medieval tale concerning the misfortunes of a virtuous queen who was foully done to death by a Machiavellian villain. After her death he was apprehended and hanged, most realistically, in full view of the camera, with his tongue choked out of his mouth. There was a stone head on a building near my house which ever afterward reminded me of this character; perhaps this is one of the reasons I never forgot the picture. It was more important, however, that I had been touched, for perhaps the first time in my life, by a kind of romantic tenderness, when I saw the last scene of this film, in which the dead queen's pet fawn was shown guarding her grave.

I greatly wish I might see this picture again, but alas! I cannot even remember the title, and for many years I had no idea about the source of the story. Then, in 1951, Houghton Mifflin Company published a book called *A Treasury of French Tales,* edited by Henri Pourrat, of which they kindly sent me a copy, and there, in a tale called "The Lady and the Hind," I found the source of

18

my old French film, seen more than forty years ago. All of which proves that everything comes to him who waits—provided he lives long enough.[10]

The hanging of the villain in the "Lady and the Hind" film will attest that we had our screen horror in those days—more, I suspect, than we had later, after the censorship agitation had got under way.[11] I remember a picture in which a man sank to his death in a bed of quicksand—it was the first time I had ever heard of quicksand—and I remember too the Dame Quickly-like reporting of the lady downstairs concerning a film she had seen on a night when I had chanced not to be present. The screen, she said, was covered with naked men. They crawled and they crawled, closer and closer to the audience, until it seemed as if they were going to crawl right off the "curtain," at which point several women screamed—whether in fear or ecstasy she did not specify— and Mr. Brown came rushing in "to see whether the machine had exploded." That was what we were all desperately afraid of in those days: the "machine" might blow up at almost any minute! Ever since the Charity Ball fire at Paris in 1897, which was really not caused by exploding film at all, people had had the most fantastic ideas concerning the dangerous properties of motion-picture film. I suspect that the lady had seen one of the early Indian pictures (although I do not recall ever having seen an Indian picture at Brown's), and it sounds very much as though the cameras were placed as they were later in *Ben Hur* so that when the chariots were driven over them they seemed to be passing right over the audi-

[10] However, I still lack bound Volume I of *The Motion Picture Story Magazine* and many early comic books—*Foxy Grandpa, Buster Brown, Little Nemo*, etc.

[11] One Pathé masterpiece was devoted to *Capital Punishment in Various European Countries*, thirty feet each being devoted to hanging, decapitation, etc. Another gem, *Avenging a Crime, or Burned at the Stake*, goes back to c.1903.—"This is a highly sensational film showing robbery and murder, the alarm, the chase, and final capture of the murderer, ending with the burning at the stake."

ence. This, however, would be very advanced camera technique for those days—more advanced, it would seem, than the nerves of this particular audience could take.

The Passion Play which came along while I was still attending Brown's was probably Pathé's 1907 version, which the theater spread out over a week, during which time the neighborhood was flooded with dodgers decorated with lurid pictures of Jesus on the Cross. There was considerable difference of opinion over whether it was proper to show the life of Jesus in the nickel show. My mother at first thought not, and we did not see the picture at the Family Electric Theater; but later, when we found the entire film being shown on a single bill at the Bijou Dream, we weakened and went in. This film was no more troubled by considerations of mystic harmonies than the medieval drama. The angels were quite as solid as the human characters portrayed in it, and I am sure that the star of Bethlehem moved on wires. Yet its technical simplicity suited the matchless sincerity of the story it had to tell, and there was more religious uplift about it than often appeared in later, more pretentious treatments of the same subject.

The thing that must be remembered first of all, if you who read in these later days are even to begin to understand how my contemporaries and I reacted to these early films, is the now almost incomprehensible fact that what we were fascinated by primarily was mere movement itself. It did not make very much difference what moved or why; the important thing was that movement occurred. Nobody had ever seen a picture move before, and unless you keep this in mind you will be puzzled by our response to the Empire State Express rounding a curve or R. W. Paul's pictures of the surf breaking upon the shore at Dover. "It was motion alone that intrigued the spectators," writes Albert E. Smith; "they exclaimed over clouds that floated, branches that waved, and smoke that puffed." So the Lumières set up their cameras to photograph workers leaving a factory, or a baby being fed, or men playing cards, and when complications were needed they might be furnished by a mischievous boy (strayed out of the contemporary comic strip) to upset a woman's washtub or step on the gardener's hose to block the flow of water and then relieve the pressure just when the poor man peered into the nozzle to try to find out what was wrong. But before you decide that we were altogether simple souls, you might do well to ponder what learned modern film aestheticians have to say about movement on the screen, and of how the essential film quality is undercut when it is neglected. "If there is an aesthetics of the cinema . . . ," says René Clair, "it can be summarized in one word: movement." And in 1960, Siegfried Kracauer devoted a whole elaborate *Theory of Film* to expounding this thesis.[12]

[12] Published by Oxford University Press. I must not leave the impression that I accept Mr. Kracauer's film theory as a whole. It seems to me vitiated by a materialistic outlook, a narrow-minded determination to limit film and the film experience to the kind of film he happens to prefer, and a generally dogmatic and authoritarian cast of mind. What could be sillier than to accept *The Seventh Seal*, which is a religious film, on the ground that both the knight and the squire "manifest a down-to-earth attitude" toward "the mediaeval beliefs and superstitions" which the film features, and that this "results in confrontations which in a measure acclimatize the film to the medium"? Kracauer objects to historical films in general on the ground that they are "finite" and "obstruct the affinity of the medium for endlessness." But there is nothing more "finite" than the passing moment, which is never more than a bridge from the past into the future, while anything in the past that we can still be interested in has, in a sense, defied time and escaped finiteness. From another point of view, historical films save us from our imprisonment in the present and give us a chance to view the world from a wider ground of vantage. Kracauer is of course quite right when he contends that we cannot reproduce the past exactly, but this does not strengthen his argument. Just to the extent that it thus fails in accuracy, the historical film *is* a contemporary document; it reveals the modern man's conception of the past, and this is as much a part of his experience as his adventures in the street. "The cinema is materialistically minded," says Mr. Kracauer; "it proceeds from 'below' to 'above.'" But this is not materialism at all, not if you really "proceed." On the contrary, it is an excellent indication

Next after the fascination of movement itself, the most important thing the film did for us was the way it enlarged our horizons. It is hard to realize how little the average man knew about the world he lived in before the movies came, or even more before photography was invented. Most Americans got their visual impressions of the Civil War mainly from line drawings. Is it any wonder that Washington Irving was bowled over as he was by Church's picture of "The Heart of the Andes"? Kracauer quotes a German critic Herman G. Scheffauer, who predicted in 1920 that through film man "shall come to know the earth as his own house, though he may never have escaped the narrow confines of his hamlet." Jane Addams was not a trained film aesthetician but she knew this intuitively, as she knew nearly everything else that was worth knowing. In the Hull-House neighborhood, she wrote, during the years of which we are now thinking, "the function of release . . . is marvelously performed by the movies."

But in all this where were the players? The amazing answer

---

of the way Christianity works. (God *became* man.) Kracauer is fighting a battle which echoes that fought by those early American critics who demanded that American literature confine itself to American themes. This view was rejected by every first-rate critical intelligence in the country, and it soon became clear that any subject in which Americans can be interested, or which can be treated from an American point of view, is an American subject. By the same token, any subject which the camera can handle creatively is a film subject. Even Mr. Kracauer admits these things when he finds it impossible to reject that whole side of the screen which goes back to Méliès. Lumière was the only important film man who ever adhered completely to Kracauer's theory; this is why Lumière's career was limited and short. Man needs the cinema to explore actuality, but he also needs the cinema to escape from actuality (which is not to be equated with reality); the popularity of history and fantasy on the screen can never be understood by those who fail to realize the depth of this need. What Herman Melville wrote long ago of fiction is worth recalling here. A work of fiction, he said, is a kind of theater between covers; men go to it, as they go to the theater, for glamour; at the same time they go to it for truth; from it they expect, in a sense, "more reality than life itself can show."

is that the players were literally nowhere, nor did they really begin to be important to me until after the first fan magazine, then called *The Motion Picture Story Magazine,* was founded in 1911. Vitagraph established it as a house organ, but it caught on immediately and went to the newsstands; at first it confined itself to "licensed" plays and players, but soon even the independents were admitted. My cousin and I have recalled with amusement the day when, while we were watching a Kalem Civil War picture together, I briefed him upon the leading actor's first appearance. "That's Jack J. Clark," I said. My cousin pondered. "Wasn't he president once?" he asked thoughtfully. "Of course not," I replied scornfully (I was a year and a half older than he). "Do you suppose that a man who had been president would pose for the movies afterwards?" Whereupon my cousin, who had evidently seen more films than I had given him credit for, countered triumphantly, "Why not? Didn't Lincoln?"

I fear I showed little intellectual humility upon this occasion, yet not too long before I myself might have been capable of something very like this. Strange as it now seems, I don't think it ever occurred to me in the days when I attended the Family Electric Theater that there were actors in motion pictures. It may be that in the beginning I thought the pictures drawings, but it is more likely that I did not think about it at all but simply accepted everything in an attitude of wonder and worship as I accepted the trees and the sun. I can still remember the Sunday afternoon when, sitting in another and a later theater, and watching Maurice Costello, as I later discovered him to be, I was struck with the fact that I had seen that face several times before in other pictures. It was an Irish film in which he was appearing, I remember, for he wore the traditional Irish costume and carried a shillelagh. I turned and remarked upon the circumstances to a boy sitting near me, who thereupon became one of the most effective and important of my teachers. "Of course," he said, "that man poses for the pictures." (It was always "posing" in those days, never "acting.")

23

And immediately a great light began to dawn, and many things grew clear together. I remember, too, the day when I paused before a motion-picture theater in an unfamiliar part of the city and scrutinized a hand-made poster suspended from the ceiling of the outer lobby. It gave the name of the film that was being shown and then added: "Miss Lawrence in the Leading Role." And that, I am sure, was the first time I ever heard of Florence Lawrence or any other film actress.

She was not the last I was to hear of by any means, and she and her successors will play a considerable role in this book. In those days, however, the play was the thing, and it was the films which drew me to the players, not the players to the films. And this too should be said of this book of mine: that it differs from many books about the movies in being almost exclusively concerned with the pictures themselves. Even when I write about the players my concern is with what happens on the screen, not behind it. I am not fanatical about this: where I happen to know something about a player's private life which I think illuminates his art, I have not hesitated to make use of it; but this kind of thing never, with me, becomes an end in itself.

I am not interested in the theaters for their own sake, either (Rachael Low, in her great history of the British film,[13] devotes a considerable portion of her space to them); but it has not been possible to avoid them altogether, for it was through particular theaters that the films came to me, and in many cases the theater is bound up with the film. In some aspects too the theatrical angle accents the representative character I hope my book may have. All the theaters I have spoken of so far were located east and south of Douglas Park (I lived across the street from the park, on California Avenue, between Eighteenth and Nineteenth streets). The

[13] Three volumes of *The History of the British Film* have so far appeared, covering, respectively, 1896–1906, 1906–14, and 1914–18. The London publisher is Allen and Unwin, 1948, 1949, and 1950. The first volume was written in collaboration with Roger Manvell.

Victoria was very handy and remained important to me all through my grade-school years, but increasingly, as time went on, I came to patronize the theaters in Lawndale, west of the park, where my aunts lived and I often visited. I can remember six different houses there, on and just off Ogden Avenue, within a range of about six blocks, and this was by no means unusual for the time. The most elaborate, by all means, was the White Palace, on Kedzie Avenue. I played in it as a small boy while it was being built, and I have lived to see it, after many years' service, an abandoned ruin in a ruined slum district. On election night in 1912—a cold, wet, drizzly night, real Democratic weather—we stood at the corner of Ogden and Kedzie watching election returns on a screen across the street, and I ran the half-block down to the White Palace to see what they were playing; there was a Vitagraph Civil War picture with Edith Storey on the bill, I remember. But the theater I loved best was the little Acme, on Ogden Avenue, near Homan, which still stands but has long devoted itself to the activities of an automotive repair shop. The reader should not be surprised to learn that theaters had more individuality in those days than they generally have now, for different theaters ran different programs—the "licensed" program in one theater, the Universal in another, and the Mutual in a third. The Acme ran licensed films at a time when, in general, the licensed companies were making better pictures than their competitors, and it was there that I really began to know my movies.

If all this seems to reflect a prodigious amount of movie-going for a small boy, it should be remembered that in the early days film shows cost five cents and ran about half an hour; you could go to an early show, get home before eight o'clock, and still have time to do other things during the evening. Even after features came in, you could get out by nine; in my college years, I always went to a movie the night before an examination, came home early, got a good sleep, rose early the next morning for a final review of the material, and wrote my examination rested and refreshed. During my early years of teaching I recommended this method to my own students (none of whom, I think, ever accepted the suggestion) ; then the curse of the double feature came upon us, and anybody who attempted to use this method today would be too tired to write anything. In the old days women would refresh themselves upon a shopping expedition by stopping in to see a film, and an uncle of mine used to go to the movies during his lunch hour. Now all this wonderful, recreative, refreshing faculty that the film once possessed has been thrown away, and going to the movies has become a job in itself, as well as a capital operation upon your bank account.

It must be remembered too that in those days motion-picture theaters changed the bill every day and did not advertise in advance. Sometimes on Sundays the Acme ran two bills (one in the afternoon and another in the evening.) You went to the "nickel show" as opportunity afforded and hoped that you would see something or somebody that you wanted to see. I suppose one of the great nights of my life was the Saturday my mother and I walked through the park to the Acme and, when we got there, found, to my intense delight, that they were showing Vitagraph's production of *A Tale of Two Cities,* which I already knew about and dearly wished to see. But it was by the merest chance that I did not miss it altogether. When Helen Gardner, who played Becky Sharp in Vitagraph's *Vanity Fair,* which shortly followed upon *A Tale of Two Cities,* left Vitagraph and made her own independent six-reel production of Sardou's *Cleopatra* (1912), I much desired to see this also, but it never came my way until the summer of 1961, when, preparing for this book, I had it screened for me at George Eastman House.[14]

---

[14] I am sorry to add that it turned out to be not worth waiting forty-nine years for, since Miss Gardner was as inexplicably bad in *Cleopatra,* in which she merely did an unsuccessful imitation of Sarah Bernhardt, as she was good in *Vanity Fair.* I had an experience in connection with this film which illustrates, effectively though trivially, what John Livingston Lowes writes

My memory of the Acme, the night of *A Tale of Two Cities,* may well be the most precious of those I cherish from my early years, but it is not the only one. There was, for example, the summer the Acme ran open-air movies right next door to itself, and here, one night among the trees, I saw the Edison *Mary Stuart,* with Mary Fuller, Miriam Nesbitt, and Marc McDermott. There were even times when a much-loved film refused to leave its glamour behind me in the theater but insisted on walking home with me afterward, so that it filled the world itself with color and excitement. Finally there are the generalized memories which are quite as important to me as the recollection of any particular occasion. If seven o'clock in the evening is still something of a magic hour to me, it is because, so many years ago, this was the time when the pictures began. And I can still stand off and see myself, during the last film at the Victoria, when I was beginning to get sleepy, with my legs crossed and my chin in my hand, my eyes glued upon the tearful Reliance melodrama on the screen, while the pianist wrung the last tear out of Edwin Kendall's "Charme

in *The Road to Xanadu* (Houghton Mifflin, 1927) about the difference between what we think we have remembered and what we have created. When *Cleopatra* was a new film and I was practically burning to see it, a boy came to school one day with a copy of *The New York Dramatic Mirror* whose entire back cover was devoted to an advertisement for this picture. It seemed to me surpassingly beautiful, and there has never been a time since when I could not achieve, as I supposed, a complete recall of it. It was printed in blue ink, and it showed Miss Gardner in character, seated on the floor, with her white robes spread out around her. When I decided to write this book, it occurred to me that it might be well to look up that advertisement and have it reproduced as an illustration. I found it in the Theater Collection at the Houghton Library. It *was* printed in blue ink; it *did* occupy the back cover of the *Dramatic Mirror;* it *did* show Miss Gardner on the floor with her white robes spread out around her. But the position of the head and the expression of the face were completely different from what I thought I had remembered. Yet the changes which I myself had unconsciously made were still so vivid to me that, even with the actual picture before me, I could still see what I had carried in my mind for so long.

d'Amour," which he always played on such occasions, and Mary Herwig, the prettiest girl in school, who was quite as lovely as anybody on the screen, would come in with her brother and take a seat somewhere up in front for the second show.

Motion pictures changed for me, as many other things did, when we moved from the Douglas Park district to Oak Park in the spring of 1915. Without the Oak Park High School and the Oak Park Public Library and the First Congregational Church during Dr. William E. Barton's pastorate, I am sure my life would have been very different but it would not have been better. If the Oak Park Theater (now the Lamar) does not quite rank with this trio of influences, it still occupies its high and honorable place. The first film I saw there was Mary Pickford in *Fanchon the Cricket,* for features had now definitely arrived; when the theater was rebuilt the next year, it reopened with a gala bill comprising Marguerite Clark in *Molly Make-Believe*, Chaplin in *The Floorwalker,* and Billie Burke in the first chapter of *Gloria's Romance.* The Oak Park was the most elegant and genteel motion-picture theater I had yet encountered and the most intelligently managed, and they *reserved* seats for their 7:30 show each evening. General admission to a section in the rear cost fifteen cents, but you could have a reserved seat for twenty, or a place in the first four rows, which were considered undesirable, for ten. There was also a good deal in the way of asking special prices for special films. The tariff was high for the period, and when Lubliner and Trinz took the place over and added it to their theater chain in 1917, they abolished the reserved seats and set a uniform admission price of fifteen cents. This soon rose to twenty-five, however, plus a three-cent war tax, which remained standard for most neighborhood motion-picture theaters for a good many years.

Such was the first impingement of the movies upon one mind. From here on there will be considerably more about the impinger and less of the impinged-upon. Chapters I and IV of this book contain general but selective surveys of the pre-feature and the feature era of silent films respectively. Chapter II deals with D. W. Griffith, greatest of all directors, and Chapter III with Mary Pickford, whose dominance among female stars was so long uncontested. In Chapter V, I have discussed the motion-picture actress both generally and specifically, the specific examples being chosen primarily because I think I have something to say about them. I may add that I wish I could send a copy of this volume, published by a university press, to all the people who, in days gone by, used to think I was wasting my time when I went to the movies. Some of these copies, alas, would have to go by messengers whom I cannot command.

CHAPTER ONE

"Came the Dawn"

"A R T," Bernard De Voto once remarked, "is the terms of an armistice signed with fate." Spiritual in essence, it depends for its expression upon physical means, but I know of no other art which requires so much physical equipment and presupposes so much mechanical achievement as the motion picture. Its pre-history traces back at least to 1640, when Athanasius Kirchner invented the magic lantern, changing from one slide to another by means of a revolving drum. The nineteenth century had various devices, many of them children's toys, in which motion could be simulated, first in drawings, then in photographs; and some of these pictures may, in a manner, have been projected. But not until after photographic film became available at the end of the century could any of these other inventions carry us far toward the motion picture as we know it today.

The early history of the motion picture is extremely complicated, due partly to the fact that so many different people were working on similar devices in different places, each often in complete ignorance of what the others were doing. In this country it has been customary to call Thomas A. Edison the "inventor" of motion pictures, but informed persons have always known that this was a great simplification, and Gordon Hendricks has now argued that the actual work at the Edison plant was done by the Englishman William Kennedy Laurie Dickson, who was later associated with the Biograph Company.[1]

[1] *The Edison Motion Picture Myth* (University of California Press, 1961). The fullest accounts of motion-picture prehistory are in Martin Quigley, Jr., *Magic Shadows: The Story of the Origin of Motion Pictures* (Washington, D. C., Georgetown University Press, 1948); in Vol. I of Georges Sadoul, *Histoire Générale du Cinéma* (Paris, Editions Denoël, 1945); and in Vol. I of Terry Ramsaye, *A Million and One Nights: A History of the Motion Picture* (Simon and Schuster, 1926). See, further, Leslie Wood, *The Miracle of the Movies* (London, Burke Publishing Company, Ltd., 1947); Fulton, *Motion Pictures;* Maurice Bessy and Lo Duca, *Louis Lumière, Inventeur* (Paris, Prisma, 1948); also the following articles: Georges Sadoul, "Lumière—The Last Interview," *Sight and Sound*, Vol. XVII (1948), 68–70; Kenneth MacGowan, "The Coming of Camera and Projector," *Quarterly of Film, Radio, and Television*, Vol. IX (1954–55), 1–14, 124–36; and Raymond Spottiswoode, "The Friese-Greene Controversy: The Evidence Reconsidered," *Quarterly of Film, Radio, and Television*, Vol. IX (1954–55), 217–30. See also, on the American film, Benjamin B. Hampton, *A History of the Movies* (Covici-Friede, 1931), which is excellent on the early business affairs with which Hampton was closely connected; Lewis Jacobs, *The Rise of the American Film* (Harcourt, Brace, 1939); Gilbert Seldes, *The Movies Come to America* (Scribners, 1947); and the pictorials: Deems Taylor *et al.*, *A Pictorial History of the Movies* (Simon and Schuster, 1943); Daniel Blum, *A Pictorial History of the Silent Screen* (Greenberg, 1953); Richard Griffith and Arthur Mayer, *The Movies* (Simon and Schuster, 1957); Joe Franklin, *Classics of the Silent Screen* (Citadel, 1960). American films also play their part in the world histories of cinema, which include Paul Rotha, *The Film till Now*, originally published by Cape and Smith in 1930, and since twice enlarged and brought up to date by Richard Griffith; Maurice Bardèche and Robert Brassilach, *The History of Motion Pictures*, translated and edited by Iris Barry (Norton, 1938); Arthur Knight, *The Liveliest Art* (Macmillan, 1947). World pictorials are Paul Rotha, *Movie Parade* (Studio Publications, 1936, 1950), and Ernest Lindgren, *A Picture History of the Cinema* (Macmillan, 1960). The third volume of René Jeanne and Charles Ford, *Histoire Encyclopédique du Cinéma,* which has four volumes thus far (1947–58), is devoted wholly to the American film. (Vol. I was published by Robert Laf-

There can be no doubt that Edison held patents, however, nor that in February, 1893, he opened the first American motion-picture studio, the Kinetographic Theater, popularly known as the Black Maria. Open-roofed, it was swung, bridge-fashion, from a pivot, to follow the sun, and cost $637.67 to build. Its purpose was to produce films not for projection but for Edison's peep-show machine, the kinetoscope, in which a fifty-foot roll ran endlessly from one spool to another (Edison feared that if films were pro-jected too many people would be able to view them at the same time, and this would reduce profits). The kinetoscope had a bar-bershop scene, a Chinese laundry scene, and such celebrities as Buffalo Bill, Annie Oakley, Annabelle the dancer, the World's Columbian Exposition strong man Eugene Sandow, and Ruth St. Denis (then plain Miss Ruth Dennis) doing their stuff; the 1894 catalog listed sixty such subjects. In 1894, too, Grey and Leroy Latham exposed one thousand feet of film making prize-fight pic-tures at the Black Maria. The popularity of dancers and prize fighters in early times was not planned, nor necessarily an evi-dence of public taste, but primarily determined by the fact that prize fights and solo dances were action subjects which could easily be accommodated to the space which the bulky, immovable camera of those days could comfortably take in. The first top-flight stage celebrity to make a film was Joseph Jefferson, who went through some scenes from *Rip Van Winkle* for Biograph in 1896.

Edison-sponsored films were projected in 1890 and 1891,[2] but the movies' celebrated first night on Broadway occurred on April 23, 1896, when Edison's "Vitascope" was demonstrated on a twenty-foot screen at Koster and Bial's Music Hall. The New York *Times* reported:

---

font, Vols. II–IV by S.E.D.E.) Wholly concerned with the silent period, and including 250 illustrations, is Heinrich Fraenkel, *Unsterblicher Film: Die grosse Chronik von der Laterna Magica bis zum Tonfilm* (Munich, Kindler Verlag, 1956).

[2] Hendricks, *The Edison Motion Picture Myth,* Chap. XV, 91–92.

When the hall was darkened last night a buzzing and roaring was heard in the turret, and an unusually bright light fell upon the screen. Then came into view two precious blonde young persons of the variety stage, in pink and blue dresses, doing the umbrella dance with commendable celerity. Their motions were all clearly defined. When they vanished, a view of an angry surf breaking on a sandy beach near a stone pier amazed the spectators. The waves tumbled in furiously and the foam of the breakers flew high in the air. A burlesque boxing match between a tall, thin comedian and a short, fat one, a comic allegory called "The Monroe Doctrine," an instant of motion in Hoyt's farce, "A Milk White Flag," repeated over and over again, and a skirt dance by a tall blonde completed the views, which were all wonderfully real and singularly exhilarating. For the spectator's imagination filled the atmosphere with electricity, as sparks crackled around the moving lifelike figures.

Biograph put on a show at Hammerstein's Olympic Music Hall in October of the same year. Among other things, the pictures showed William McKinley in a parade at Canton, Ohio, and "at home. . . . Major McKinley was seen to come down the steps of his house with his secretary. The secretary handed him a paper which he opened and read. Then he took off his hat and advanced to meet a visiting delegation." To an America which had never before seen a Presidential candidate in action, all this was sensational.

In the beginning Edison was at war with all his competitors, claiming violation of patents, but in 1907 he began to make peace with some of them, and in 1908 the Motion Picture Patents Company was formed. This finally comprised Edison, Biograph, Vitagraph, Essanay, Selig, Lubin, Kalem, Méliès, and Pathé (which in 1910 began producing in America as well as in France), together with the importer and exchange man George Kleine of Chicago. Beginning in 1910 they distributed their products through the General Film Company, which also imported Gaumont and

Urban-Eclipse films from France. Buying up exchanges all over the country, General Film collected a license fee of $2.00 per week from each exhibitor and refused him permission to show films distributed through other exchanges.

Because it was based upon the protection of patents, this arrangement was regarded as an airtight monopoly, safe from prosecution under the Sherman Act. The license fee alone brought in about $1,250,000 a year. That it was not permanently successful was due among other things to the courage and leadership of such "independents" as Carl Laemmle and William Fox.[3] It was a great day for the independents when Fox won a suit against Edison in 1912. In January, 1913, the federal government itself opened suit, and on February 24, 1915, the General Film Company was restrained from enforcing license patents and other interconnecting agreements, the costs of the long-drawn-out litigation being assessed to the Patents companies, with the exception of Méliès, which was specifically exempted from conspiracy charges.

In 1910, however, this was all for the future. Let us take a look at the Patents companies in their hour of glory.

We may begin, for a very special reason, with one of the least distinguished—Méliès. This firm was headed not by Georges Méliès but by his brother Gaston, who was sent here to protect his interests after any number of Americans including Edison had stolen from him by "duping" his "Star Films" and distributing them in the United States without one cent of profit to their creator. The American Méliès firm produced, of all things, "Western" pictures; their principal players were William Clifford, Mildred Bracken, and Edith Storey, whom they had "borrowed" from Vitagraph. If noth-

[3] For Laemmle, see John Drinkwater, *The Life and Adventures of Carl Laemmle* (Putnam, 1931), and Laemmle's "From the Inside," *Saturday Evening Post*, (Aug. 27, Sept. 3, and Sept. 10, 1927). *Upton Sinclair Presents William Fox*, published by the author at Los Angeles in 1933, contains some information about Fox's life and personality but very little about his films. Sinclair's primary interest is in how Fox was wronged by the money masters.

ing needs to be said of these films, something does, most emphatically, need to be said of Georges Méliès, who, although he never
came to America, profoundly influenced both Porter and Griffith
and through them the whole course of American film-making.

Méliès was the first real artist of the screen. His career has been
described in detail elsewhere,[4] and the details belong to the French
rather than the American film; here I can do little more than indicate the character of his work and assess his influence.

Méliès began, like the Lumières, by photographing actualities,
and it is said that he got the idea for the wonderful transformations with which his films abound when his camera jammed one
day while he was photographing a street scene, so that when the
picture was developed a bus seemed to have changed into a hearse.
But since he was a magician and a theatrical producer, he must
surely have hit upon transformations shortly even if this accident
had not occurred. His famous studio at Montreuil set the pattern
for film studios throughout the world, and his repertoire ultimately included the whole stock-in-trade of the film tricksters—
"double exposure, stop motion, fast and slow motion, animation,
fades, dissolves," etc.[5] "Artificially arranged scenes," he called his
pictures—he was making something happen for the purpose of
photographing it, or, at his best, bringing it into being by photographing it—and they were "scenes" in the theater sense, one following another as in the case of a play and shot from a stationary
camera at eye-level. For all that, Méliès was the Walt Disney of
the early cinema, and he used his camera not to reproduce reality
but to create a world of illusion. Machines fascinated him as did
magic, and his pictures are full of weird contraptions, some of
which startlingly anticipated the electronic monstrosities of today,
but show girls pop out even from the stars of heaven to remind

[4] Most elaborately in Maurice Bessy and Lo Duca, *Georges Méliès,
Mage; et "Mes Mémoires" par Méliès* (Paris, Prisma, 1945). See also Jacobs,
The Rise of the American Film, and Fulton, *Motion Pictures*.

[5] Griffith and Mayer, *The Movies*, 6.

us that he was after all a Frenchman. In *Merry Frolics of Satan* there are dancing girls in hell. In *The Conquest of the Pole* the scientist's machine travels through very literal, animated signs of the zodiac and finally rides the axel of the Pole itself. There is no denying that Méliès *thought* in terms of the theater, calling attention to the importance of Bluebeard's key not by giving a close-up of it, as Griffith was to do, but by making the article itself a dozen times as large as it would have been in life. For all that, he often *functioned* in terms of the cinema, overprinting the end of each scene on the beginning of the next, and, as Kracauer has accurately observed, although "he did not take advantage of the camera's ability to record and reveal the physical world, he increasingly created his illusions with the aid of techniques peculiar to the medium."

Méliès' early films photographed magic tricks he had created on the stage. He also made pictures like *The Dreyfus Affair* and *The Coronation of Edward VII,* reconstructing contemporary events; but he did not really find his way until he produced *Cinderella* (1899), in twenty scenes, totaling 410 feet of film. He went on to *Faust, Robinson Crusoe, The Arabian Nights, Little Red Riding Hood,* and much besides, but his most famous film was *A Trip to the Moon* (1902)—825 feet long—based on a story by Jules Verne and satirizing the pretensions of professors and scientific societies while simultaneously appealing to man's sense of wonder in the face of an unexplored universe.[6] *The Impossible Voyage* (1904) was more elaborate—it ran 1,233 feet and cost $7,500—but it was much less successful, for by this time public interest had shifted to a more realistic type of film. Méliès continued production until the war put him out of business in 1914, after which he was for a time nearly destitute, but he was rescued and petted by film *aficionados* until he died in 1938. He was a man of great humor and *élan vital,* and his films are still wonderful to see though sometimes

[6] See Fulton's full and careful description of *A Trip to the Moon* in his *Motion Pictures,* 36–43.

hard to follow. The highest tribute we can pay him is to say that he developed a mechanical art, and made the mechanics themselves foster a sense of wonder.

I have said that he influenced Edwin S. Porter, and Porter was the Edison Company's great gift to the screen. He began as a mechanic and general handyman,[7] became a cameraman, and first revealed his gift for picture-making when he made *The Life of an American Fireman* in 1902. The picture is patchwork, for Porter used the stock shots of fire equipment, etc., that he found in the Edison vaults and photographed only what they didn't have. It opens on a picture of a fire chief dreaming of his wife and baby, who are shown in a "balloon," not by means of crosscutting. Next comes a close-up of a fire-alarm box; a hand moves into the picture and gives the alarm. The firemen are now shown swinging into action at the station, and from this point we intercut freely between the woman and child in the burning house and the fire engines dashing to the rescue. It is true that Porter misses some opportunities and displays a certain lack of imagination in depicting the actual rescue,[8] and for this reason *The Life of an American Fireman* is not a very interesting film to watch today. In its time it was very startling.

But *The Great Train Robbery,* which came along only a year later, *is* still an exciting film, for much of the essential screen syntax can be illustrated from it. The attack on the telegraph operator, the holdup of the passengers on the train, the escape of the bandits with the engine, their pursuit and capture, the Western dance-hall scenes, the little girl who comes to the station with her father's lunch to find him tied up on the floor—all this makes up a much more varied dish than anything that had been seen before. The interiors are stagy and all shot from the same angle, but

[7] See the sketch of Porter's career, *National Cyclopaedia of American Biography,* XXX, 407–408.
[8] See Fulton, *Motion Pictures,* 50–51.

there is considerable fluidity in the outdoor scenes, where the camera is not only mounted on a moving train but even "pans" to follow the bandits down the grade from the railroad tracks and into the woods. *The Great Train Robbery* was the *Birth of a Nation* of the early film days. It gave the movies a new lease on life just as the first novelty was wearing out, and revealed fascinating glimpses of new, unexplored possibilities. For years it remained the most famous of all films, and new motion-picture theaters (then springing up like mushrooms all over America) often used it as their opening attraction.[9]

How well Porter understood what he had created is something of a question. His aesthetic sensitiveness was never equal to his mechanical skill. He used contrast and parallel construction in two 1905 films, *The Ex-Convict* and *The Kleptomaniac,* which were impressively described by Lewis Jacobs in 1939.[10] I have not seen *The Ex-Convict,* but Jacobs' description of *The Kleptomaniac,* which was probably made from the Edison catalog rather than from the film, is considerably more interesting than the picture.

Méliès' influence upon Porter appears clearly in *Uncle Tom's Cabin* (1903) and *The Dream of a Rarebit Fiend* (1906), which was probably suggested by Winsor McCay's cartoons, but there is nothing in either film which suggests the creator of *The Great Train Robbery. Uncle Tom's Cabin* is a "primitive" of great charm, but it reverts completely to Méliès' "scenic" method, and it lacks Méliès technical bravura. It is developed in terms of a series of tableaux, without even an attempt at continuity. Topsy dashes in without an introduction and goes straight into a jig. The boats on the river (wholly unconnected with Mrs. Stowe's story) are children's toys. St. Clair is killed in a saloon brawl while defending

---

[9] Fulton, *ibid.,* 51–57, gives a detailed analysis of *The Great Train Robbery.*

[10] *The Rise of the American Film,* 46–48. Chapter V of this work is excellent on the social consciousness in early American films. Chapter IX contains interesting material on the pre–World War I moral outlook.

Uncle Tom, and Marks shoots Simon Legree. Uncle Tom, dying, sees visions of Lincoln and John Brown in "balloons."[11]

The Dream of a Rarebit Fiend is much more cinematic. At times the audience sees the swaying world through the hero's disturbed eyes, a device which was considered startlingly new when Murnau used it in *The Last Laugh* in 1925. Yet when the rarebit fiend steps out of his room for a moment the camera does not go with him; instead it focuses on the empty space until he comes back into it.

In 1911, Porter left Edison to found his own firm, Rex. One of his first Rex pictures, *By the Light of the Moon,* was done entirely in silhouette. At the foundation of Famous Players he became Zukor's principal director, directing all of Pauline Frederick's early films and some of Mary Pickford's. He died at seventy-one, after a long period of contented retirement, on April 30, 1941.

Except for Porter, the Edison Company contributed little to screen progress. They did, however, have some attractive players: Mary Fuller, whom we shall meet again; Miriam Nesbitt and her husband Marc McDermott; Mabel Trunnelle and Herbert Prior, one of the first husband-and-wife teams in domestic comedy; and others.

Biograph must be mainly considered in the next chapter in connection with D. W. Griffith, but it should be understood that the Mack Sennett "slapstick" comedies (generally, in this period, "split" reels)[12] began with Biograph; *Comrades* (released March 13, 1911) was the first film Sennett directed, and his *One-Round O'Brien* (1912), with Fred Mace, was so popular that sequels were called for. Sennett began as an actor, although he was never a very

[11] In A. Nicholas Vardac, *Stage to Screen: Theatrical Method from Garrick to Griffith* (Harvard University Press, 1949), stills from Porter's *Uncle Tom's Cabin* are placed side by side with stills from William A. Brady's 1901 stage production. They are virtually indistinguishable.

[12] It should perhaps be explained that this term applies to a reel (1,000 feet) of motion pictures which contains more than one subject.

good one. He was never able to convince Griffith that policemen were funny, and though he did direct Mabel Normand in *The Diving Girl* (August 21, 1911), the real development of his "bathing girl" comedy belonged to a later period. He left Biograph in the summer of 1912, when the bookmakers Kessel and Bauman agreed to back his "Keystone Comedies" on the Mutual program—the trade-mark was borrowed from the Pennsylvania Railroad—and he took Mace, Ford Sterling, and Mabel Normand with him. They went to California, set up their camera within thirty minutes after arriving at the railroad station, and turned out 140 pictures the first year. Later Sennett was associated with Griffith again on the Triangle program; later still he made some of his best pictures, including such masterpieces as *East Lynne with Variations, Uncle Tom without the Cabin,* and *Salome vs. Shenendoah,* as "Mack Sennett Comedies" for Paramount; although slapstick farces in general are still popularly spoken of as "Keystones," actually Sennett had to leave this brand-name behind him when he broke with Triangle.

Sennett's work has already been described so well, first by Gilbert Seldes and later by James Agee,[13] that it is not necessary for me to consider it at length here. According to Sennett himself, he derived his inspiration from the early Pathé films ("I have been posing for many years as the inventor of slapstick motion-picture

[13] For Seldes, see especially *The Seven Lively Arts,* originally published by Harper, 1924, and in an enlarged edition by The Sagamore Press in 1957. James Agee's "Comedy's Greatest Era," originally published in *Life* (Sept. 3, 1949), has been reprinted in *Agee on Film* (McDowell, Obelensky, 1958) and in Daniel Talbot, *Film: An Anthology* (Simon and Schuster, 1959). For Mack Sennett, see his autobiography, *King of Comedy,* written with Cameron Shipp (Doubleday, 1954), and Gene Fowler's book about him, *Father Goose* (Covici-Friede, 1934). See, further, Buster Keaton and Charles Samuels, *My Wonderful World of Slapstick* (Doubleday, 1960); Harold Lloyd and Wesley W. Stout, *An American Comedy* (Longmans, 1928); and John McCabe, *Mr. Laurel and Mr. Hardy* (Doubleday, 1961). Finally, see John Montgomery's comprehensive account of *Comedy Films* (London, Allen & Unwin, 1954).

comedy and it is about time I confessed the truth. It was those Frenchmen who invented slapstick and I imitated them") and the Bowery burlesque:

> The round, fat girls in nothing much doing their bumps and grinds, the German-dialect comedians, and especially the cops and tramps with their bed slats and bladders appealed to me as being funny people. Their approach to life was earthy and understandable. They whaled the daylights out of pretension. They made fun of themselves and of the human race. They reduced convention, dogma, stuffed shirts, and Authority to nonsense, and then blossomed into pandemonium. . . . I especially enjoyed the reduction of Authority to absurdity, the notion that Sex could be funny, and the bold insults that were hurled at Pretension.

Sennett films were compounded of attractively diverse elements. There was a slight touch of madness about them—they defied both logic and gravity and hovered on the edge of fantasy— yet down to earth as they were, the girls who appeared in them glorified them with a touch of beauty. The result should have been a hodgepodge, but it was not, somehow; it was a world. How this was achieved was Sennett's secret, and this constitutes his final claim as an artist, for nobody else has ever been able to do it so well. The terrible punishments which his characters received and inflicted, for example, were saved from sadism by the exhilaration they exuded; you felt that the people on the screen—and you, for the moment—were superior to the hazards of life.

Vitagraph, a Brooklyn concern in which J. Stuart Blackton, Albert E. Smith, and William T. Rock held the controlling interest, has been neglected by film historians[14]—Norma Talmadge says the firm burned many of its negatives for lack of storage space— but it loomed very large in the lives of contemporary movie fans,

[14] The fullest account is in Albert E. Smith and Phil A. Koury, *Two Reels and a Crank* (Doubleday, 1952); cf. Smith's addendum in *Films in Review*, Vol. IV (1953), 232–35, and J. Stuart Blackton's "Yesterdays of Vitagraph," *Photoplay* (July, 1919). But the most intimate picture of life at

and by 1912–13, its profits were in the neighborhood of $1,250,000 a year. Next to Biograph, Vitagraph had the most impressive stock company, and it anticipated Biograph by several years in publicizing its players. I should say that the first real approach to the star system among the Patents companies was made at Essanay with the Broncho Billy pictures, which were produced and acted by G. M. Anderson, the "A" or "ay" of that concern (George K. Spoor was the "Ess"); not only was the name Broncho Billy generally a part of the name of the picture, but it became the custom to print a circled photograph of Mr. Anderson, with his name under it, in one corner of the poster. Vitagraph approached this, however, with the John Bunny comedies, generally directed by George D. Baker, which often carried such titles as *Bunny's Birthday, Bunny in Disguise,* and *Bunny Dips into Society.* The first great comic of the screen, Bunny (1863–1915) had had rather more success on the stage than most of the early film stars, having played Bottom in Annie Russell's production of *A Midsummer Night's Dream,* and when he first approached Vitagraph they were very doubtful of their ability to use him, simply because they did not think they could pay him what he was worth. He agreed to start at $40 per week; according to Norma Talmadge, he rose to $200, thence to a percentage, being the only Vitagraph player to be so treated. "This is my work," he told an interviewer, after he had established himself in the new medium. "Here every day is a first night. It keeps you alive, stimulates your imagination, and compels a constant thinking out of new ideas."

How good was Bunny? Not much of his work is available for reinspection, but what I have seen leaves me with the impression that he was an artist of considerable gifts. "When Mr. Bunny laughs," observed the London *Spectator,* "people from San Fran-

Vitagraph is in the reminiscences of Norma Talmadge, "Close-Ups," serialized in *Saturday Evening Post* (Mar. 12, 26, Apr. 9, May 7, 21, and June 25, 1927).

cisco to Stepney Green laugh with him. When Mr. Bunny frowns, every kingdom of the earth is contracted in one brow of woe. When he smells a piece of Gorgonzola cheese there is no doubt whatever that his nose has been seriously offended. His despair is incredible. His grief is unendurable. His wrath is apoplectic. His terror is the terror of a whole army."

His materials were generally quite unliterary. It is true that in 1913, Vitagraph sent him to England to do a *Pickwick Papers* and that in 1914 he made a picture of Ellis Parker Butler's *Pigs Is Pigs*. He sometimes appeared in minor roles in serious pictures; he was, for example, the Jos Sedley in Vitagraph's big production of *Vanity Fair* at the end of 1911. But in the typical comedies which he made his own, he simply devoted himself to high jinks, often in association, for purposes of contrast, with Flora Finch, "in all her Scrawny, Skinny Majesty," as she was later billed when, after his death, she tried a starring career of her own. Like "Fatty" Arbuckle a little later, Bunny was fond of disguising himself as a woman, and they both did it extremely well; in *Bunny's Dilemma* our hero became a maid to avoid meeting a woman visitor and then found himself greatly attracted to her. There was a great deal of flirting and other extramarital shenanigans in the Bunny films; there was also considerable drinking and smoking (this was also true of the domestic comedies produced by Mr. and Mrs. Sidney Drew with which Vitagraph found another profitable "line" after they had lost Bunny); in this respect they conformed to the Age of Innocence pattern less than one might have expected. In spite of his enormous bulk, however, Bunny had considerable charm as well as great vitality, and those who worked with him generally remembered him affectionately.[15]

The great dramatic stars at Vitagraph were Maurice Costello

[15] There are many pictures of Bunny in an article by Henry W. Lanier, "The Coquelin of the Movies," *World's Work*, Vol. XXIX (1915), 566–77. See also Joyce Kilmer's tribute in *The Circus* (Doran, 1921).

and Florence Turner. Costello, who may be identified for a later generation as Dolores Costello's father—both Dolores and her sister Helen played with him as children in Vitagraph films—was the first great matinee idol of the screen, and Florence Turner was "The Vitagraph Girl" before anybody knew her name. Costello won the first popularity contest conducted by *The Motion Picture Story Magazine* in 1912 with 430,816 votes. I myself was mad about him in those days; when I recently, somewhat shamefacedly, mentioned my enthusiasm for him to Zena Keefe, who played with him, she replied, a bit reproachfully, I thought, "Well, he *was* very good, you know." So I think he was, not only in the big roles, like Sydney Carton in *A Tale of Two Cities* (1911), which roused Rex Ingram's interest in motion pictures and caused the British press to speak of Costello in the same breath with Martin Harvey, but in hosts of now completely forgotten one-reelers. Obscene as I find the kind of psychological slang now in vogue, I suppose it would not be too far beyond the mark to speak of Costello as a "father image." Already a mature man when success came to him (he had been on the stage in stock), Costello did not go in for "sex appeal." Neither did he try to overwhelm you with his athletic prowess, and I am sure he would have felt nothing but disgust for the "sullen slobber" kind of thing, as it has been called, associated with some later screen idols. He may sometimes have been slightly conscious of his charm, but there was always a relaxed friendliness in his exercise of it.

Florence Turner was, I suppose, a more serious artist, and a more ambitious one, and nobody in my generation could have had any difficulty in understanding the young Norma Talmadge's enthusiasm for her even before she herself had become a Vitagrapher: "I would rather have touched the hem of her skirt than to have shaken hands with Saint Peter." Miss Turner's ambition finally proved her undoing, for she left Vitagraph early in 1913 and went to England, with Lawrence Trimble as her director, to produce independently. Her films were at first very successful, and Rachael Low, the authoritative historian of the British film, speaks of them with great enthusiasm,[16] but the war intervened and brought hardship and failure. Miss Turner returned to America, but she never regained her old position on the screen.

From 1907 on at Vitagraph, however, she played everything from Lucie in *A Tale of Two Cities* and Elaine in *Lancelot and Elaine* down to broadest farce. She loved "mugging" and never considered it beneath her; this, no doubt, was one of the reasons why she was so successful in English music halls. In her serious work she never overacted, however; unsatisfactory though *The Deerslayer* is as a motion picture, I was much impressed, when I saw it recently, by the fine restraint with which she played Hetty. In 1911 she did a solo performance as a discarded harem favorite whose life ends in murder and suicide in a one-reeler called *Jealousy;* this of course antedated Chaplin's solo film *One A.M.* by a number of years.[17] Miss Turner had enthusiasm and a quick, eager mind which addressed itself to every aspect of film-making. When I met her in 1945, only a year before she died, I asked her, "Do you remember a film called *The Closed Door?*" This was an oppressively moral Vitagraph of 1910 in which Miss Turner played an unfaithful wife who ran off with Leo Delaney from her husband (Maurice Costello) and her child (Adele de Garde). I can still see the radiant smile on her face as she looked up adoringly at

[16] See especially her third volume, 1914–18, in *The History of the British Film.*

[17] In 1915, Miss Turner appeared in a one-reel MinA, *Florence Turner Impersonates Film Favorites.* Here a slavey falls asleep in the kitchen and dreams she is a film star. There follow impersonations of Ford Sterling, Mabel Normand, Broncho Billy, and Sarah Bernhardt in the death scene of *Queen Elizabeth.* In 1914, King Baggott appeared in a two-reel Imp, *Shadows,* in which he played all ten characters—mother, son, uncle, merchant, Chinese servant, villain, prostitute, jailor, policeman, and detective—with two or three characters sometimes appearing on the screen together.

Delaney when they passed down the street together, and I can see her too, broken and white-haired, as she returned on the eve of her daughter's wedding to be self-righteously shown the door in one of Costello's most theatrical gestures. It was of course the *East Lynne* motif, which was used again and again in early films, but this time it had not come from *East Lynne* directly. "Do I *remember* it?" Miss Turner exclaimed in answer to my question. "I *wrote* it. I went to see *Madame X* one night, and the next morning I came down to the studio and said to Mr. Smith, 'I have a *wonderful* idea for a picture!'" She was a lovely, idealistic, and unselfish woman, and such she remained, through good fortune and bad, to the end.

The Vitagrapher who came closest to her was probably Helen Gardner, but she left six months or so before Miss Turner did and also took on independent production. Because she began with *Cleopatra* and went on to such works as *The Wife of Cain*, "An Original Drama of the Primal," *A Sister to Carmen*, and *A Princess of Bagdad*, she is often called the screen's first "vamp." I doubt that she planned it that way, for she too was an idealist, and her predilection for this type of character was probably due to her fancying herself as a kind of Bernhardt of the screen. "Every one of these pictures contains an idea, and is builded upon a motive," proclaimed one of her many many display advertisements in the *Dramatic Mirror*. "THERE IS SOMETHING DOING IN AMERICA AS WELL AS IN ITALY, GOOD AMERICAN CITIZENS." Her venture must have thrived for a time, but by the end of 1914 both she and her producer-director Charles L. Gaskill were back with Vitagraph, where they remained until the next fall, when it was announced that she had gone to Universal, and at this point I lose track of her. I shall never forget a dreadful Vitagraph two-reeler of February, 1915, *The Still Small Voice*, in which she played a dumb, half-witted girl who committed murder and then killed herself over the ravages of conscience; I can still see her roaming—as it seemed, endlessly—through the woods, searching for a place to hang herself, a dreadful exhibition on the part of a star who for me always had considerable glamour.

In speaking of Miss Gardner in connection with Florence Turner, I do not mean to slight that fine actress Julia Swayne Gordon, who survived into feature pictures, appearing in both *Wings* and *Monsieur Beaucaire*. But Mrs. Gordon was primarily a character woman, and she often played the older roles for which her great dignity and distinction of presence so eminently qualified her. Vachel Lindsay praised her as Julia Ward Howe in *The Battle Hymn of the Republic;* she was equally impressive in *Rock of Ages*. Ralph Ince was the Lincoln of the *Battle Hymn;* Ince specialized in Lincoln as William Humphrey did in Napoleon; the latter, who hailed from the Castle Square Stock Company in Boston, is said to have made his first connection with Vitagraph because the company wanted his fine collection of Napoleonic costumes. They were all used in the oddly titled *Napoleon Bonaparte and the Empress Josephine of France* and *Napoleon, the Man of Destiny,* both released in April, 1909. Humphrey was the Napoleon and Mrs. Gordon (she was then still Miss Julia Swayne) the Josephine. In 1912, Clara Kimball Young came along with her first husband James Young, who was director as well as actor; she was a very beautiful girl in those days, and she made her first appearance as Anne Boleyn in *Cardinal Wolsey,* in which Tefft Johnson was the Henry VIII, Julia Swayne Gordon the Catherine of Aragon, and Hal Reid (Wallace Reid's father) the Wolsey. Many years later I told Mrs. Young I had seen her in her first film; she was not able to remember it, but she admitted that it had been made in 1912, and she seemed so appalled by the date that I felt very rude for having mentioned it. That same year Ralph Ince brought his sister-in-law to the studio, a fresh, distractingly pretty little slip of a girl named Anita Stewart, and Vitagraph found just the right showcase for her personality in *The Wood Violet*. Another little girl who has already been mentioned, Norma Talmadge, had arrived two years before. She made her first important

47

appearance with Florence Turner in *A Dixie Mother,* and she was the girl who held Carton's hand on the way to the guillotine in *A Tale of Two Cities.* Norma learned film-acting rather slowly, and her ability was not highly regarded at first, but Costello believed in her and championed her. She was not the kind of person to forget such a service; when in 1927 she produced *Camille* she gave Costello one of the best roles of his later years as the elder Duval.

Vitagraph even had the first dog star, Larry Trimble's beautiful collie, "Jean the Vitagraph Dog." Trimble was a wizard with animals; I have heard it said that to know him was to have no difficulty in crediting what has been written about Saint Francis of Assisi and the Wolf of Gubbio; after his picture career was over, he carved another for himself as a trainer of "seeing-eye" dogs. As Miss Turner remarked, Jean did not do tricks; she was simply an actress! She appeared in innumerable Vitagraphs; she even shared with Bunny the distinction of having some of them carry her name—*Jean the Matchmaker, Jean Goes Foraging,* etc.—and when she reproduced herself she was given part of a reel to display her proud family. Vitagraph's idea of a very poetic final fade-out in those days was Jean silhouetted against the sunset on a seaside rock, and Miss Turner told me a delightful anecdote of what happened one day when she, Trimble, Charles Kent, and others were out on location making such a scene. "Do you suppose," Kent asked Trimble, "that you could get that dog to do something you told her *not* to do?" "I don't know," replied Trimble. "I never thought of that. Let's try it." Then he turned to her. "Jean," he said, "go over and sit on that rock, and when I call you, *don't come.*" Jean went over and sat on the rock, and Trimble proceeded to wear out his lungs shouting to her. She did not come, and she did not even condescend to turn her head. Then Trimble changed his tone. "Jean," he said, "come here to me, *and this time I mean it.*" Jean trotted obediently to his side.

Essanay and Selig were Chicago firms, though both began

producing in California also at a very early date. Essanay's great Chicago star was Francis X. Bushman, who with Beverly Bayne later formed one of the screen's legendary teams of "great lovers." Bushman's last big role was as Messala in the 1925 *Ben Hur,* though he has appeared occasionally since then in sound films, still looking very much as he always did—and he might have appeared more frequently if he had not preferred his own self-respect to the kind of kowtowing that is favored in the film industry today. Bushman always did have a mind of his own; it is said that he broke with Essanay when he was asked to "support" Viola Allen when she was brought in from the stage for *The White Sister.* Like Bunny, he came to films because he loved them, becoming a fan while he was still in stock, and describing pictures as "the only practical Esperanto that is understood by the whole world" and a greater influence for good than press or pulpit. They keep men "from the saloon," he declared, "the pool parlor and the cabaret and other forms of amusement that are not agents for health or morals." He also believed that pictures would break down barriers between nations and make us realize "that we are all brothers of God's family." Such were the high hopes we had for the films in the early days. They turned out, alas! no better than the men who controlled them.

Gloria Swanson and Wallace Berry also began their careers at Essanay's Chicago studio, and of course Chaplin went to Essanay for a year after leaving Keystone. But perhaps the name one thinks of first of all in connection with Essanay is that of G. M. Anderson, who was born Max Aronson and became world-famous as Broncho Billy.

Anderson did not confine himself entirely to cowboy films. In 1911 he appeared as a prize fighter in *"Spike" Shannon's Last Fight;* in 1914 he was in a four-reeler, *The Good-for-Nothing,* wherein he impersonated both "a man of a large eastern metropolis and a man of the far and unsettled West"; in 1914–15 he appeared in a whole series of multiple-reel "mystery plays." Anderson is recorded as having established an Essanay studio at Niles, California, as early as the fall of 1908, and it is said that he got his screen name from a Peter B. Kyne story, "Broncho Billy and the Baby." But the earliest Broncho Billy film title recorded seems to be *Broncho Billy's Redemption,* which was released July 30, 1910.

He was a heavy-set, rather stolid actor, with amazing, white-gleaming eyes. He was not exactly a romantic figure, and at the beginning of his career as the first great cowboy hero of the screen, he could not even ride a horse. He himself says that he never became more than a fair rider, and he claimed even less for his marksmanship. Nevertheless his contemporaries loved him, and if I were ever tempted to forget it, I should have to recall the old German lady, mother of many children, who lived downstairs in my aunt's house on Sawyer Avenue. "Ach!" she would say as often as occasion warranted, "ich muss tonight nach der White Palace. Der Broncho Billy ist da. Ach, der ist zu schön!"

When you have to think up a story a week, it does not pay to be fussy about consistency, and Broncho Billy's admirers could never be quite sure which side of the law he was going to be on. In *Broncho Billy Reforms* (1913) he was an outlaw who refused to join his fellows in robbing a store kept by the local schoolteacher, and in *Why Broncho Billy Left Bear County* he not only reformed but got religion. In *Broncho Billy's Scheme* he was a medical man, but in *Broncho Billy's Mother* he was a "booze fighter" who shot up the town. In *"Alkali" Bests Broncho Billy* he was teamed with the diminutive Augustus Carney, who had a series of his own, and whose name had to be changed from "Alkali Ike" to "Universal Ike" when he deserted Essanay for Carl Laemmle. In *Broncho Billy's Conscience* he was even killed, but few of his followers can have entertained any real fears that he would turn out to have been "kilt entoirely." Anderson was probably most popular in the films in which he exemplified the spirit of renunciation, like *Broncho Billy's Christmas Spirit,* where he sacrificed his horse for a destitute family. Frequently he gave up a girl, and then we might see

SCENE IX (*Continued*)—THE TRANSFORMATION.   CLOSING TABLEAU.

Jack and the Beanstalk. Copyright, 1902.

We send this sheet of half tones to our customers for the purpose of illustrating the excellent photographic and spectacular qualities of our great moving picture production, JACK AND THE BEANSTALK. The accompanying pictures were taken from the film itself, and, therefore, must readily demonstrate the perfection of this production from a photographic standpoint. We offer this production as positively the greatest motion picture that we have ever turned out. When selecting a special film as a headline attraction to your entertainment REMEMBER this fairy story is known to every child throughout the civilized world. It has been printed in every language, read in every nursery, and appeals to every boy and girl, because they have recently read it and dreamed of it. It appeals to every man and woman, because it awakens memories of their childhood. Space does not permit us to enter into a lengthy description of JACK AND THE BEANSTALK. It is the most popular fairy tale extant, and the story is known to every one. The subject has been carefully studied and every scene posed with a view to following as closely as possible the accepted version of JACK AND THE BEANSTALK. The story is illustrated complete, from the time of the trading of the cow for the hatful of beans until Jack scrambles down the beanstalk into his mother's yard with the captured hen that laid the golden eggs, the bags of the giant's gold, and cuts down the beanstalk and kills the giant.

Sold in one length only. Supplement No. 150 contains complete description.

Length of complete film, 625 feet. Code *Unmeasured.* Class A. $93.75.

JACK AND THE BEANSTALK offers great opportunities for color effects. The price for coloring the film complete, including background, figures and all details, is $140.00 extra, and the price for coloring the figures only is $85.00 extra.

Page 4 of a four-page flyer for Edwin S. Porter's *Jack and the Beanstalk* (1902). Notice that the picture might be had either plain or colored. Color was applied by hand in each copy; with film running sixteen exposures to the foot, this must have been a tedious process. The NOTICE on page 1 proclaims that "this film is sold subject to the restriction that it shall not be used for duplicating or printing other films from it" and that "all infringements of the Edison copyrighted films will be prosecuted at once and stopped by injunction." But such warnings were often disregarded.

These frames from *At the Altar* (Feb. 25, 1909) illustrate Griffith's use of the close-up. Griffith also used crosscutting in this film, the third such use which George Pratt of Eastman House has so far been able to establish, the earliest instance being in *The Fatal Hour* (Aug. 18, 1908).

PICTURE 2

Florence Lawrence was at her radiant best in *Lady Helen's Escapade* (Biograph, 1909).

PICTURE 5

orence Turner, wearing Lucie Manette's
onde wig from *A Tale of Two Cities* (1911).
bove left and below center are from *Lancelot
·d Elaine*; above center and below left, *A Dixie
other*; left center, *Jealousy*; all the others, *A
ile of Two Cities*. From *The Motion Picture
ory Magazine*, Vol. III, No. 2 (Mar., 1912).

cture 6 *(right)*, Maurice Costello as Sydney ▶
arton, with William Shea as Mr. Lorry, in
itagraph's *A Tale of Two Cities.*

cture 7 *(below)*, Darnay asks Dr. Manette for
ucie's hand (Charles Kent, Leo Delaney, Flor-
ce Turner). Note the stage-type garden scen-
y and the painted background.

Two early covers of *The Motion Picture Story Magazine:* Picture 8 *(left),* Vol. II, No. 6 (July, 1912); Picture 9 *(right),* Vol. IV, No. 11 (Dec., 1912). The cover at the right shows Mary Pickford in a scene from *The Informer,* a D. W. Griffith Biograph film.

Picture 10 *(above),* a scene from Vitagraph's 1909 production of *A Midsumm* *Night's Dream,* showing Gladys Hulette as Puck. Picture 11 *(below),* Char) Kent as Christ saves Julia Swayne Gordon as Mary Magdalene in one of Vi(graph's early religious films, *Tho Your Sins Be As Scarlet* (1911).

PICTURES 10, 11

Helen Gardner as Cleopatra in one of the earliest (1912) and most elaborate of American "features," as advertised in *The New York Dramatic Mirror*.

him gazing in upon her happiness with his rival from the wrong side of a lighted window and trudging out into the night with his traps as sadly as Chaplin ever walked down the lonesome road.[18]

Selig is best remembered for its features, the three-reelers *Cinderella, The Two Orphans,* and *The Coming of Columbus;* for the first of many productions of *The Spoilers* which opened the Strand Theater, New York, in 1914, and permitted William Farnum and Thomas Santschi to set a standard for screen pugilism which endured for years (Colonel Selig said he could have retired on the profits from this film alone); for the first serial, *The Adventures of Kathlyn,* which will be considered later; and for the early Tom Mix films. Mabel Taliaferro was brought from the stage to play Cinderella; Vachel Lindsay praised this film as a prime example of fairy beauty on the screen. But *The Two Orphans* was a very crowded picture, and *The Coming of Columbus* seems to have been made in order to photograph the Columbus caravels which had been built for the World's Columbian Exposition in 1893 and anchored in Lake Michigan off Jackson Park ever since. Kate Claxton, who had done the play so many times on the stage, was consulted for *The Two Orphans* as Griffith was later to consult her for *Orphans of the Storm.* Kathlyn Williams was Selig's big feminine star, famous for her scenes with wild animals in her serial days, and for many years thereafter as a *grande dame* in heaven knows how many "society" films. They also had Hobart Bosworth and, until he was murdered in California by a crazed Japanese gardener, the director Francis Boggs, whom some old-timers rate very high.[19]

Lubin was a Philadelphia concern with the Liberty Bell for its trade-mark. Sigmund ("Pop") Lubin, a kindly man, was long a

[18] There is an interesting but not entirely accurate discussion of Broncho Billy in Ezra Goodman, *The Fifty-Year Decline and Fall of Hollywood* (Simon and Schuster, 1961), 340–44.

[19] See Hobart Bosworth, "The Picture Forty Niners," *Photoplay* (Dec., 1915); William N. Selig, "Cutting Back," *Photoplay* (Feb., 1920).

power in motion pictures, but though his films were very enjoyable in their time, it is hard to isolate any separate, distinguishing qualities as one seeks to describe them in retrospect. The ones I remember best teamed Arthur Johnson and Florence Lawrence. Johnson, as we shall see, began with Biograph; Miss Lawrence had played with Edison, Vitagraph, Biograph, and Imp before coming to Lubin; she was the original "'Biograph Girl," but the company had dispensed with her services upon learning that she and her husband Harry Salter had sounded out Essanay on a possible opening. Laemmle delightedly grabbed her, announcing his acquisition in the trade journals with advertisements which proclaimed that "The Biograph Girl is now an IMP." Whether it was he or another who started the story that she had been killed by a streetcar in St. Louis, he certainly played it for its full publicity value, so that Miss Lawrence had to make a personal appearance in that city, to prove that she was alive and to be mobbed by her fans with such ardor that she was nearly killed in earnest. She later went back to Laemmle under the Victor banner, but Johnson stayed on with Lubin, now generally playing with Lottie Briscoe, until he died at forty in 1916.

The cause of Johnson's death was given as tuberculosis, but alcoholism was well known to have played its part in his collapse. Miss Lawrence's end was even more tragic, for though she lived until the end of 1938, she took her own life. In 1915 she was badly injured in a studio fire, from which she might easily have escaped if she had not turned back to help a fellow player, and after which she was first paralyzed and then, for a number of years, invalided. She worked again—with Florence Turner she was a member of the M-G-M stock company at the time of her death—but she had no more real opportunities. Salter died in 1920, and two later marriages were unsuccessful; finally she developed a bone disease. Florence Lawrence was not exactly a beauty, but she was a vivid, gallant little person—a Canadian girl, she had been on the stage as "Baby Flo" since her earliest years—and she was the last kind of person one would have thought a promising subject for suicide. Only a few days before her death she sent a photograph to a collector who had requested it. "I only wish," she wrote, "that the producers thought as highly of me as you do."[20]

Kalem was founded in June, 1907, by George Kleine, Samuel Long, and Frank J. Marion, and the name formed out of a combination of their initials. Kleine soon withdrew, leaving Long and Marion, both of whom had come from Biograph, in charge. Kalem's trade-mark was a sunburst with the name "KALEM" in the middle in white letters, and after a time they ended their films with a shot of the sunburst revolving about its center while a white pencil wrote the word "Kalem" across the screen. This anticipated the Mutual trade-mark showing the rapidly revolving hands of a clock with the motto "Mutual Movies Make Time Fly," and I was always annoyed when projectionists cut it short. According to their gifted leading woman Gene Gauntier they had no studio for the first three years, depending upon exteriors exclusively. In the winter of 1908–1909 they sent their director Sidney Olcott and a company of players to Jacksonville, Florida, where they produced *A Florida Feud, The Seminole's Vengeance, Hunted through the Everglades, In Old Florida,* and many other local color films, often completing a picture in a day. Yet *A Florida Feud* was widely praised for its photography, and in Chicago it increased Kalem's business by 1,000 per cent.

Gene Gauntier credited Olcott with psychic powers and a virtually hypnotic control over his actors; however this may be, there can be no question that in turning to locale pictures the Kalem forces had found their métier. It was not that they neglected standard literature, for Miss Gauntier, who did most of their scenarios, was a young lady of literary tastes. In 1924, she said that she had appeared in some five hundred films, of which she herself had

[20] See Adela Rogers St. John, "The Return of Florence Lawrence," *Photoplay* (May, 1921); Frederick James Smith, "Unwept, Unhonored, and Unfilmed," *Photoplay* (July, 1924).

written all except half a dozen. When you are sometimes required to turn out three scenarios during a single day, it is a great help to have standard literature to draw on. Miss Gauntier began by drawing on *Tom Sawyer*. She adapted *As You Like It, Evangeline, Hiawatha,* and *The Scarlet Letter;* since the censors required, in the last-named instance, that Hester and Dimmesdale must be married, one wonders what the story can possibly have been about. She got a film out of *Way Down East* and turned *Polly of the Circus* into *Dolly the Circus Queen.* But you are less likely to remember Kalem for these masterpieces than for such films as *Maggie the Dock Rat,* which was set on the New York waterfront. With *The Sponge Fishers of Cuba* and many other pictures they furnished a printed lecture, and the *Dramatic Mirror* complained bitterly that so few New York theaters made use of this service. In 1913 they did a picture called *The Invaders,* about the Wyoming Rustlers' War of 1892, and in 1914 there was a four-reel *Wolfe, or the Conquest of Quebec,* said to have been filmed in the authentic locations. There were also a good many Civil War films, including a whole series on *The Adventures of the Girl Spy,* which ran on for two years until Miss Gauntier got so sick of it that she married herself off and ended the war.

In 1910 the Kalem people invaded Ireland. The first trip produced only one-reelers, but they returned the following June, and this time they came out with productions of such works as *The Colleen Bawn* and *Arrah-na-Pogue,* by Dion Boucicault, which were very beautiful pictorially. The O'Kalems, as they were now facetiously called, had hardly got back when they were hustled off again, in December, for the Near East; it was on this trip that they made, in Egypt and Palestine, the most famous of all Kalem films, the five-reel *From the Manger to the Cross,* which ran for a generation and more and was enthusiastically praised by both Dean Inge and the Bishop of London, who thought it superior to the Oberammergau Passion Play. The idea for this film came to Gene Gauntier in delirium while she was recovering from sunstroke—

the front office had originally forbidden the company to make a picture about Christ—and even though, as she says, it became "a heavy factor in making millionaires of the Kalem officials," the company's attitude toward it remained so equivocal that both Olcott and Miss Gauntier left Kalem. Viewed today, the crowd scenes in *From the Manger to the Cross* seem to lack focus, but those involving a smaller number of persons are for the most part pleasantly grouped, and the very absence of elaborate staging makes the Crucifixion seem more stark and terrible. Gene Gauntier played the Madonna with the sure, quiet intensity which was her hallmark, and the British actor R. Henderson-Bland was both moved and moving as the Christ. Besides being an actor, he was a very minor poet of strong mystical tendencies—Olcott engaged him over the telephone (heaven only knows why!); there was something odd about the making of this film from the beginning—and there can be no question that for him, and in lesser degree for the other members of the company also, *From the Manger to the Cross* was a genuine spiritual experience. It was surely a bitter piece of irony that within a few years he should have become one of the great military heroes of World War I; perhaps the extraordinary naïveté which lay alongside his extraordinary sincerity made it easier for him to make the necessary adjustment.[21]

[21] Consider the amazing climax of Henderson-Bland's account of his meeting with Queen Mary when she attended a showing of *From the Manger to the Cross* upon its being reissued with sound in 1938: "The seal was put on the delightful informality of everything by a lady-in-waiting coming over and offering the Queen a cigarette which she smoked." He discussed the film first in *From Manger to Cross: The Story of the World-Famous Film of the Life of Jesus* (London, Hodder and Stoughton, 1922), later in his autobiography, *Actor—Soldier—Poet* (London, Heath Cranton, 1939). Gene Gauntier's autobiography, "Blazing the Trail," was serialized in *Woman's Home Companion*, issues of Oct., 1928, to Mar. 1929, inclusive. Sidney Olcott's career is covered by George Mitchell in *Films in Review*, Vol. V (1954), 175–81—note the letter of George Geltzer, p. 251. See, further, Gerald D. McDonald, "U. S. Filmmaking Abroad," *Films in Review,* Vol. V (1954), 257–62.

Sidney Olcott also directed the first *Ben Hur* (1907), which has considerable extrinsic if not intrinsic importance since it established the principle that literary works could no longer be filmed without payment and permission. The situation had hitherto been very fluid and contradictory. In 1907, Mark Twain gave his blessing to Vitagraph's production of *A Curious Dream;* two years later he even made a brief introductory appearance in Edison's production of *The Prince and the Pauper,* in which Cecil Spooner played both boys. But when Biograph filmed *The Death Disk* (1909), their advertisement did not even bother to mention him; neither did they mention Frank Norris when they issued *A Corner in Wheat,* nor, for that matter, did the *Dramatic Mirror* review name him. On *Ben Hur,* however, Harpers, Klaw and Erlanger, and the author's heirs tried a test case. Kalem fought it through to the Supreme Court, lost, and in 1911 was required to pay $25,000, which made *Ben Hur* the most expensive one-reel scenario in motion-picture history.

The Kalem Company was very rich in directorial talent. Besides Olcott, they brought forward such directors as Robert G. Vignola, George Melford, and Marshall Neilan, all of whom had noteworthy careers. Carlyle Blackwell and Jack J. Clark were accomplished leading men, while Ruth Roland and Helen Holmes were destined to signal success in serials. But the Kalem player best remembered today is the serene Alice Joyce, former artist's model, who began with them in 1910 and stayed for five years. Later she was a Vitagraph star; still later she played many and varied roles in both silent and sound films. She was in *Beau Geste;* she was Clara Bow's mother in *Dancing Mothers;* she supported George Arliss in the sound version of *The Green Goddess* and John McCormack in *Song of My Heart.*

The American branch of Pathé centered in Bound Brook, New Jersey. They had Paul Panzer, a good actor of German extraction who had been with Vitagraph; Charles Arling; Octavia Hand-worth for the society women; and a tiny, blue-eyed, vivacious blonde named Gwendolen Pates, who must surely have been one of the most charming ingénues of screen history. Gwendolen dropped out very early; I do not recall ever having seen her in more than one two-reeler, *The Great Steeplechase;* I have never seen her name in any film book, and I sometimes wonder whether I am the only person left on earth who remembers her. (When in 1912–13, *The Motion Picture Story Magazine* distributed twelve special colored portraits of outstanding players with the magazine, she was one of the twelve selected.)

But of course the Pathé people who contributed most to screen history were Max Linder and Pearl White. Miss White was the serial queen par excellence. She had an imperturbable, almost mask-like type of (artificial) blonde beauty; she was fearless, gay, and untroubled by inhibitions, and she was idolized in Europe, particularly in France; when the Spanish novelist Vicente Blasco-Ibáñez came to the United States after World War I to celebrate the triumph of his novel *The Four Horsemen of the Apocalypse,* she was high on the list of those he wished to meet.[22]

Linder was more important; since he was probably the first actor to develop a distinct motion-picture style, he was very important indeed; he even influenced Chaplin. Beginning in 1905, he never played in this country for Pathé, although Essanay did bring him over briefly in 1917, in an attempt to replace Chaplin, which attempt was a disastrous failure. But in the early days when the French film was dominant his pictures went all over the world. His screen character was that of a French *boulevardier,* complete with cane, spats, silk hat, and all the other accouterments;

[22] Pearl White's *Just Me* (Doran, 1916) must have been the first autobiography ever published by a film star; unfortunately it is completely unreliable. For the facts of her colorful career, see Wallace Davies' articles about her in *Dictionary of American Biography, Supplement Two* and *Films in Review,* Vol X (1959), 537-48.

he had a devilish sense of humor and a dazzling technique. He too died a suicide, in Paris in 1925, together with his young wife, under circumstances of indescribable poignancy.[23]

I lack the space to consider the independent companies seriatim. In May, 1910, the Motion Picture Distributing and Sales Company was organized to distribute films produced by companies not belonging to the Patents group. The Sales Company split in 1912, and Universal organized, distributing Imp, Nestor, Champion, Republic, Gem, and 101 Bison, along with the Itala importations (*The Fall of Troy,* 1910, was perhaps the first important revelation to America of the glories of the Italian film), leaving Thanhouser, American, Majestic, Reliance, Lux, Solax, Eclair, and Comet with the Film Supply Company, along with the French Gaumont, which shifted its releasing outlet from time to time, and the Danish Great Northern films. But in July, Charles Bauman withdrew from Universal, leaving the brand name 101 Bison behind him (after which his pictures were known as Kay-Bee); in December, Mutual supplanted the Film Supply Company, releasing Kay-Bee, Keystone, Broncho, Thanhouser, American, Reliance, Majestic, and Punch.

Carl Laemmle, producer of Imp, later Universal, films, had originally been an exchange man in the Middle West. Laemmle refused to buckle to the dictates of the trust, and when they cut off his supply of films, he was forced into production on his own. The first Imp, *Hiawatha,* was released October 25, 1909: "Length 988 feet. Taken at the Falls of Minnehaha in the Land of the Dacotahs. And you can bet it is classy or I wouldn't make it my first release." In 1910 there were one hundred more Imps. From the trust's point of view they were well named. Laemmle used the same brash, often ungrammatical, ill-mannered style in vaunting his own films as he did in attacking his enemies, but he fought a good

[23] See Bardèche and Brasillach, *The History of Motion Pictures,* 79–82, 120, 166–67; Montgomery, *Comedy Films,* 75–78; Georges Sadoul, *French Film,* 12–13.

fight, and his advertisements in the trade journals had fire and brimstone in them.

Not, to be sure, that the case was quite open and shut. I know no wars between God and the devil, and this certainly was not such a war. The Patents companies were establishing a monopoly; they were also protecting their "rights," and in the beginning at least they certainly introduced order and reason into a chaotic business. As it turned out, the independents were fighting for the freedom of the screen, and the wave of the future was on their side, but later screen history was not to reveal them as less greedy than their opponents.

Perhaps in the early days Thanhouser was the most distinctive of the independent companies; they undertook ambitious things, and they had some delightful players—Marguerite Snow, celebrated for her *Carmen,* and her husband James Cruze, later the director of *The Covered Wagon,* and the ravishingly lovely Florence LaBadie, who remained with them until her tragic death at the age of twenty-three, on October 13, 1917, just before her intended marriage, from injuries received two months before in an automobile accident.[24] (Charles J. Hite, Thanhouser's president, had

[24] I am sure that Thanhouser's *Miss Robinson Crusoe,* released October 8, 1912, in two reels, with the second reel appropriately filled out with *Specimens from the New York Zoological Park,* does not deserve to be memorialized; it must have been a terrible picture. I, however, shall never forget it. The heroine (Florence LaBadie) was wrecked on a desert island, after which she appeared attired in a leopard skin (as I remember it) and nothing more. A large brown snake approached her, and she picked it up and played with it, in what must have been a very long scene for those days, lifting it above her head and much besides, until finally a rescuer approached her and she put the reptile aside. And that was it. Only it wasn't quite. I suspect that judged by present-day standards Miss LaBadie was probably fairly well covered. But to eyes that were not accustomed to seeing bare legs even on little girls she seemed startlingly and wonderfully naked, and her beautiful body combined with the horror of the snake to create an impact that was unforgettable. Later an interviewer asked her about snakes, among

gone before her, three years earlier, by the same route, while his company's hit serial, *The Diamond from the Sky,* was cleaning up the country.) Among Thanhouser's adaptations from the classics were *Undine* and *Nicholas Nickelby* and *Little Dorrit,* the only American productions these particular Dickens novels have ever had. Miss LaBadie was the Undine, but Maud Fealy, whom Thanhouser brought from the stage to play *King René's Daughter,* was the Dorrit. She remained a successful film star for a number of years.

The informality of early film-making is hard to realize today. "In those days if there was a fire or a procession or a circus," wrote Hobart Bosworth, "we 'grabbed' it and wrote a story around it afterward." Vitagraph, according to Albert Smith, wrote no contracts until 1916, and seasonal layoffs were so common that they used a form letter to announce them. Biograph worked more systematically and carefully. "On Mondays," writes Mary Pickford, "we would rehearse. Mr. Griffith would call the company round him and assign our parts. Then and there the story would be written or built up. Tuesdays we took interior scenes and Wednesdays we took exteriors." But even Biograph improvised, as one may tell by reference to Miss Pickford's own account of the making of *Wilful Peggy.*[25] Thanhouser used a Siberian locale in one film because a sudden snowstorm had buried the New Rochelle studio; when the snow melted before the picture was finished, they simply inserted a subtitle: "Later—A Warmer Clime." In one early Vitagraph, *The Life of Washington,* William Shea played fifteen parts and died twice in one scene; in *The Servant Girl's Problem* he was a Jew, a Dutchman, and three old maids. When in 1911 somebody asked *Motion Picture's* "Answer Man" how long it took to make a

other things, and she exclaimed, "Don't speak to me of snakes! Ugh! I hate them!" Perhaps she had learned how much she hated them from *Miss Robinson Crusoe,* and who could blame her? At Christmas of the same year she was a radiant young Madonna in Thanhouser's two-reel production, *The Star of Bethlehem.*

[25] Mary Pickford, *Sunshine and Shadow* (Doubleday, 1955), 119–22.

film, he replied that "a week to ten days should cover the ordinary production." But Bosworth said the early Seligs were made in two days, and Gene Gauntier claims to have ground out Kalems at the rate of one a day. Warren Kerrigan, the first player to be engaged by American, testified in 1914 that for three and a half years he played the leads in two pictures a week, or everything that the company produced. When Herbert Brenon and Annette Kellerman were hurt while filming *Neptune's Daughter* in the Bahamas, *The Moving Picture World* conjectured that other members of the company would probably make other pictures while waiting for them to recover. All this made for roughness of course, but it also made for spontaneity, and Gilbert Seldes reports so meticulous a worker as Chaplin eyeing his elaborate equipment during the filming of *Modern Times* and remarking wistfully, "We used to go into the park with a stepladder, a bucket of whitewash, and Mabel Normand, and make a picture."[26]

Kracauer speaks of "hunger for people" as one of the forces which drove audiences into picture theaters, yet in the beginning all players were anonymous; sometimes the actor himself insisted upon anonymity, lest he ruin his standing in the theater. In the early days of Biograph, Griffith did not want Mary Pickford to read her own mail, lest the evidence of her popularity should cause her to ask for more money. In the beginning, too, until Costello rebelled, the men were expected to act as handymen about the studio and the women to sew costumes; Vitagraph's Romeo (Paul Panzer) helped to build his own balcony. Frank Woods says that Kalem was the first company to identify players; Vitagraph followed, and all the others except Biograph (which held out until 1913), fell rapidly into line. Most inquiries to *Motion Picture's*

[26] Good descriptions of improvising in early films will be found in Sennett and Shipp, *King of Comedy*, 87, 131–32, 156. See especially the use the Sennett forces made of their knowledge that the Los Angeles Water Department was about to drain the lake in Echo Park (p. 194) and the account of the flinging of the first custard pie (pp. 136–37).

"Answer Man" concerned the identity of players. "The 'little lady' you mention is a Biograph player," he told one inquirer, "and there is a legend to the effect that Biograph players have their names locked in a big safe and only get them back when they leave the company." Names were given only sporadically in trade-paper advertisements, although Vitagraph stepped it up sharply after August, 1913. Yet as early as April, 1912, Imp was advertising "King Baggott in *The Loan Shark*," and Lubin put Arthur Johnson's name in large letters with the two-reeler *The Stolen Symphony*. At one time Universal ran a series of quarter-pages in the *Dramatic Mirror* listing Florence Lawrence films and featuring one of them: "Florence Lawrence in . . ."; there was also a medallion of the lady as a kind of Victor trade-mark. By 1913 the New Empire Theater in Detroit was setting up in electric lights "TODAY John Bunny & Flora Finch," without bothering to mention the name of the film.[27]

[27] The winners in the first popularity contest conducted by *The Motion Picture Story Magazine*, and completed in June, 1912, were, in order, Maurice Costello, Dolores Cassinelli, Mae Hotely, Francis X. Bushman, and G. M. Anderson. In October, 1913, the second contest was won by Romaine Fielding, Earle Williams, Warren Kerrigan, Alice Joyce, and Carlyle Blackwell. Just one year later Earle Williams, Clara Kimball Young, Mary Pickford, Warren Kerrigan, and Mary Fuller won the third contest. It should not be forgotten that in silent pictures the director often acted by remote control, the player being required to do what he was told, frequently without even understanding the situation in which he was placed. See King Vidor's autobiography, *A Tree Is a Tree* (Harcourt, Brace, 1953), for some interesting data on this point, connected with the filming of *The Big Parade*; and cf. *Agee on Film*, 401, for John Huston's testimony, showing that it has not been completely abandoned even in sound films. Lindgren, *The Art of the Film*, 78–79, cites a striking example of how editing can be substituted for acting. A famous case was that of Thomas Meighan in George Loane Tucker's great film *The Miracle Man* (1919), in which Meighan, playing a crook, was required to weep to signalize his conversion and redemption. First Meighan could not get himself to weep; then, having once started, he could not stop. Tucker photographed his breakdown, and on the screen the effect

Of course all these people were working for a low-price market. The higher admission prices charged for films in Europe early irked American producers. Returning to the United States in the fall of 1913 after six months of picture-making abroad, Herbert Brenon saw Berlin as leading the world in film presentation, with performances starting at 9 P.M., running three hours, and costing one dollar to one dollar and a half. When Florence Lawrence went to Victor in 1913, exhibitors were warned of her first film that "IT IS GOING TO COST YOU EXTRA MONEY" and exhorted in Laemmle's inimitable prose not to "fuss about price." When in 1914 a theater in Syracuse got fifty cents for a week of Thanhouser's *Joseph in the Land of Egypt,* the fact rated an "I TOLD YOU SO" headline in a trade-journal advertisement. Announcing *Samson* in six reels with Warren Kerrigan in 1914, Universal declared that they would "have to charge the exchanges the highest price ever charged for a film; that the exchange in turn will have to get a record price from the theatres; and that the theatres will have to RAISE THEIR PRICE OF ADMISSION." Vitagraph, which got one dollar for *The Christian* at the Manhattan Opera House in 1914, took a whole page to explain that they opened the Vitagraph Theater "to demonstrate that Vitagraph Features, when presented in the right way, will not only draw record crowds, but will bring Higher Class Patronage at Higher Prices." Yet when in February, 1917, two houses in Portland Maine, raised the tariff from ten to fifteen cents, the fact was big news in *The Moving Picture World,* with a subhead assuring the reader that there were still plenty of five-cent houses left in Portland; and in the summer of that year

was that of wonderful "acting." It is true that similar methods are sometimes used by stage directors (see David Belasco's account of how he worked on Frances Starr when *The Easiest Way* was in rehearsal, in *The Theatre through its Stage Door* [Harper, 1919]); but an actor who creates an effect "naturally" in rehearsal always knows that he must be able to reproduce it artificially in performance, and that what he does at 9:20 tonight he must repeat at 9:20 every night and at 3:20 every matinee.

Mutual's president John R. Freuler was still pleading for a general price raise of from ten to fifteen cents' admission.

But ambitions were in evidence from the beginning. General Film resisted features, with Kalem more reluctant than many; yet when W. W. Hodkinson pulled out and started his own exchanges, both Samuel Long and Frank J. Marion invested in his new business. George Kleine backed the 1913 *Quo Vadis?* as an independent venture. Passion Plays and prize fights ran into multiple reels from the beginning; in 1909, too, Vitagraph did *Les Miserables* in four reels and in 1910 *The Life of Moses* in five.

Nor was the use of standard materials confined to feature films; I am afraid nobody in these latter days can possibly realize how many of the great historical figures or great literary masterpieces first crossed the horizon for children of my generation by way of a motion-picture screen. It is true that they sometimes kept strange company; when Vitagraph did *Elektra* in one reel with Mary Fuller in 1910, exhibitors were exhorted to "BILL IT LIKE A CIRCUS—IT WILL DRAW BIGGER CROWDS THAN ANY FILM YOU HAVE EVER HAD." Both Edison and Selig were making American-history films as early as 1908, but the history was not always reliable. The *Dramatic Mirror* pointed out that in Edison's *In the Days of Witchcraft* (1909), a Puritan girl burned as a witch was given a cross to kiss, and in Pathé's *Oliver Cromwell* (1907), the Protector was supplied with a daughter who disguised herself and enlisted with the Royalists to protect the King against her father. The *Dramatic Mirror* criticized Thanhouser severely for the lack of period feeling in their *Paul and Virginia* (1910), whose poster, I recall, was a reproduction of Cot's beautiful painting *The Storm* in the Metropolitan Museum. (I saw it then, I am sure, for the first time and fell in love with it on sight, and my infatuation has endured.) But the *Dramatic Mirror's* own erudition was not always above reproach. When Selig did a one-reel *Tale of Two Cities* in 1908, the *Dramatic Mirror* attributed the novel to Ouida, and it described Vitagraph's *In the Days of the*

Pilgrims as "an Indian story represented as having taken place in the fifteenth century in New England." There would not be much point in attempting a representative listing of the "classics" that were filmed; the safest thing is simply to say that they tried everything. One might have thought that the silence of the medium would rule out musical subjects, but even this did not happen. Perhaps Thanhouser owed it to itself to do *Tannhaeuser,* but a great many operas were done without such excuse. Biograph's *A Fool's Revenge* (1909) was the *Rigoletto* story. American, of all firms, had a two-reel *Footsteps of Mozart* in 1914; Ambrosio did both *Parsifal* and *Siegfried* in 1912; in 1916, Lois Weber and Phillips Smalley made for Universal a costly production of *The Dumb Girl of Portici,* with the great dancer Anna Pavlova.

Of the early productions of Shakespeare we have an authoritative survey by Professor Robert H. Ball.[28] The earliest Shakespeare filmed seems to have been a scene from Tree's production of *King John* in 1899. The next year Clément Maurice photographed Sarah Bernhardt in the duel scene from *Hamlet* for the Paris Exposition. In 1907, Méliès made *Shakespeare Writing "Julius Caesar"* and *Hamlet, Prince of Denmark, or Hamlet and the Jester's Skull.*

In this country G. W. Bitzer photographed a fifty-foot *Duel Scene from "Macbeth"* in 1905, but the first attempts to film whole plays date from 1908, when no fewer than nine of them went before the cameras. At Biograph, Griffith did *The Taming of the Shrew* with Florence Lawrence; Kalem had an *As You Like It;* Vitagraph was responsible for all the rest—*Romeo and Juliet, Macbeth, Othello, Richard III, Antony and Cleopatra, Julius Caesar,* and *The Merchant of Venice,* all directed by William V. Ranous. In 1909 they followed these with *King Lear* and *A Midsummer*

[28] "Shakespeare in One Reel," *Quarterly of Film, Radio, and Television,* Vol. VIII (1953–54), 139–49. See also *Films in Review,* Vol. VII, 247, 543.

Night's Dream, in 1910 with *Twelfth Night,* and in 1912 with *Cardinal Wolsey.*[29] All these were directed by Lawrence Trimble. Selig had a *Merry Wives of Windsor* in 1910, and Thanhouser offered both *The Winter's Tale* and *The Tempest* in 1911.

Of these films I remember seeing *King Lear* and *Cardinal Wolsey* as a child, and I saw the George Eastman House print of *A Midsummer Night's Dream* while working on this book. It is an enchanting little primitive, with Costello as Lysander and the child Gladys Hulette as a sweet little bare-legged Puck. *King Lear* I recall as containing the most heroic piece of exposition I have ever encountered in a theater. In the very first scene all the characters were introduced in a single shot—the actors, costumed, standing on a flight of black stairs, with the name of the character each was to represent painted under him in large white letters. Julia Swayne Gordon was the Goneril, and I think Charles Kent was the Lear. In the mad scenes, Lear wandered before a painted stage drop, representing a wave-battered seashore, and at the end, while Edgar and Edmund fought their duel, a tinted sun came up over the cliffs behind them.

In some of their "High Art Films," as they liked to call them, Vitagraph apparently adopted a somewhat more leisurely method of introducing the characters, since the *Dramatic Mirror* commented on the 1909 *Saul and David*: "At the opening of the picture the Vitagraph Company again follows the plan of introducing all the principal characters with individual pictures before the commencement of the story proper." Cultivating its Biblical researches further, Vitagraph did both *Jephthah's Daughter* and

[29] If Professor Ball is right in seeing this as an adaptation of *Henry VIII.* I am not quite sure myself that it was not a straight historical film. I do not recall any Shakespearean claims being made for it when it appeared, nor do any appear in the March, 1912, number of *The Motion Picture Story Magazine,* where it is one of the featured films. Vitagraph's most ambitious Shakespeare film was of course the three-reel *As You Like It* of 1912, in which Costello played Orlando to the Rosalind of the distinguished but sixty-two-year-old Rose Coghlan, imported from the stage for the purpose.

The Judgment of Solomon the same year, announcing the latter as "A Grand Biblical Reel for Sunday Shows." Pathé had a *Samson and Delilah* in 1908, "ending with his entrance into Paradise," which I witnessed, there first encountering the great story. I could think of nothing else all the next day, but went about babbling of "Simpson" to anybody who would listen to me.

"Classical" material naturally brought the movies closer to the theater. Film historians sometimes give the impression that this influence began with Sarah Bernhardt's success in *Queen Elizabeth* and Zukor's organization of Famous Players; but it was as early as 1908 that Le Film d'Art was organized in France, and their first production, *The Assassination of the Duke of Guise,* for which Saint-Saëns composed a musical score, and which moved Charles Pathé to tears of admiration and homage, has all the characteristics of *Queen Elizabeth* except that it is not nearly as good.

Moreover, American producers did not need Le Film d'Art nor any other exemplar to incline them toward the theater. Vitagraph's very first story film was *Raffles* (1905). Later Imp used a theater curtain rising on all its main titles. As has already been suggested, there were many unacknowledged adaptations of stage successes: Vitagraph's *'Twixt Love and Duty* (1908) was, for example, *The Squaw Man.* As I have already indicated, the movies had always been crazy about the devil. On his way to California for Selig in 1908, Francis Boggs stopped off in Indiana and made a one-reel *Faust* with Thomas Santschi. The next year the same firm's *Mephisto and the Maiden* modified the *Faust* motif, and there was a kind of burlesque of the theme in Pathé's *Miss Faust* in 1909. But when on the night of August 18, 1908, George Arliss made his great success on the New York stage in Ferenc Molnár's play *The Devil,* the whole film world was inspired. On September 19, Edison's *The Devil* was already being reviewed, and Biograph's identically titled masterpiece was considered on October 2. Vitagraph's contribution was *He Went to See the Devil Play,* about a man who actually visits the theater to see Arliss, after which everybody he meets turns into a devil, including his wife, who had natural gifts in that direction. But the prime example of this influence is Selig's *The Devil, the Servant, and the Man,* in which was achieved a combination of *The Devil* and Charles Rann Kennedy's play *The Servant in the House;* the erring husband in the film saw both plays, and each contributed elements to the dream which led to his reformation. Selig did *The Devil, the Servant, and the Man* three times —in 1910, 1912, and 1916—and Kathlyn Williams was in all three productions. In Biograph's *A Drunkard's Reformation* (1909), Arthur Johnson was reclaimed after taking his little daughter to see Zola's *L'Assommoir;* all these reformations, however unconvincing, were nice little compliments to the moral influence of the theater.

Nor was the legitimate theater the only institution toward whose personnel the early cinema was hospitable. The swimming star and physical-culture expert Annette Kellerman, who later made a great hit in *Neptune's Daughter* and *A Daughter of the Gods,* appeared as early as 1909 in a Vitagraph split-reel called simply *Annette Kellerman,* "doing her physical culture exercises, diabolo playing, fancy swimming and doing displays" (the syntax is Vitagraph's). The same firm made a successful screen player out of the dwarf Marshall P. Wilder, who, in a short bearing merely his name (1912), was shown "in his famous vaudeville act of funny stories and impersonations," though how the funny stories could have come across in a silent film is something of a mystery. Nearly all the comic-strip characters of the time appeared on the screen— as cartoons, as regular movies, or as both, sometimes under the supervision of their creators.[30] In 1910, Selig made four films based on the work of the most popular American writer for children, L. Frank Baum—*The Wizard of Oz* (March 24), derived from the musical-comedy version, not the book; *Dorothy and the Scarecrow in Oz* (April 14), which drew elements from both *The*

[30] See Jack Spears, "Comic Strips on the Screen," *Films in Review,* Vol. VII (1956), 317–25, 333.

Wizard of Oz and *The Land of Oz;* a film called *The Land of Oz* (May 19) ; and *John Dough and the Cherub* (December 19). Later Baum himself formed a company for the purpose of filming his works, but after a brave start this finally proved unsuccessful.[31]

The exploitation of current events—real and faked—long antedated the establishment of regular newsreels. In 1909, Vitagraph had both genuine pictures of the Messina earthquake and *Teddy in Jungleland,* in which the animals met Theodore Roosevelt in Africa with a flag of truce, presented him with a big stick, stole his rifles, etc. In this case there was of course no intent to deceive, but this was not always the case. Both Biograph and Selig made films showing the workings of the Salvation Army—the *Dramatic Mirror* judged both to have been inspired by Mrs. Fiske's success in Edward Sheldon's play *Salvation Nell*—and the Army itself cooperated in making the Biograph film. Essanay used and advertised "THE CHICAGO FIRE DEPARTMENT" in *Napatia, the Greek Singer,* with Francis X. Bushman and Dolores Cassinelli, in 1912, and Vitagraph put their own studio and the process of moviemaking on the screen in *A Vitagraph Romance.* In 1914, Kalem brought out *A Passover Miracle,* "produced with the assistance of the Bureau of Education in the Jewish Community of New York," with titles in English and Yiddish. In *A Million Bid* (1914), Vitagraph even flirted with the idea of the subconscious mind, and American advertised *The Town of Nazareth* as "Driving Home with Astounding Emphasis a Fundamental Principle of Psychology"—they did not specify which one. In Monopol's *The Seed of the Fathers* (1913), Marion Leonard long anticipated *The Bad Seed* when she killed her son, the third generation of worthless males. Unlike the play on which it was based, *The Bad Seed* (1957) did not quite dare this; it put the job up to God by having the little monster killed by lightning, but movie (and stage) genetics were quite as unscientific in 1957 as they had been forty-four years before.

[31] See the article by Baum's son, Frank Joslyn Baum, "The Oz Film Co.," *Films in Review,* Vol. VII (1956), 329–33.

There was also a tendency to bring people to the screen because they had attracted attention to themselves by becoming involved in some scandal or misfortune. This continued as late as 1918 when Essanay brought out the Butte exhibitionist Mary Mac-Lane, self-styled literary genius, in *Men Who Have Made Love to Me*. For a time indeed, while any film player who became involved in scandal must promptly be kicked out, it seemed that the very fact of being mixed up in a scandal before you came to the screen was the one sure way of getting in. Yet the only one of these people who made anything like a success was Evelyn Nesbit, who, in 1906 and after, by her testimony in the Thaw-White murder case, had for a time divided the whole country into pro-Evelyn and anti-Evelyn factions. Miss Nesbit first appeared with her son Russell Thaw in a Lubin feature; in 1917, Julius Steger presented her in *Redemption,* which played at the George M. Cohan Theater, and inspired *The Moving Picture World* to declare that she must "strike a responsive chord in every heart" and that with "the requisite amount of experience" she must take her place "in the front rank of screen favorites." Later she made a number of films for William Fox, and in 1956 she advised Twentieth Century–Fox on a very good picture about her stormy life called *The Girl in the Red Velvet Swing*.

Pornographers too early discovered that it was easier to work with film than on the stage, and there was some film pornography from the very beginning—some of it openly circulated, some sold only on the black market. Nakedness too is, for obvious reasons, easier to handle on screen than on stage, and it has been used from time to time in both legitimate and illegitimate ways. The famous model Audrey Munson posed after famous nude statues and paintings in *Purity,* and *Diana's Inspiration* was nothing but a series of "art poses" by "Baroness Von Dewitz." Who could question the actions of a lady of title, even when she appeared as naked as she was born? But the boldest use of nakedness on the open market was probably Lois Weber's in *Hypocrites* (1914), in which a nude woman, representing Truth, walked, in somewhat veiled photography, throughout the film. On the other hand, Vitagraph rigged up the first enclosed set they had ever used for Julia Swayne Gordon's *Lady Godiva,* and, not satisfied with having arrayed the lady in a pink union suit and a long blonde wig, they suspended all other production for the day and sternly ordered everybody who was not needed to make the picture off the lot.

A more respectable type of popular screen fare, toward the close of the pre-feature era, was the serial. Because they are generally considered trash, film historians have in general had little to say about serials,[32] yet they were better adapted to the medium than many more pretentious films. The first serials were probably French.[33] Over here the business is generally said to have begun when, at the very end of 1913, Selig released the first chapter of *The Adventures of Kathlyn,* with Kathlyn Williams.[34] This was a

[32] But see Edward Connor, "The Serial Lovers," *Films in Review*, Vol. VI (1955), 328–32, and Frank Leon Smith, "The Man Who Made Serials, *Films in Review*, Vol. VII (1956), 374–83.

[33] They began, perhaps, with Jasset's *Nick Carter* series (1908). The most famous French serial was *Fantomas* (1913 ff.) by Louis Feuillade, and the best known (though not the best) American serial, *The Perils of Pauline*, had a French director, Louis Gasnier. See Bardèche and Brasillach, *The History of Motion Pictures*, 68–70.

[34] It is sometimes difficult to draw a line between a serial and a series-picture. Series-pictures go back to the very early days. At Vitagraph, J. Stuart Blackton was making Happy Hooligan pictures back in 1897, with himself in tramp costume (see Jacobs, *The Rise of the American Film*, 18), and even Griffith did a Mr. and Mrs. Jones series at Biograph. Essanay had the Snakeville comedies, the Broncho Billy pictures, and the Alkali Ike pictures. But *Kathlyn's* most important series predecessor was Edison's *What Happened to Mary*, with Mary Fuller, which began in the summer of 1912, the stories being published in *The Ladies' World*. It was followed in 1914 by *Who Will Marry Mary?* and *Dolly of the Dailies*, both with Mary Fuller. Edison had gone series-mad. Besides the Mary Fuller films, the company had in 1914 a Marc McDermott series, *The Man Who Disappeared*, the stories by Richard Washburn Child appearing in *Popular Magazine*, and *Olive's Opportunities*, with Mabel Trunnelle as Olive the Gypsy Girl; and at the end of the year

Chicago *Tribune* publicity stunt; the story, written by Harold Mac-Grath and serialized in the *Tribune* concurrently with the exhibition of various chapters of the film in the theaters, is said to have boosted the paper's circulation by 10 per cent. There followed *The Million Dollar Mystery,* also sponsored by the *Tribune* and written by MacGrath but produced by Thanhouser, which was a tremendous commercial success; from there the *Tribune* moved on to *The Diamond from the Sky,* written by Roy L. McCardell and directed by William Desmond Taylor for American—for which they tried desperately to get Mary Pickford but finally settled for her sister Lottie—and Thanhouser produced *Zudora,* with Marguerite Snow, which promised "more scenes than in all the plays of Shakespeare."

By this time serials were big business. They drew the film theater and the newspaper closer together and stimulated motion-picture advertising and reviewing. Using Pathé plays and players, early in 1914, Eclectic got under way *The Perils of Pauline,* which was to make Pearl White one of the legendary figures of the twentieth century and keep her for most of the rest of her career hanging over cliffs, lashed to steel girders, and dangling on ropes out of

---

they announced their new star Gertrude McCoy in *The Stenographer.* Kalem tried to eat their cake and have it too by announcing Alice Joyce in a weekly two-reel series beginning with *Nina of the Theater,* but the only continuity achieved was that the exhibitor was assured of a new two-reel Alice Joyce picture every Monday; concurrently, however, they were producing *The Hazards of Helen,* a railroad serial with Helen Holmes. In February, 1915, Kalem announced a series of three-reelers "showing the application of the Ten Commandments to present-day conditions." *The Second Commandment* was a Christian Science film. In the fall they began a series of single-reelers, *The Virtues of Marguerite,* with Marguerite Courtot. (A modern producer would certainly have made it "vices.") Lubin had Arthur Johnson and Lottie Briscoe in *The Beloved Adventurer*—"Each part forms a complete dramatic picture—nevertheless the complete series forms a consistent and continuous narrative." Essanay undertook weekly releases of George Ade's *Fables in Slang.* And so it went.

72

airplanes from this week's episode to the next. Vitagraph climbed on the band wagon in the spring of 1915 with *The Goddess,* written by Gouverneur Morris and Charles W. Goddard, starring Anita Stewart and Earle Williams, and directed by Ralph Ince. *The Goddess,* said the grandiloquent announcement, "will have no more in common with the ordinary melodrama than a story in the Century magazine with the fiction prepared for circulation among messenger boys." Miss Stewart was to be "a modern Joan of Arc, who is reared on a desert island in the belief that she is a goddess, and who escapes . . . and comes in contact with all the social forces that go to make up our complex civilization." Later they seem to have settled for a cave in the wilderness instead of the desert island, but by August, Vitagraph was quite drunk on its own publicity. "From the standpoint of literature . . . [*The Goddess*] may be classed with the works of Charles Dickens. From the standpoint of artistry it may be compared with the work of Sir Joshua Reynolds. From the standpoint of continued photoplays *it is in a class by itself."* In 1916, George Kleine presented Billie Burke, who had made her screen debut for Thomas H. Ince in 1915 in *Peggy,* in Rupert Hughes's *Gloria's Romance,* which cost a great deal of money but was too tame for the serial audience. Hearst ventured into the occult with *The Mysteries of Myra,* written by no less an authority on such matters than Hereward Carrington, and Costello returned to the screen with Ethel Grandin in *The Crimson Stain Mystery.* The year 1916 also produced the most vicious of all serials, Hearst's *Patria,* written by Louis Joseph Vance and starring Irene (then Mrs. Vernon) Castle, which whipped up war fever, glorified the munitions makers, and so openly attacked Japan that President Wilson personally requested that it be withdrawn.

A good many of the pictures I have latterly been discussing were necessarily multiple-reelers, but even though the ultimate triumph of the "feature" had been assured by the beginning of World War I, the single-reeler died hard. In August, 1913, Pathé announced that their Friday release would thereafter be "a multiple reel feature." Selig followed with the announcement of a two-reeler every Monday; Vitagraph, Saturday; Lubin, Thursday. With the issue of September 6, 1913, *The Moving Picture World* began to use a separate heading for "Specials," meaning pictures in more than one reel. (Biograph's *The Mothering Heart* was described as "a big picture. An evidence of this is the fact that it is in two parts.") In May, 1915, even Keystone announced that after June 14 all their pictures would be two-reelers. By the week of March 27, 1916, General was releasing only fifteen single-reelers—one an Essanay split between a cartoon and a scenic, one a Biograph revival. Universal had ten single-reelers that same week, and Mutual, nine.

In 1915, Vitagraph, Lubin, Selig, and Essanay formed VLSE to produce feature films. (It reminded the wags of "Vaseline.") Essanay and Selig soon withdrew, and for a time there was a KESE (Kleine, Edison, Selig, Essanay). General Film was falling apart even before the government finally ruled against it. Pathé had seceded in high dudgeon in 1914, irked because the Hearst-Selig newsreel was being circulated in competition with the *Pathé News*. Vitagraph bought out Lubin and announced that VLSE and Vitagraph were now one and the same. Later they also acquired Kalem. Vitagraph was indeed the only one of the old Patents companies that really made a success of features, continuing in business until 1925, when they sold out to Warner Brothers, whose primary interest was in acquiring their far-flung system of exchanges.

Yet even while VLSE was being set up, Albert Smith was proclaiming that the one- and two-reel film was the foundation of the industry. Both Laemmle and Kalem's William Wright urged consideration for those "who drop in at odd times and for short stays—men with an hour between engagements, women who want rest after a tour of the shops." When Thanhouser's *Uncle Tom's Cabin* was playing against a two-reeler controlled by another company, they advertised, "You can see the whole thing in one reel—why buy two?" Universal advertised *Captain Kidd as* "Ten Reels of

Action Condensed into Three." As late as 1913, Eclectic's nine-reel *Les Misérables* was being distributed in four sections; and though Monopol proudly advertised *The Sins of the Fathers,* in six reels, as the longest American film yet, they added reassuringly that "for convenience of exhibiting it, it is divided into three acts." At the beginning of 1915, Lubin was releasing three-reel features on every alternate Wednesday and Thursday, yet they were still using Arthur Johnson, Lottie Briscoe, and Ethel Clayton not only in one-reelers but in one-reel comedies. In 1914–15, Biograph was still taking only two reels apiece for *Martin Chuzzlewit, Felix Holt,* and *Gwendolin (Daniel Deronda).* In 1916 the Unicorn Film Service was set up, supplying mostly one-reelers, with nothing longer than two; that same year Paramount itself began to advertise single-reelers to "Lend Variety to Your Program."

More surprising still was the late survival of the split-reel. Toward the end of 1911, Imp even made special announcement of "A Split IMP Every Saturday," and the advertisement showed the little devil who was their trade-mark cleft down the middle. Some producers achieved amazing combinations. Keystone's offering of September 1, 1913, was *Fatty's Day Off* with *Los Angeles Harbor, California.* In December, Thanhouser issued a two-reel *Jack and the Beanstalk,* with *The Bush Leaguer's Dream* "on the last half of the second reel." In 1914, Chaplin's *Recreation* was coupled with *The Yosemite,* while Vitagraph presented Maurice Costello and Clara Kimball Young in *Some Steamer Snooping* on the same reel with *Niagara Falls.*

During the early days, too, European films—mostly French, Italian, and Danish—were shown more freely in the United States than they were ever again until recent years; it was not until World War I interfered with European production and distribution that American film makers secured their monopoly not only in America but everywhere else except in central Europe. *The Moving Picture World* thought foreign films superior to American productions; the *Dramatic Mirror* heatedly denied this, thus inaugurating a debate which still rages. There can be no question, however, that the Italian films greatly stimulated the production of features. In 1913 we had Enrico Guazzoni's *Quo Vadis?* and in 1914, Giovanni Pastrone's *Cabiria. Quo Vadis?*, in which Nero peers at the Christians in the arena through a kind of lorgnette, is not very impressive today; but *Cabiria* still inspires respect, and this not wholly because of its amazing "dolly shots," with the camera moving in as if to create a third dimension or attract the attention of the spectator to particular characters, as Theodore Huff observed, and thus providing a substitute for close-ups and changing camera angles. *Cabiria* is set, as everybody knows, against the war between Rome and Carthage—it opens with Hannibal crossing the Alps, elephants and all—and while it is often cited as an example of the turgid confusion of the great Italian screen spectacles, the complexity of the story has been greatly exaggerated; no normal person should have any difficulty in following it, though it is certainly hard to remember.

After *Intolerance* the scenes of ancient battle in *Cabiria* may have begun to look pretty tame—Archimedes in Syracuse trying to burn the attacking fleet with the sun's rays; the long, long shot of a pyramid of soldiers building up beside the city wall; boiling oil poured over the walls for defense; and much besides—but certainly the settings and the sacrifices to Moloch are still theater in the grand manner, and nobody ever forgets the gentle giant Maciste, who protected the heroine, "the Guitry of the biceps," as Louis Delluc was to call him. An almost illiterate dock hand, Bartolomeo Pagano was thenceforth known only by the name of the character he had played in *Cabiria;* in *Maciste against Death, Maciste in Hell, Maciste in the Lion's Den,* etc., he was a continuing figure of heroism.[35]

[35] For Italian films, see Vernon Jarratt, *The Italian Cinema* (London, Falcon Press, 1951), and a vast pictorial, *Fifty Years of Italian Film,* first published in Rome by Carlo Bestetti, Edizioni d'Arte, 1954. The American edition, which carries an introduction by Richard Griffith, has no title page.

We should remind ourselves, however, that *Cabiria* was not shown in the United States until after Adolph Zukor had imported Louis Mercanton's production of Sarah Bernhardt in *Queen Elizabeth,* and that this latter picture had led to the establishment of the Famous Players Film Company, whose success ensured the establishment of the feature and for a considerable period dominated the film trade of the world. In Chicago, I remember, *Queen Elizabeth* was shown during the dull season in that sanctum sanctorum of the spoken drama, Powers' Theater, where no film had ever been seen before. It was not Bernhardt's first picture, but it was by all means her most influential.[36] The greatest actress in the world had accepted the lowly movie. Who could hope to hold out after that?

[36] On Bernhardt's connection with films, see Charles Ford, "Sarah Bernhardt: Notes on a Dying Legend," *Films in Review,* Vol. V (1954), 515–18.

77

CHAPTER TWO

"D. W. Griffith Presents . . ."

"D. w. G R I F F I T H presents *Broken Blossoms."* As I write the words, time's flight recoils upon itself, and it is again the spring of 1919. Incense hangs heavy in the air, and girls in Chinese regalia trip up and down the aisles of the Illinois Theater in Chicago, distributing souvenir first-night programs with decidedly American assurance. The clang of Chinese gongs is heard in the orchestra pit; there is all the hubbub and excitement of a characteristic Griffith *première.* Finally the red lights are dimmed; the orchestra begins its plaintive, pitiless melody; the curtain rises on a screen bathed in the richest blue ever seen in a theater, and the unreeling of the noblest achievement yet vouchsafed to the cinema has begun.

I met Griffith only once, but I saw him also upon two other occasions. Our meeting was in January, 1922, on the stage of the Great Northern Theater in Chicago, where Lillian Gish introduced me to him on the first night of *Orphans of the Storm.* His curtain speech was already behind him; he had made that, in response to insistent applause, during the intermission. Wearing a sack coat, and with his hair none too recently shorn, he stood at the extreme right side of the stage, toward the rear, resting his weight on one foot, rubbing his long fingers together, and spoke in a trembling voice. He had influenza, he said, and ought to be in bed, and he looked it. Whether it was genuine or simulated, nothing could have been more modest than what he said. He tried to place credit for the picture upon Lillian and Dorothy Gish—who were there in the box right behind me—upon the photographer, upon everybody except himself. If D. W. Griffith had put anything good into his work, it all went back to the day when, as a struggling young actor in Chicago, "I, a Southerner," was called upon to impersonate "your Abraham Lincoln." His always sharp profile seemed unusually prominent against the dead black of the stage drop. He was either a very lonely man or, for some reason best known to himself, he was giving a good imitation of one.

Backstage he was much more assured, decidedly alert now, comparatively relaxed, smiling, friendly, with the courtesy of the old South about him. There was still the suggestion of loneliness, but it was not pathetic now. If he was alone, that was the way he wanted to be. He took you in, and then he dropped you; you were not quite sure whether he heard what you were saying or not. Chicago did not hold all there was of him, nor the *Orphans première* either; part of him, perhaps the more important part, was somewhere else. As Henry James might say, you were all there for him but he was not all there for you.

The first time I saw him without meeting him had been almost three years earlier at the Chicago opening of *Broken Blossoms.* He made a speech on that occasion also, but all I remember is that it was in the same high-flown, deeply earnest style of the *Orphans* speech; I cannot remember what he said. On this occasion my closest view of him was on the sidewalk, where my mother and I were standing for a few moments before the performance began, and he came along on foot and went into the theater. I said, "There's Mr. Griffith," and he heard, looked in our direction and smiled. He was well dressed, his manner was one of quiet dignity, and he was obviously in very good humor and exercising all the charm of which he was capable, which was considerable.

My last glimpse of him was at the Roosevelt Theater—a motion-picture theater this time—to which he had brought Carol Dempster in the summer of 1925 for the first local showing of *Sally of the Sawdust;* but now he was a different man. There was nothing high-flown about him on this occasion; instead, he was so bluff and hearty that he was a little brash. The principal bit of enlightenment he now conveyed to us was that he hoped we had liked the picture but that he himself "didn't have a damn bit of brains." Then he called Carol Dempster out from the wings. "Say good evening to the ladies and gentlemen," he told her, as if she had been a little girl appearing at the last-day-of-school exercises in the second grade. Carol responded in character by piping, "Good evening, ladies and gentlemen," and that was about it. It was a strange Griffith to contemplate, but one thing was quite clear. He was well aware that he was bringing no *Broken Blossoms* to Chicago this time, nor any *Orphans of the Storm* either.

D. W. Griffith was born at Crestwood, Kentucky, on January 22, 1875, and died at Hollywood, California, on July 23, 1948.[1] A

[1] The best and most reliable account of D. W. Griffith's career in book form is still Iris Barry's sketch, *D. W. Griffith: American Film Master* (Museum of Modern Art, 1940). The first Mrs. Griffith, Linda Arvidson, preserved many memories of Biograph days in *When the Movies Were Young* (Dutton, 1925). Robert Edgar Long's *David Wark Griffith* (D. W. Griffith Service, 1920) is press agentry. Henry Stephen Gordon's "The Story of D. W. Griffith" ran serially in *Photoplay*, June through November, 1916.

Among work published under Griffith's own by-line, see *The Rise and Fall of Free Speech in America* (Los Angeles, Privately printed, 1916); "Pictures vs. One-Night Stands," *Independent*, Vol. LXXXVIII (1916), 447–48; "Motion Pictures: The Miracle of Modern Photography," *Mentor* (July, 1921); "Are Motion Pictures Destructive of Good Taste," *Arts and Decoration* (Sept., 1923); "The Real Truth about Breaking into the Movies," *Woman's Home Companion* (Feb., 1924); "How Do You Like the Show?" *Collier's* (April 24, 1926); "The Motion Picture Today—and Tomorrow," *Theatre Magazine* (Oct., 1927). Frederick James Smith, "He Might Be the Richest Man in the World," *Photoplay* (Dec., 1926), is an important interview. A. Nicholas Vardac, *Stage to Screen: Theatrical Method from Garrick to Griffith* (Harvard University Press, 1949), is a valuable critical study.

sensitive, ambitious boy, in his own mind destined to greatness, he grew up with little formal education, his soul nourished on Elizabethan and Victorian literature and the old South's memories of the lost, sacred cause. "I felt driven to tell the story," he afterwards

Miss Lillian Gish is currently at work on a book about Griffith; see also her articles: "The Birth of an Era," *Stage* (Jan., 1937); "D. W. Griffith: A Great American," *Harper's Bazaar* (Oct., 1940); "Beginning Young," *Ladies' Home Journal* (Sept., 1942); and the interview, "Conversation with Lillian Gish," *Sight and Sound*, Vol. XXVII (1957), 128–30. There is also much Griffith material in Albert Bigelow Paine, *Life and Lillian Gish* (Macmillan, 1932).

Seymour Stern reportedly plans a plethoric, definitive work on Griffith which does not seem to move any closer to publication as the years pass, but he has published some important Griffith material, including "An Index to the Creative Work of D. W. Griffith," *Sight and Sound*, Index Series, No. 8, II (Sept., 1946); "The Birth of a Nation: A Monograph," *Sight and Sound*, Index Series, No. 4 (1945); "The Griffith Controversy," *Sight and Sound*, Vol. XVII (1948), 49–50; "11 East 14 Street," *Films in Review*, Vol. III (1952), 399–406; "The Cold War against D. W. Griffith," *Films in Review*, Vol. VII (1956), 49–59; "The Soviet Directors' Debt to D. W. Griffith," *Films in Review*, Vol VII (1956), 202–209.

See Stern, again, "Biographical Hogwash," *Films in Review*, Vol. X (1959), 284–96, 336–43, for the mistakes in Homer Croy's inept *Star Maker: The Story of D. W. Griffith* (Duell, Sloan and Pearce, 1959); for corrections of Stern's corrections, see the letters on pages 274–76, 441–46, including Stern's reply. When Stern calls *The Ten Commandments* (1923) Cecil B. deMille's first spectacle, he ignores both *Joan the Woman* and *The Woman God Forgot* (both 1917). There is no excuse whatever for his attempt to make a mystery of the death of Clarine Seymour; she died after an operation for strangulation of the intestines, and there was no mystery about it. Neither had she "been assigned the leading feminine role (Anna Moore) in *Way Down East*." Nobody was ever Anna Moore except Lillian Gish; Clarine played the role afterward taken over by Mary Hay, and can still be seen in some of the long shots. Finally, Stern states that *Intolerance* "never played so-called neighborhood houses. There was no 'second run.'" I saw it at the Oak Park Theater, however, and when I became a student at the University of Chicago in the fall of 1917, it was playing in the Hyde Park neighborhood also.

said of *The Birth of a Nation*—"the truth about the South, touched by its eternal romance which I had learned to know so well." The Shakespearean readings of his father, Colonel Jacob Wark Griffith, C.S.A., influenced him importantly in the direction of the theater; so did the glamorous Julia Marlowe when the impressionable youngster had the good fortune to see her on the stage. Griffith's values, derived from his reading and his family background, were, at their worst, mawkish and chauvinistic; at their best they had idealism and high aspiration about them, and though he did not always live up to them, he believed enough in them so that he could not betray them even to woo the bitch goddess success when, after World War I, he heard all the fools shouting that "moral values had changed" simply because there were more tramps in the world than there had used to be.[2]

Young Griffith worked in a dry-goods store and a bookstore; he was employed on a newspaper; he took subscriptions in the Kentucky hills for *The Baptist Weekly* and the *Encyclopaedia Britannica;* he played in stock and on the road; one year he was even with that fine actress Nance O'Neil. But he wanted to be a great poet, and *Leslie's Weekly* published in 1907 a free-verse effusion called "The Wild Duck." He also wanted to be a great playwright,

[2] The third and last of Lewis Jacobs' chapters on Griffith in *The Rise of the American Film* ("The Decline of D. W. Griffith") is as bad as his first chapter is good; it is inaccurate factually and confused in its evaluations. Mr. Jacobs is determined to make everything Griffith did during his final period illustrate the thesis announced in his chapter title; consequently he must dismiss *Isn't Life Wonderful* on the wholly irrelevant ground that "people of the twenties were concerned chiefly with physical sensations [which is of course nonsense] and had little time for honest appraisals of social conditions." Does this mean that Mr. Jacobs believes Griffith would have made better pictures during these years if he too had concerned himself "chiefly with physical sensations" and abandoned "honest appraisals of social conditions"? See, in this connection, Peter John Dyer, "The Decline of a Mandarin," *Sight and Sound*, Vol. XXVIII (1958–59), 44–47, which, though left-slanted, makes some excellent points, correcting easy generalizations about Griffith in other books and articles.

D. W. Griffith   PICTURE 13

Pictures 14, 15 *(above, center)*, *The New York Hat* (1912)—Lionel Barrymore, Mary Pickford, and Charles H. Mailes; Picture 16 *(below)*, *The Battle at Elderbush Gulch* (1914)—Kate Bruce and Lillian Gish.

Picture 17 *(above)*, *Judith of Bethulia* (1914)—Henry B. Walthall and
Blanche Sweet; two scenes from *The Birth of a Nation* (1915): (Picture
18, *below center*) the departure of Confederate troops from Piedmont,
showing Henry B. Walthall as the Little Colonel, and (Picture 19,
below) one of the scenes of battle.

es from D. W. Griffith's *Intolerance* (1916): Picture 20 *(left above)*, the an story; Picture 21 *(left center)*, the French story; Picture 22 *(left below)*, Marsh and Robert Harron in the modern story; Picture 23 *(below center)*, is in camp; Picture 24 *(below)*, one of the battle scenes. Pictures 23 and e from the Babylonian story.

Scenes from *Broken Blossoms* (1919): Picture 25 *(above left)*, Lillian Gish in the famous closet scene; Picture 26 *(above right)*, Lucy (Lillian Gish) on the Limehouse wharf; Picture 27 *(below)*, Cheng Huan (Richard Barthelmess) and Lucy in his chamber.

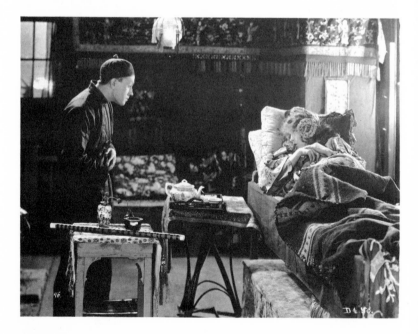

PICTURES 25, 26, 27

Scenes from *Way Down East* (1920): Picture 28 *(above left)*, Lowell Sherman and Lillian Gish before the mock marriage; Picture 29 *(above right)*, the ice scene (Lillian Gish); Picture 30 *(below)*, David and Anna (Richard Barthelmess and Lillian Gish) after her rescue.

PICTURES 28, 29, 30

Picture 31 *(above)*, Lillian and Dorothy Gish as the two orphans in *Orphans of the Storm* (1921); Picture 32 *(below)*, Henriette is befriended by Danton while Robespierre looks on disapprovingly (Lillian Gish, Monte Blue, and Sidney Herbert).

and James K. Hackett produced his play called *A Fool and a Girl* —Griffith had got the material through working as a hop picker in California between periods of more congenial employment—at Washington, D. C., also in 1907; Fannie Ward and Alison Skipworth were in the cast.

Like Mary Pickford, Griffith saw his first film in Chicago; he never could remember what it was, but he thought it "silly, tiresome, and inexcusably tedious," a waste of time. The literary in-·fection still had possession of him; long after he was a successful director, he was ashamed of his connection with films; for a long time he was "Lawrence Griffith"; he was saving "David Wark Griffith" for higher things; as late as October 11, 1913, after he himself had dropped the distinction, *The Moving Picture World* announced that "Lawrence Griffith" had severed his connection with Biograph. Acclaimed all over the world for his film achievements, Griffith would not have been human had he not at times seemed to accept them at his admirers' evaluation; but even when he was at the height of his career, he fluctuated between arrogance and disparagement, and often managed to give the impression that he was condescending to a minor art. After Hollywood threw him out and he fell upon evil days, he was of course sure that he had been right about this all along; and until hope died in him altogether in his lonely and somewhat embittered old age, he again found himself toying with grandiose, impossible literary achievements.[3]

[3] To complete the personal record, or as much of it as there is room for here, Griffith was married first, in 1906, to Linda Arvidson, who appeared in many of his Biograph films. They parted before *The Birth of a Nation*. In 1936 he finally divorced her and married a charming, unselfish young woman, Evelyn Marjorie Baldwin, who gave him the kind of home he had always glorified in his films; but though they seemed very happy at first, Griffith finally decided perversely that he was not a family man. In 1947, Mrs. Griffith opened divorce proceedings, and the old master spent his last years alone in Hollywood hotels and bars. There is an appalling picture of him in this aspect in Ezra Goodman's *The Fifty-Year Decline and Fall of*

Griffith's first contact with films came in 1907 when he played the rough-and-ready father who saved his child from a property eagle in the strange combination of realistic and romantic materials which Edwin S. Porter achieved in *Rescued from an Eagle's Nest*. But we soon find him under Wallace McCutcheon at Biograph, where he both acted and furnished stories. When he was offered a directorship he would not take it until he had been assured that if he did not make good he could have his acting job back again. His first picture was *The Adventures of Dollie,* released July 14, 1908, in which a little girl is stolen by gypsies and recovered from them, but not until the water cask in which they have hidden her has fallen "off the wagon and into the water, where it is carried by a strong current downstream, over a waterfall, through seething rapids, finally to enter the quiet cove of the first scene." Long unavailable, *Dollie* has now been printed up from the paper roll in the Library of Congress and exhibited. It has much the same kind of quaint, fresh charm as the English producer Cecil Hepworth's *Rescued by Rover* (1905). Linda Arvidson played the wife; the husband was Arthur Johnson, whom Griffith stopped in the street because he seemed to be the type. It was the beginning of Johnson's distinguished but all too brief film career; as late as 1926, Griffith was still remembering him as the finest of all screen actors.

In a full-page advertisement in *The New York Dramatic Mirror* (December 3, 1913), Griffith declared that "for two years from the Summer of 1908" he had "personally directed all Biograph mo-

---

Hollywood; I do not understand how a community can begin to "decline and fall" before it has risen. Much less detailed but more sympathetic candid-camera shots of Griffith during his final period may be found in René Clair, *Reflections on the Cinema* (London, William Kimber, 1935), and Daniel A. Lord, S.J., *Played by Ear* (Hanover House, 1936). Hedda Hopper did her utmost during these same years to get Griffith a foothold in Hollywood again; see the references to him in her autobiography, *From under My Hat* (Doubleday, 1952). Erich von Stroheim's impassioned tribute to him may be read in Peter Noble's *Hollywood Scapegoat* (London, The Fortune Press, 1950), 23–28.

tion pictures. Thereafter as general director he superintended all Biograph productions and directed the more *important* features until Oct. 1, 1913." There followed a list of about 150 titles. Let us try to analyze some of the material it contains.

First of all, there are numerous "classics": *The Taming of the Shrew, Leatherstocking, The Cricket on the Hearth, Enoch Arden* (first in one reel as *After Many Years* in 1908, then in two, under Tennyson's own title, in 1912), *Pippa Passes, A Blot on the 'Scutcheon,* etc. This classification can be extended on the one hand to take in near-classics like Helen Hunt Jackson's *Ramona* and drafts upon the bank of contemporary and near-contemporary literature, like *A Corner in Wheat,* from Frank Norris, and *For Love of Gold,* from Jack London's story, "Just Meat," which is a modernized version of the story Chaucer told in "The Pardoner's Tale,"[4] and on the other to films suggested by literary works or even by quotations from literature, like *The Song of a Shirt, The Sands of Dee, Lines of White on a Sullen Sea,* and *Edgar Allan Poe,* in which data drawn from the writer's personal history are arranged in a fictional pattern to show how he wrote "The Raven."

Griffith turned also to history. *The Sealed Room,* for example, had a medieval setting; the king (Arthur Johnson) had the guilty lovers, his beloved (Marion Leonard) and the court singer with whom she was carrying on a flirtation (Henry Walthall), walled up until they suffocated. (One need not be much of a literary detective to suspect that Griffith was remembering Poe's "The Cask of Amontillado.") But he might even use prehistory, as he did

---

[4] *Money Mad* (released Dec. 4, 1908) seems to have been still another variation on the "Pardoner's Tale" situation. "An old miser hoards up gold only to have it stolen by a couple of thugs, who in turn lose it and their lives in a fight over the division of spoils. It falls into the hands of an old hag, who in a delirium of money-madness upsets a lamp, setting fire to the place and incinerating herself." *The New York Dramatic Mirror* commented: "We doubt if the best French actors, acknowledged masters in moving picture pantomime, could have improved on the work of the Biograph players in this subject."

in one of his most famous Biographs, *Man's Genesis*. All Griffith's strength and weakness went into this "Psychological Comedy Based upon the Darwinian Theory of the Evolution of Man"—his daring, his genuine interest in ideas, his intellectual pretentiousness, and the whole pedantic, "culture-vulture" side of his personality. The setting of the story proper is in the days of the cavemen, and there are only three characters: Bruteforce (Wilfred Lucas), Weakhands (Robert Harron), and Lilywhite (Mae Marsh). Miss Marsh, then a newcomer, got the role, incidentally, and her foothold in pictures along with it, because Griffith's already established actresses balked at being cast in a "barelegged role," and he showed his appreciation by also giving her the lead in *The Sands of Dee,* which all the rest of them *did* very much wish to play! The yarn itself is only an anecdote, in which Weakhands is able to save Lilywhite from Bruteforce because it occurs to him to use a club while Bruteforce is still relying upon the strength of his own body. There was a frame in which an old man (W. Christie Miller) told the story to his two grandchildren after the boy had taken a stick to his sister, and it ended with the expression of the pious hope that now that man had devised yet more terrible weapons, he might also have learned how to be wise in their use. It was pretty heady stuff for 1912, and many audiences found it queer; but it was sufficiently popular to call forth a two-reel sequel, *Brute Force,* in which Lilywhite was stolen again, this time by another tribe with clubs as powerful as those of Weakhands and again rescued, by him after he had invented the bow and arrow.

In general, however, the important historical pictures were American. We fought the Civil War again in *The Informer* and *The Battle* (which anticipated Ince's *The Coward*), and *The Massacre* and *The Battle at Elderbush Gulch* applied to Indian-fighting the epical methods which Griffith was so impressively developing.[5]

[5] If I were asked which is the greatest Biograph picture I have seen (excluding *Judith of Bethulia*), I think I should specify *The Battle at Elder-*

86

By an extension of the term, such pieces as *The Last Drop of Water* and *The Female of the Species* may be included in this group also, for though they do not deal with historical incidents, they use similar backgrounds and require identical techniques. It is clear too that Griffith shared the contemporary interest in Indian pictures, of which he made a number including *The Redman and the Child, The Mended Lute, The Indian Runner's Romance, An Indian's Loyalty, Iola's Promise,* etc.; but he came a serious cropper with his most ambitious Indian picture, the two-reeler called *A Pueblo Legend,* which was produced at Albuquerque in order to make use of the genuine Indian remains in the museum there. Not only was it a dull film, in which the characters got quite lost in their backgrounds, but some of the detail so offended the Indians that the company was very nearly run out of town.[6]

Some of Griffith's literary and historical films have already had considerable attention in motion-picture history. *Pippa Passes,* the first film ever to be reviewed in *The New York Times* (October 9, 1909), has been praised for the lighting innovations which showed the progress of the day from dawn to dusk; and there is a very pleasant firelight effect in *The Cricket on the Hearth,* when the candle is put out and Herbert Prior sits down before the fireplace. *Ramona* is supposed to have contained the first extremely long shots, and the two versions of *Enoch Arden* have even occasioned controversy in connection with the use of the flashback contained in them. In general, however, there is a feeling, sometimes resulting from a confusion between critical judgment and personal taste, that Griffith did his best work when he took his materials bush Gulch; but *The Informer* and *The Battle* are also fine films by any standard, and *The Massacre* and *A Feud in the Kentucky Hills* are not far behind them. It is of course difficult to weigh films like these, with their trend toward crowd action, against such quiet, intimate pictures as Mary Pickford's last Biograph, *The New York Hat,* or *The Mothering Heart,* in which Lillian Gish gave her fine first performance in a grown-up role.

[6] See Mary Pickford's account of this matter in "My Own Story," *Ladies' Home Journal* (Aug., 1923), 121.

directly from contemporary life. In the sense that some of the pictures he based on literature were not well suited to cinematic representation, there is some justice in this. I do not see how either *Leatherstocking* or *The Cricket on the Hearth* could possibly be intelligible to anyone who did not have the original work well in mind; and good as Florence Lawrence and Arthur Johnson are in *Resurrection,* the film is rather a series of illustrations for Tolstoy's novel than a dramatization of it. Fortunately Griffith was not quite so cultured as, in some of his moods, he thought he was—not too much so, at any rate, as not to be able to look around him at the life of his time and take his material where he found it. I must confess that, except for Lillian Gish's performance in it, I do not admire *The Musketeers of Pig Alley* (1912) so much as it is fashionable to admire it. It may have begun the gangster film, but that in itself strikes me as a doubtful service, and the sets were too small to enable Griffith to develop the tension he might otherwise possibly have secured from his shots of the two rival gangs wandering endlessly through them in search of each other. But who would have wished to miss *A Beast at Bay,* with its curious anticipation of *Intolerance* in the race between the engine of a railroad train, a touring car, and a racing auto? Both *The Lonely Villa* and *The Lonedale Operator* are primitive little stories, but the first represents Griffith's crosscutting at an interesting stage of its development, while in the second it has nearly reached perfection. Equally primitive was *The Lesser Evil,* in which Blanche Sweet stood ready to die at the hands of the friendly smuggler-captain rather than fall into the hands of his libidinous crew which was trying to break into the cabin. This time too the situation was heightened by the really overwhelming vision of blonde loveliness which the heroine presented—I wonder if there was ever another film in which Blanche so *glowed* upon the screen—and there was a fascinatingly teasing moment at the end when, after having been restored to her lover (Edwin August), she gazed longingly after her champion through a telescope, a subtle touch of ambiguity in such a direct and straightforward melodrama.

That D. W. Griffith was the greatest and most influential of all film directors has become an axiom; as late as 1959, Frank Capra declared uncompromisingly that there had been no major improvement in film direction since his time. His contemporaries accepted his pre-eminence unquestioningly. When Maurice Tourneur was asked why he had come to America, he replied that it was because he wished to learn from Mr. Griffith. "Griffith," wrote Cecil B. deMille in retrospect, "had no rivals. He was the teacher of us all." "He was my day school," said Mack Sennett, "my adult education program, my university." At the other end of the world, the whole post-revolutionary school of Russian cinematography stemmed from him, and Sergei Eisenstein wrote a brilliant article in his praise.[7]

Although his full greatness was not appreciated until *The Birth of a Nation,* the time of his work for Biograph was his most richly creative period. Even we children sensed that Biograph pictures were "different," though we could not, for the life of us, have told you wherein their difference might consist, and sometimes I think we felt more at home with the less adventurous and disturbing Vitagraphs. "This progressive film company," declared the *Dramatic Mirror* as early as May, 1909, "follows one high-class feature production with another so rapidly as to make us wonder when and where the upward advancement is to end."

To be sure, not everybody liked the Biographs. Sometimes, even, the front office did not like the Biographs, and we have been told often enough how Griffith had to fight to use close-ups, his employers insisting that every actor must walk into the set in full view of the audience, just as he would on the stage, and arguing that spectators certainly would not wish to pay for half an actor

[7] "Dickens, Griffith, and the Film Today," in his *Film Form* (Harcourt, Brace, 1949).

when they might have a whole one at the same price. In 1912 a writer in *The Moving Picture World* complained bitterly because *The Sands of Dee* was broken into sixty-eight scenes. He could find only three other current one-reelers which exceeded forty; he himself thought eighteen to twenty the right number. The Biograph methods made jumping jacks of the actors; the director had clearly been "bitten by the lightning bug"; there was "lots of action, but no acting and no chance for any."[8]

Such complaints were not completely unechoed during later years. When Burns Mantle became motion-picture critic of *Photoplay* in March, 1920, he opened his first article by quarreling with Griffith, his particular complaint being what he considered the director's obsession with scenes in which women and girls were beaten or attacked. But he added, with special reference to Griffith's current film, *The Greatest Question,* that he thought Griffith was "shooting birdshot in places of bullets, or scattering his dramas so full of incidental scenes that he loses all contact with the main story." This is not the same complaint as that made in 1912, but one does, I think, feel that it is allied to it. And one must feel too, I believe, that neither of these critics really likes the motion-picture way of telling a story, and that their idea of a good motion picture is one that comes as close as possible to what is good dramatic technique on the stage.

But if Biograph films were "different," what made them different? Was it entirely a matter of technique? In the *Dramatic Mirror* advertisement already cited, Griffith claimed among the "innovations" which he had introduced into pictures, "the large or close-up figures, distant views as represented first in *Ramona,* the 'switchback,' sustained suspense, the 'fade out,' and restraint in

[8] George Pratt, "In the Nick of Time," *Image*, Vol. VI (1957), 52–59. This is an important article, covering other aspects of Griffith's technique besides those referred to here and illustrated with unique and significant frame enlargements.

expression, raising motion picture acting to the higher plane which has won for it recognition as a genuine art."

In the form stated, this claim is certainly inadmissible. You may, if you like, dismiss *Fred Ott's Sneeze* and *The Kiss* of May Irwin and John Rice on the ground that being all close-up they are not close-ups, failing to achieve the dramatic contrast which is accomplished when the close-up is used for contrast as part of a longer film. You may even dismiss the bandit who fires his pistol at the audience at the end of *The Great Train Robbery* because he is not part of the action of the film but something appended to it. But there will still be a great deal of other material to consider. "Ferdinand Zecca's *The Victims of Alcohol* (1901)," writes James Card, "is an example of the early use of multiple scenes in a narrative film. Williamson's *A Big Swallow* (1901–02) contains an extreme close-up, which finally fills the entire frame. [The idea conveyed is that the camera and the cameraman are swallowed up; perhaps even the audience is swallowed as well.] Porter used an interpolated close-up to further narrative action in his *Life of an American Fireman* (1902) and his *Rube and Mandy at Coney Island* (1904–05) shows that the camera was panned without following any particular action." Hobart Bosworth claimed not only the close-up but the vignette, the silhouette against the sun, and telescope and keyhole shots for the pioneer Selig director Francis Boggs.[9] Albert Smith insisted that Blackton was shooting close-ups right and left before Griffith ever heard of motion pictures; for himself he declared, "I claim 100% to have invented Stop Motion Photography. I discovered it by accident during our early troubles with steam on the Morse Building roof." And he goes on to describe how he used it to secure magical effects in *A Visit to a Spiritualist* (100 feet, 1898), *The Humpty Dumpty Circus* (75 feet, 1901), etc.; but he seems to have forgotten that it had

[9] Hobart Bosworth, "The Picture Forty-Niners," *Photoplay* (Dec., 1915).

already been used, several years before, at the Black Maria in *The Execution of Mary Queen of Scots*. There is a true close-up in Porter's *The Gay Shoe-Clerk* (Edison, 1903), where the camera focuses on a lady-customer's shoe, after which her skirt is slowly and daringly lifted, still in close-up, to reveal her leg, and Biograph's pre-Griffith *The Lost Child* (1904) has a very different kind of close-up as the culmination of a chase scene.[10]

But none of this is very important. What matters is the use Griffith made of all these devices. He broke up his scenes into various shots, taking his pictures from different angles and various distances all the way from the extreme long-shot to the extreme close-up of a face or part of a face or some other part of the body (like Mae Marsh's anguished clasped hands in the courtroom scene of *Intolerance*), or even inanimate objects of dramatic significance, like the poison in *The Medicine Bottle* (1909) or the pistol in his seventh film *The Fatal Hour* (August, 1908).[11] He used crosscutting for suspense, for contrast, and for reference, and the flash back for remembrance and startling juxtaposition; he even used shots to build up atmosphere and establish the setting, though they might not advance the action in any way. One might even say that the Griffith technical devices were most strongly validated by the fact that others *had* used them; if this had not been so, their use would have been freakish or arbitrary on his part. *This was the right way to tell a story in film,* and Griffith had the wit to discern it. He built on the foundations his predecessors had laid and took up everything of value that they had, often accidentally and uncomprehendingly, discovered. All this he deliberately, intelligently manipulated and developed.

Insofar as this side of Griffith's work had any non-cinematic inspiration, it came straight from Charles Dickens. "Why not?"

[10] Reproduced in George Pratt's article, " 'No Magic, No Mystery, No Sleight of Hand,' " *Image*, Vol. VIII (1959), 192–211.

[11] See the illustrations in *Image*, Vol. VI (1957), 55–58, and in this volume.

Griffith himself asked when the Biograph people objected to his discontinuity. "Doesn't Dickens write that way?" And Eisenstein has now demonstrated the uncanny parallelism of the two artists' methods of development in completely convincing detail. But it is a mistake to create the impression that Griffith used crosscutting only in connection with "the Griffith last-minute rescue." In *A Corner in Wheat* the extravagant banqueting of the rich is inter-cut with shots of the poor in their bread lines, and this is taken straight out of Frank Norris. In a grim little film called *The Usurer* we intercut between scenes showing the usurer's (George Nichols') gay dinner party and his victims being evicted from their homes, etc. Walthall (in a bit part) shoots himself while the usurer is toasting his rich friends. When Kate Bruce as the mother of a sick child comes to plead with him in his office, he rudely brushes her away and steps for a moment into his vault; fainting, she stumbles against a desk which bumps against the vault door and slams it shut. Now shots of the usurer's suffocating are inter-cut with scenes showing the suffering of others which he has caused, and this crosscutting continues until his death. In *Through the Breakers* we cut from a frivolous mother on the dance floor to her sick child in bed and calling for her at home. I am not sure that when Griffith cut from Annie Lee on the seashore to Enoch on his desert island in the 1912 *Enoch Arden* he meant to say that she was thinking of him; if he did, he cheated, for Annie did not know where her husband was; he may simply have intended to contrast husband and wife in their respective situations. There is, however, an interesting suggestion of what we would now call extrasensory perception in this film when Annie screams in terror at the moment when her husband is wrecked far away.

Yet, as we went through Biograph after Biograph in the summer of 1961, both George Pratt and I were surprised to note how little there really is of this sort of thing. If one were to judge by what many film critics have written, one would conclude that all Biograph films were a tightly woven tissue of tricky, brilliant technical devices, a never-ending show of virtuosity for its own sake. The reverse is the case. The devices are used sparingly and only when they are needed; you can look at a good deal of film without encountering so much as a single close-up. And this is just as well, for it will not do to leave the impression that Griffith was merely a technician. In *The Song of the Lark,* Willa Cather had one of her characters remark that her opera singer–heroine's "secret" was "every artist's secret . . . passion." And she goes on to say that "it is an open secret and perfectly safe. Like heroism, it is inimitable in cheap materials." Passion was Griffith's secret too, passion and tenderness, and a keen eye for beauty, and a sense of values, and an interest in ideas which none of the other film pioneers possessed to the same degree. He not only titillated your nerves by bringing you to the edge of your seat in your anxiety over whether the hero would arrive in time to save the heroine or the child; he also made you care deeply about what was going to happen to the heroine or child as an individual. He used charming people, and he used them, for the most part, while the dew of the morning was still fresh upon them.

Griffith and Biograph finally came to the parting of the ways over the company's refusal to back him in a program of feature films, followed by their asinine decision, when they did go in for features, to form an alliance with the stage producers Klaw and Erlanger and entrust the (quite insignificant) productions which resulted to other directors. When Griffith made a two-reel Civil War film glorifying the old plantation Negro, Biograph insisted upon releasing it as two pictures, *His Trust* and *His Trust Fulfilled.* They tried the same trick with *Enoch Arden,* but this time exhibitors insisted on showing the two parts together. Griffith's last film for Biograph was the four-reel *Judith of Bethulia,* from the Apocryphal story and the verse-play by Thomas Bailey Aldrich in which Nance O'Neil had starred. This he produced at Chatsworth, California, in 1913 upon a scale of unprecedented splendor for Biograph, but they thought so little of it that they did not even release it until 1914, after he had left the company. *Judith* had a very luscious Blanche Sweet as the wealthy and pious Jewish widow who attires herself like a courtesan and goes to the camp of the Assyrian general Holofernes (Henry Walthall) who is besieging the city, and there, in spite of the fact that she has fallen in love with him (an Aldrichian "improvement" upon the original story), cuts off his head. Mae Marsh and Robert Harron furnished lyrical relief as a pair of young pastoral lovers, and Lillian Gish had a minor part as a young Jewish mother trying to keep her baby alive during the siege. It is interesting that Griffith turned back to history, literature, and religion for this his first large-scale effort instead of drawing upon contemporary life. He told Iris Barry that he had not seen the Italian film spectacles which were coming into America at the time, but it is hard to believe this, for they were giving him such competition as he had never faced before. *Judith of Bethulia* is heavy and ominous from the first scene; it has a rich, brooding splendor of imagination, as befits its semioriental subject; all in all, it is certainly the greatest achievement of the early American film.[12]

According to his own account, Zukor offered Griffith $50,000 a year to become principal director for the new Famous Players Film Company—Edwin S. Porter accepted the post after Griffith had turned it down—but the great man went instead to Mutual, to direct and supervise production on a salary-plus-stock-participating basis, including the privilege of making two independent productions a year. Cecil B. deMille says that Griffith also turned down Samuel Goldwyn when he tried to get him for the new Lasky company; probably he was not sure of the financial stability of the

---

[12] Biograph's principal source of income during its last years seems to have been reissues (beginning in 1915) of Griffith's and later (1916 ff.) of Mack Sennett's old films. In February, 1917, they achieved one of the curiosities of cinema history by issuing "D. W. Griffith's *Her Condoned Sin*," in six reels, "founded on *Judith of Bethulia*." The length of the film had been increased 50 per cent by adding scenes which Griffith had discarded.

newcomers. At least one of Griffith's Mutual "supervises" was a distinguished film; this was the third *Enoch Arden,* directed by Christy Cabanne, with Alfred Paget, Lillian Gish, and Wallace Reid, and with Griffith himself playing a bit role as Annie Lee's father. Annie gave Miss Gish a better role than she was to have in *The Birth of a Nation,* and she was breathtakingly lovely in it. On the whole, however, Griffith's Mutual period, like the Triangle phase into which it was soon merged (and which involved some of the same business personnel), was disappointing, probably because most of his thought and time and energies were going into the big features he was making for himself.

The four most important pictures Griffith personally directed for Mutual were *The Battle of the Sexes* (December, 1913), *The Escape* (January, 1914), *Home Sweet Home* (March, 1914), and *The Avenging Conscience* (August, 1914). I have never seen *The Battle of the Sexes* or *The Escape.* In the first, Lillian Gish was again praised as the girl who drew a bead on her father's mistress; *The Escape* was an underworld story, adapted from a play by Paul Armstrong.[13] Neither *Home Sweet Home* nor *The Avenging Conscience* now seems a very impressive film.

Home Sweet Home has been called a preliminary study for *Intolerance;* it is such no more than *Pippa Passes* was, and I should say it suggests *Intolerance* considerably less than do either *Judith of Bethulia* or Luigi Maggi's great Italian spectacle, *Satan; or, the Drama of Humanity* (Ambrosio, 1912), which was the culmination of all early devil films.[14] The frame story deals with the (fic-

[13] *The Moving Picture World* found that Griffith had not only embellished Armstrong's work "whenever and wherever an opportunity is afforded, intensifying it by methods of character contrast, and giving it a new charm," but had also "endowed a rather morbid and commonplace play with some nobility of purpose."

[14] It is the essence of *Intolerance,* not that it deals with four separate stories thematically related but that the stories are interwoven in their presentation so that all four reach their climax with tremendous, overwhelming impetus during the last two reels. *Satan* presents the Eden story, the

tionized) life of John Howard Payne (Henry Walthall); the three central episodes concern the beneficent influence of his song,[15] for which, Griffith argues in subtitles, the errors of his life must be forgiven. The allegorical endings with which Griffith embellished his films at this period were not in general well done, but this one was surely the most absurd of all. Attired in impossible garments, halfway between bed sheets and swaddling clothes, Payne is shown laboring at nothing in particular upon a smoking hillside which is apparently supposed to suggest hell, when his long-dead sweetheart (Lillian Gish) literally comes floating through the air to draw him up to heaven with her.

Vachel Lindsay's praise for *The Avenging Conscience,* which he analyzes at some length in *The Art of the Moving Picture,* seems very extravagant and can perhaps best be explained by his passion for Poe. Both "Annabel Lee" and "The Tell-Tale Heart" are important for this film, which has a pseudoliterary flavor and many

Christ story, a medieval episode in which the devil invents alcoholic beverages to debauch mankind (an achievement considerably postdated), and a rather cheap modern underworld story. The tales are no more interwoven than in *Home Sweet Home,* but the atmosphere and feeling is considerably closer to *Intolerance.*

[15] In the first, Robert Harron as an Eastern "dude" who had decided that the little Western girl Apple-Pie Mary was not good enough for him returned to her after hearing "Home Sweet Home" at the psychological moment. (Mae Marsh was adorable as the girl; it was one of her best early roles.) In the second, a fisher–life story with some nice seacoast scenes, Mary Alden was saved from suicide after her two sons (James Kirkwood and Donald Crisp) had shot each other to death; apparently she made up her mind to live for "The Dull Boy" (Jack Pickford), who had undertaken a wild ride to fetch the sheriff in an attempt to avert the tragedy but had arrived too late. In the third, separately titled "The Marriage of Roses and Lilies," Blanche Sweet, as the wife of Courtenay Foote, was saved from the tempter Owen Moore, but she would not have had time to hear the song and experience a change of heart if her husband, upon apprehending the situation, had not decided to sit down and finish his cigar before confronting her and fallen asleep!

quoted subtitles.[16] It is full of visions, not very well presented, and the characters wander endlessly through the gardens of a great estate whose use, one suspects, must have been determined by their availability. A great deal of footage is wasted on "The Party," with a long, dreadful dance for which the story stops dead as in the old French opera, and all this is so irrelevant and unprepared for that one cannot but wonder whether there was not an actual garden party going on at the time the film was made which Griffith decided to photograph. For all that, there is about *The Avenging Conscience* a brooding sense of fate which builds up as the film proceeds to give it an intensity which *Home Sweet Home* never knows.[17] Blanche Sweet's characterization is fascinating in its teas-

[16] Henry Walthall, as an ambitious young writer brought up by his uncle (Spottiswoode Aitken), is opposed in his love for Annabel (Blanche Sweet); watching spiders and ants killing (as Cowperwood had watched the lobster and the squid in Theodore Dreiser's *The Financier*), he conceives the idea of killing his uncle. Having walled the body up in the fireplace, he is tormented both by his uncle's ghost and by a detective (Ralph Lewis) who suspects him. Apprehended in a hut he has prepared for himself with a subterranean getaway, he attempts to cheat the law by hanging himself, but is cut down before he has strangled. Annabel, in despair, throws herself over a cliff. At this point the young man wakes up, horrified by his dream, and is reconciled with his uncle, who conveniently, and rather suddenly, decides to accept Annabel. The last scene shows the lovers on the hillside à la *Birth of a Nation*. He tells her about the book he is writing; Pan plays in the woods, and little naked children come out of the tree to frolic with him.

[17] There is a sense in which artists of genius are more interesting in their failures than in their successes, and Griffith's worst films all have touches beyond the reach of other directors. Surely he never made a worse picture than *One Exciting Night*, yet who could feel that an effort had been wholly wasted which could inspire an artist like René Clair to remark that its "boldness and skill . . . was not to leave us outside the drama, but to involve us in it and make it play itself out in ourselves"? The French director adds that "we have to be very careful how to judge a man of this stature. If his best work is often marred by irritating little mannerisms, his feeblest contains remarkable visual effects."

ing ambiguity, and Walthall is at his best except for his final confrontation with the detective, where he is so "corny" and melodramatic as practically to burlesque himself. Yet in a measure *The Avenging Conscience* may be said to have substituted a psychological chase (Walthall and Lewis, assisted by the former's own conscience) for the physical chase more commonly associated with Griffith.

After six weeks of rehearsing, Griffith devoted the nine weeks which began July 4, 1914, to shooting *The Birth of a Nation* from the scenario in his head; the three months following were devoted to editing. The film is generally said to have cost about $100,000; by 1939 it had grossed about $15,000,000.

It is based on the novel *The Clansman,* by Thomas Dixon, Jr. (Doubleday, 1905), and the same author's unpublished play of the same title, supplemented by additional material from another Dixon novel, *The Leopard's Spots* (Doubleday, 1902). When it opened at Clune's Auditorium in Los Angeles on February 8, 1915, *The Clansman* was the name of the film as well. On February 20 it was shown in New York to an invited audience, and it was upon this occasion that Dixon leaned over toward Griffith and declared that *The Clansman* was too tame a title for so great a film; it ought, he said, to be called *The Birth of a Nation.* It was the most inspired title in motion-picture history. A program reproduced in Long's book on Griffith shows that it was still *The Clansman* in Los Angeles as late as September 19, 1915, but it had been *The Birth of a Nation* in New York from its opening at the Liberty Theater on March 3, at regular theater prices.[18] *The Birth of a Nation* established the motion picture as a top-flight theater attrac-

[18] Many film historians give the impression that all seats for *The Birth of a Nation* cost two dollars; this is incorrect. *Best* seats were two dollars at the evening performances, but I doubt that any film was shown anywhere in America with no cheap seats available until World War II. When *Broken Blossoms* was shown at the George M. Cohan Theater, New York, in 1919, the second balcony cost fifty-five cents in the evening and twenty-eight cents for the matinee.

tion; it also led to the establishment of motion-picture advertising and reviewing in many newspapers.

Moreover, *The Birth of a Nation* made the motion picture front-page controversial material. Because of its partisan interpretation of Civil War and Reconstruction materials and its alleged misrepresentation of the Negro, it produced fear of riots in many cities and caused headaches to innumerable officials. The question was most hotly agitated in Boston, where the state legislature actually passed a special censorship bill to enable any two members of a newly created three-member board to stop *The Birth of a Nation,* and the board astonished everybody by voting in favor of the film! The State House was stormed; the Tremont Theater was picketed; there was even crazy talk of dynamite. Upon the mind of one distinguished citizen of the Boston area the film would seem to have exercised a debilitating intellectual influence at least, for Harvard's President Charles W. Eliot came out with the statement that even though he had not seen it, he knew that it presented "an extraordinary misrepresentation of the birth of this nation"! Injunctions were issued in a number of American cities; in Louisville an exhibitor was arrested under a 1906 law against exciting race prejudice; and two bills were introduced (but not passed) in Congress to prevent the film's showing in the District of Columbia; one of these was sponsored by a Pennsylvania congressman who resented Griffith's attack on Thaddeus Stevens. Ironically enough, the place where the opposition came closest to success was Lillian Gish's own home state of Ohio, where *The Birth of a Nation* was never exhibited until February, 1917.[19]

[19] President Wilson saw it at a private showing in the White House and was widely quoted as having declared that it was like writing history in flashes of lightning, and that his only regret was that it was all so terribly true. In the spring of 1915, however, Joseph P. Tumulty, in a letter to Congressman Thatcher of Massachusetts, denied that Wilson had "expressed approbation" of *The Birth of a Nation.* "Its exhibition at the White House was a courtesy extended to an old acquaintance." The old acquaintance was the author Dixon, not Griffith. See *The Moving Picture World,* Vol. XXIV (1915), 1122.

As Mary Pickford once remarked, *The Birth of a Nation* is the greatest example we have of "dramatic accumulation" on the screen. No qualified judge doubts that, aesthetically considered, it is one of the finest films ever made, and in its effect the most influential of them all.[20] Yet it inspires controversy even today. What shall be said of the charges against it? Since art does not exist in a vacuum—motion-picture art least of all—they cannot be ignored.

How *The Birth of a Nation* treated the Negro when it was first exhibited cannot now be judged, for Griffith cut many of the scenes which gave most offense, and these are not now extant. He gave every indication of being genuinely hurt and surprised by the criticisms which were made of him; indeed, *Intolerance* was partially inspired by them. Later, in *The Greatest Thing in Life* (1918) he included a touching scene in which a white American soldier in World War I kissed his dying Negro "buddy" in the trenches, so that the Negro, in his delirium, might suppose himself dying in his mother's arms. In *The White Rose* (1923) he had Mae Marsh taken in and cared for in her agony by a kindly Negro family, whom he represented as on the best possible terms with the first white families of the little Louisiana town.

Griffith was quite just when he pointed out that his criticism

[20] The most important influences were the contributions it made to the establishment of the feature film and the increased interest in film technique which it inspired. But it was also directly imitated. Its most respectable stepchild was Selig's picturization of Winston Churchill's novel *The Crisis* (1916). That same year, Dixon was out with a vicious piece of war propaganda, *The Fall of a Nation*, without Griffith but with a musical score by no less a person than Victor Herbert. A minor firm called Unicorn issued a two-reel feature, *The Rise of a Nation*, picturing American history as it impinged upon an American family. As late as 1919 there was a film called *The Birth of a Race*, "The Story of a Great Peace. In Two Parts." This played the patrician Blackstone Theater in Chicago at a two-dollar top—one of the many now totally forgotten films which, in their time, collected as extravagant encomia from weak-minded commentators as the great films have ever been able to command.

was directed not against Negroes but against the carpetbaggers and scalawag whites who led them astray. The subtitles at the beginning of Part II declare that the film is not meant to reflect upon any race or people of today, and they are followed by quotations from Wilson's *History of the American People* about the carpetbaggers' having aimed to "put the white South under the heel of the black South." Stoneman's (Thaddeus Stevens') "stooge," Silas Lynch, is called a traitor to his white patron and even more of a traitor to his own people. When the Negro guerrillas raid Piedmont, we are told that "the scalawag white captain influences the Negro militia to follow his orders." Moreover, there are good Negroes in the film as well as bad. We see them in their slave quarters during the two hours they have off in "their working day from six to six." They are happy and gay in the cotton fields and on excellent terms with their masters. The slaves (later, servants) of the Camerons are faithful to them, scornful of the "trash" that serve the carpetbaggers, zealous and brave in assisting the Camerons when they are in danger, and none grieve more than they when the Little Sister is killed.

So far the defense can and should justly go, but it must stop here. Negroes who keep their "place" are admired in *The Birth of a Nation*—Negroes who never give the whites any trouble. Race prejudice is naked and unashamed in such scenes as that in which Negro troops rudely brush the Little Colonel (Henry Walthall) before his own door—"This sidewalk belongs to us as much as to you, Colonel Cameron," says the loathsome Lynch—and I have heard applause when the Little Colonel folds his arms and looks away upon being introduced to Lynch by Stoneman. Stoneman has a mulatto mistress, hatefully portrayed by Mary Alden; Lynch nearly rapes Elsie Stoneman (Lillian Gish); Flora, the Little Sister (Mae Marsh), learns the "stern lesson of honor" and throws herself over a cliff, through "the opal gates of death," to get away from Gus, one of Lynch's minions. The Negro members of the 1871 House of Representatives in South Carolina pass a bill legalizing mis-

cegenation; they are shown as almost animals, and there is las-
civious rejoicing both on the floor and in the gallery when the bill
is carried. We are told that the Ku Klux Klan saved the South
from anarchy, though not without the shedding of more blood than
was lost at Gettysburg; but the force of the qualification is weakened through its ascription to "Judge Tourgée of the Carpetbaggers."[21] When the Little Sister dies, the Klansmen seek out Gus
to give him "a fair trial in the halls of the Invisible Empire," and
when they have killed him, they dump his body at Lynch's door.
When the Camerons finally take refuge in the hut occupied by the
two Union veterans, former foes are united in support of "their
Aryan birthright." At the close the Klansmen ride through the
streets shooting the Negroes down like vermin, after which they
preside, in their ghostly robes, over the next election, where all the
blacks are disqualified.[22]

[21] It may be worth noting that two years before *The Birth of a Nation*,
Gene Gauntier had made a three-reel film, *In The Clutches of the Ku-Klux
Klan*, in which that organization was presented most unadmiringly.

[22] I would recommend a careful reading of *The Clansman* in both its
novelized and dramatized versions (there is a typed copy of the latter in the
Harvard Theater Collection) and also of *The Leopard's Spots* to those who
wonder why Griffith was hurt that his moderation went unappreciated. Dixon saw Negroes as human degenerates, incapable of civilization, and said
so frankly.

There is no Little Sister in the novelized form of *The Clansman*. Instead there is a girl named Marion Lenoir, to whom Ben Cameron (the
Little Colonel) is engaged. Gus (the same character responsible for the
death of the Little Sister in the film) invades her home and rapes her, whereupon she *and her mother*, at her instigation, by jumping off a cliff, commit
suicide together to wipe out her shame, a sickly, morbid, and disgusting
episode.

The film has closer affinities at this point to both the dramatic version
of *The Clansman* and *The Leopard's Spots*. In the latter, Ron Camp's daughter, also named Flora, is raped and her skull crushed by a Negro when she
goes to a spring for water, but she does not jump from a cliff. She is brought
home, where doctors work vainly to save her, and the Negro who menaced
her is burned alive! In the stage play, on the other hand, Ben's little sister

103

In its attitude toward war, *The Birth of a Nation* is much fairer than in its racism. Griffith claimed to have pictured war so that war might be held in abhorrence, and in this case the evidence is all on his side. One subtitle reads: *"War* claims its *bitter, useless sacrifice."* The caption "War's peace" precedes a shot of corpses on the battlefield, and the allegorical ending pictures war as a beast and pits him over against Christ. When we read "while women and children weep, a great conqueror marches to the sea," Flora does appear, and she jumps from the cliff to escape Gus when she goes to the spring on her birthday, over her brother's objection, to feed her ground squirrel. While this is going on, Elsie Stoneman learns of Ben's connection with the Klan and rejects him. General Forrest has just come to town to organize a local K.K.K.; Dr. Cameron is opposed but Ben welcomes the idea. After Flora's death, Dr. Cameron joins the Klan to avenge his daughter, and Gus is made to confess through the doctor's hypnotic power over him. Called upon by her father to testify against Ben, Elsie refuses; he is court-martialed nevertheless and sentenced to be shot. While he is awaiting execution Elsie has her big scene with Lynch, but the crisis is precipitated by her hysterics rather than by any attack from him. After she has been carried into the next room her father arrives and hears and rejects Lynch's proposal of marriage with her, but Lynch declares that unless they can be married at once, he will have Elsie shot! Both she and Ben are saved by the Klan.

It is interesting to note that in *The Leopard's Spots* some of Lynch's functions are performed by George Harris out of *Uncle Tom's Cabin* (Simon Legree is also a character). George is patronized by the Hon. Everett Lowell, Boston congressman, but repudiated and thrown out when he asks for his daughter's hand; finding work closed to him in the North, he becomes a criminal.

Incidentally, the title of the film was first suggested when Dixon wrote of Elsie Stoneman (in the novel *The Clansman*): "She began to understand why the war, which had seemed to her a wicked, cruel and causeless rebellion, was the one inevitable thing in our growth from a loose group of sovereign States to a United Nation." Passionately as they sympathized with the old South, both Dixon and Griffith were uncompromisingly pro-Lincoln and pro-Union. As a subtitle in *The Birth of a Nation* puts it: "The soul of Daniel Webster calling to America, 'Liberty and union, one and inseparable, now and forever.'" Dixon later considered Lincoln at greater length in his stage play *A Man of the People* (Appleton, 1920).

we understand that the South still hates General Sherman too much to speak his name. Even at home, among the Cameron girls, war is "the breeder of hate." So famous are the battle scenes in *The Birth of a Nation,* and so carefully is the spectator's eye guided, that one can well understand why, visiting the Western front in 1917, Griffith should have found little excitement there and caught himself feeling crazily that he had put all this stuff on himself. For all that, there are not many battle scenes in the picture; the only real battle is that occasioned by Lee's ordering an attempt to break through the Union lines to save a food train, and these scenes are anything but brutal, judging by what the screen has shown since. The emphasis throughout is upon what war costs and destroys; the real focus of interest is on the people who suffer at home and the lasting evil which follows war. All this is from the film itself, but the program notes underline it unmistakably:

> Great care has been taken not to glorify battle. Even the music stops in its motif of glorification to sound the note of terror and desolation which is the real truth of WAR.
>
> Armies seldom settled disputed questions of state. But where they accomplish this much, in the wake of conflict arise newer and more terrible questions. But for the hatred engendered in the Civil War, the sufferings of the Reconstruction period would never have been known.

I have sometimes been tempted to feel and to say that a great masterpiece was lost to the world when *The Birth of a Nation* went into its second half. The first part, with the Civil War scenes, the return of the Little Colonel to his ruined home,[23] and the assassi-

[23] There would, I think, be universal agreement that this is one of the great moments in motion-picture history. It culminates when, after the poignant scene between the Little Colonel and his sister, his mother's arm reaches out through the door, the rest of her person unseen, to encircle his neck and draw him into the house. James Card once remarked to me upon the interesting anomaly that even those enthusiasts who insist most fanatically upon separation between stage and screen always single out this scene for

nation of Lincoln, is almost consistently great historical epic;[24] the second, which is the Reconstruction portion, with its hard riding, its attacks on women, and its appeal to prejudice and passion, has received a much stronger infusion of melodrama. Yet this is over-simplification, for, as Gilbert Seldes has said, "the second half of the picture is filled with a kind of idyllic poetry" in spite of its melodrama. "The whole countryside is peopled with characters who come to life no matter how briefly we see them." Although it may seem absurd to say it, the terrible scenes leading up to the death of the Little Sister are drenched in poetry; nothing in pictures has ever been more brilliantly edited than the closing sequences; and whatever one may think of the Klan, their activities do provide superb motion-picture material.

---

praise; there is nothing in it, he said, that might not have been done on the stage. Mr. Card, of course, was not disparaging the scene but merely rebuking those who insist upon confining the scope of the motion picture to what he considers too restricted a field.

[24] The principal exception to this statement, aside from Griffith's always besetting sins of making his girls flutter and the trying combination of the flowery and the pedantic in his subtitles, is the shadowy characterization of the younger Camerons and the Stoneman boys. Some of the sets look cheap and flimsy (it had always been an idiosyncrasy of Griffith's to spend a great deal of footage on people passing through hallways, but there is no other film in which so much action takes place in a hall as in *The Birth of a Nation*), and, unlike the rest of the war scenes, the pictures of the burning of Atlanta, with their technically daring divided screen, now seem very crude. I do not think it fair, however, to criticize Griffith, in *The Birth of a Nation* and elsewhere, because so many of his characters are more types than individuals. He lived closer to the world of *The Faerie Queene* than to that of *Madame Bovary,* and his films often hover on the verge of allegory: even his fluttering heroines are intended more to suggest the spirit of youth than to document the observed behavior of this particular girl in this particular situation. As Lillian Gish once confided to Mae Tinée of the Chicago *Tribune:* "Mr. Griffith makes me do it. He says that all young people behave that way." This, too, is the explanation for the rather silly labels he sometimes pinned on his characters—The Dear One, The Friendless One, The Musketeer of the Slums, etc.

For so active a film, *The Birth of a Nation* opens with surprising quietness, and there is a good deal of the tableau type of development characteristic of some of the Biographs about it, the action being announced in a subtitle, then illustrated in the following scene.[25] Lincoln, for example, hardly appears in action at all: if ever the term "posing for the movies" was justified, it might be applied to Joseph Henaberry here. After signing the call for troops, he turns to his desk, wipes his eyes with a huge handkerchief, then folds his hands in prayer. This scene, Ford's Theater on the night of the assassination, the surrender of Lee, and the 1871 South Carolina legislature are all "set" pieces, historical reconstructions.[26] Obviously all this contrasts very effectively with the rush of furious action after the war begins, as in the scenes showing the departure of the Camerons from Piedmont or the ball after Bull Run. Even here, however, the principle of contrast is recognized, as when the Little Colonel leaves the dancing to go in and fondle the Little Sister, who has been asleep on a couch.

We badly need a book which shall contain a complete scene-by-scene description of *The Birth of a Nation* and *Intolerance*, re-

[25] *The New York Hat* even opened, without a subtitle, on Kate Bruce's deathbed, which was not a part of the story but was necessary to create the conditions under which it could move. Griffith repeated this effect at the beginning of so elaborate a film as *The Avenging Conscience*, where the baby's mother dies in the first scene, leaving him to be brought up by his uncle. Sometimes he employed somewhat similar devices after a film had got under way. Take the subtitle in *The Battle*: "Later. Chance places her alone in her home with the battle outside." Some may consider this crude. To me it seems an example of admirable economy. The director simply accepts the time limitations of the short film and secures his effects within them.

[26] The legislature scene even opens on an empty chamber, after which the people "dissolve" into it, an effect Griffith repeated in *Intolerance* when showing the offices of the Jenkins Foundation. In some of the early Biographs, notably *A Corner in Wheat*, he had opened on "frozen" actors, not permitting them to come to life until after a few frames had passed, a focusing device of at least questionable cinematic value which was afterward completely discontinued.

producing at least one frame from each shot. Meanwhile, we should be thankful for what Lewis Jacobs has printed of Lynch's encounter with Elsie Stoneman[27] and for A. R. Fulton's record of the whole Ford Theater sequence.[28] Fulton writes cogently:

> If the scene were done like Porter's there would be only a single shot, or two at the most, to show parallel action in the passage outside the President's box. However, by breaking the scene down into fifty-five shots, Griffith obtains effects that would not be possible in one or two long shots. He establishes a relationship between Lincoln and Booth—showing Lincoln's unconsciousness of danger and Booth's intention; between Lincoln and the play—showing where Lincoln's attention is directed; between the bodyguard and the play—showing why the bodyguard leaves his post; and even between Lincoln and the audience in Ford's Theatre, particularly Elsie and Ben—showing that the audience too is unconscious of the terrible deed about to be committed. Griffith emphasizes Booth's murderous intention by the close shot of the revolver. He interpolates shots of the stage not only to indicate where all the characters except Booth are centering their attention but also to create suspense. This suspense is heightened by having Elsie direct Ben's attention to the balcony at the side of the box, and then cutting to Booth—his first appearance in the film: will anything come of his thus being noticed? These and other details, such as Lincoln's premonitory gesture of drawing the shawl over his shoulders,[29] would be ineffective if done in the manner of *The Great Train Robbery*.

The sequence devoted to Sherman's march to the sea begins with a shot showing only the refugees huddled on the hillside at

---

[27] *The Rise of the American Film*, 180–85. See also pages 193–97 for a section of *Intolerance*.

[28] *Motion Pictures*, 91–97.

[29] There may be a suggestion of premonition here, but the implied irony is more important. Lincoln protects himself against the draft a moment before Booth's bullet is to plow its way into his brain, making him thereafter indifferent alike to drafts and creature comforts forevermore.

the left side of the screen, after which the camera opens out to take in a vast panorama showing the Union soldiers marching in the valley below. Another masterly shot shows refugees streaming up the hill in the foreground; they are followed by others, much smaller, seen from afar off. The unforgettable close shot of the parched corn served to Confederates in the trenches during the last days of the war exemplifies the kind of detail later developed by Eisenstein. Crosscutting is masterly throughout. The Camerons in the South get news of the death of their son, then the Stonemans in the North; in both cases the reaction is the same. From the battle scenes we cut to the Camerons at home, the father, with clasped hands, passionately engaged in leading family prayer. The "War's peace" scene is inserted between scenes of furious fighting. When Lynch tells Stoneman "I want to marry a white woman" and receives his blessing, we crosscut to all the persons involved in the problem before we come back to the completing subtitle "The lady I want to marry is your daughter" and the consequent shift to fury on Stoneman's part.

The Birth of a Nation hammered the sensibilities of its audiences as no film had ever hammered them before, and at the same time it made them think as no film had ever done it before. In both aspects, as in all others, it was topped by *Intolerance,* first shown at the Liberty Theater in New York on August 5, 1916, and still incontestably the greatest motion picture ever made. *Intolerance* began with the modern story, at first entitled *The Mother and the Law;*[30] it was not until after the *Birth of a Nation* controversies had begun that Griffith conceived the idea of combining and interweaving this with three other stories showing the operations of intolerance all through history, or selectively and representatively in Christ's Judea, Belshazzar's Babylon, and Paris at the

[30] This title actually appeared on the screen when in 1919 the modern story of *Intolerance* was reissued as a separate film. The Babylonian story similarly became *The Fall of Babylon,* with the Mountain Girl this time saved from death.

time of the Massacre of St. Bartholomew. This not only tremendously enlarged the scope of the film—the ruins of Belshazzar's banquet hall, the greatest ever built for a motion picture, whose presentation involved the greatest "crane" or "trucking" shot in motion-picture history, stood for years in Hollywood, and it has been estimated that the $2,000,000 film would cost $30,000,000 to duplicate today[31]—but it also gave Griffith the opportunity for a dazzling technical achievement, the creation of the only film symphony or fugue. As A. Nicholas Vardac expressed it:

> The addition of the three complementary stories served to carry the film out of the present and to color it with a significance beyond that of temporary interest. And each of these stories was, in itself, a spectacle. In other words, through the addition of three parallel spectacles, the simple melodrama was raised far above its original level. The young wife rushing to save her unjustly condemned husband from the gallows was entirely melodramatic and of only contemporary importance, but its dramatic and thematic significance was lifted out of all time and presented as an eternal verity through the intercutting of the culminating events of the other three spectacles: Christ struggling toward Calvary, the Babylonian mountain girl racing to warn Belshazzar that his priests had betrayed him, and the Huguenot fighting his way through the streets on St. Bartholomew's Day to save his sweetheart from massacre by the French mercenaries. The melodrama of *Intolerance* achieved its dramatic significance and thematic structure through graphic integration with breath-taking spectacle, thus bringing to a culmination the melodramatic editorial syntax emanating originally from the popular nineteenth-century stage and demonstrated years previously by Porter in *The Great Train Robbery*.

Griffith himself added that in *Intolerance* "events are not set forth

[31] William K. Everson, "Film Spectacles," *Films in Review*, Vol. V (1954), 459–71. Details concerning the filming of *Intolerance* have been given in many film books, including Jacobs, *The Rise of the American Film*, Griffith and Mayer, *The Movies*, and Fulton, *Motion Pictures*.

in their historical sequence, or according to accepted forms of dramatic construction, but *as they might flash across a mind seeking to parallel the life of the different ages."* And once more he might have asked his critics, "Why not? Doesn't Dickens write that way?"

Even more than *The Birth of a Nation,* then, *Intolerance* is a glorified Biograph, or in other words a perfect motion picture. This has nowhere been better expressed than by the amazingly erudite critic who wrote in the Boston *Evening Transcript*:

> The [general] effect is naturally a stunning departure from the customary moving picture, developed though it is from Mr. Griffith's own invention, the "flash back." But it is not so much of a departure from Mr. Griffith's past as many will think. Just as the two different stories told, one following another, in the two halves of *The Birth,* may be traced technically to his earlier Biograph films, *The Battle* and *The Battle at Elderbush Gulch,* so you may find "studies" for the various parts of *Intolerance* in other films made in those almost prehistoric but immortal days when the future of the photoplay and of Mr. Griffith was being made at the old Biograph studios. The slum life of the modern story in *Intolerance* was handled in half a dozen films like *The Musketeers of Pig Alley,* blending the romance of the "gunman" with an intimate realism of treatment. The fall of Babylon had its prototype in *Judith of Bethulia.* The Christ story has figured in a dozen bits of allegory in photoplays of other periods. The Renaissance of Charles IX is almost wholly novel to the screen but Griffith has handled Italian costumes of that period in *The Perfidy of Mary* and *The Blind Princess and the Poet.* There is even a bit of Griffith's old "Pickford stuff" . . . in the girl from the mountains who descends upon Babylon, displays her tempestuous talents in the marriage market, and ends by driving a rocking chariot to the relief of the city.

The element of propaganda was just as evident in the old Biograph days.[32] Mr. Griffith has always been fascinated by the ability

[32] One of Griffith's very earliest film stories, *Old Isaacs the Pawnbroker,* written before he had begun to direct, attacks the foundations, and reformers get a rough handling even in so light a film as *Muggsy's First Sweetheart.*

of the film to show, both in action and in printed "leaders," an ethical point of view. He taught a sort of cave-man pathology in *Man's Genesis* . . . he showed the eternal struggle of the scholar-husband and the light-minded dancer-wife in *Oil and Water*; he made a sort of *Everywoman* of the films in *The Blind Princess and the Poet*; and the list might be continued almost indefinitely.

Yet for all the training the Biographs ought to have given them, audiences of the time were not up to *Intolerance;* financially the film was a disastrous failure. Worse still, later critics have sometimes been quite as stupid, chattering about the difficulty of following four different stories, and much besides. I had no difficulty in following them at the age of sixteen, and I do not believe that I should have experienced any if the film had been shown to me in a prenatal state. If, as has been stated, spectators were confused by the woman out of *Leaves of Grass* who rocked the cradle marking the transition from one age to another, they must all have been mental defectives. John Howard Lawson says that nothing happened to her. What was supposed to happen to her? In a deeper sense everything that took place in the film happened to her, for all the characters were her children. Much as I respect Julian Johnson as a film critic, he seemed to me quite absurd when he wrote in *Photoplay* (and Lewis Jacobs quotes him approvingly): "The fatal error of *Intolerance* was that in the Babylonian scenes you didn't care which side won. It was just a great show." Didn't care whether Belshazzar and Nabonidus continued to maintain peace and the arts of civilization in Babylon or whether the barbarian Cyrus overran it with his savage hordes? Didn't care whether religious toleration survived under Belshazzar or whether the treacherous, intolerant priest of Marduk succeeded in his treason? Didn't care whether Belshazzar and the Princess Beloved lived out their happy lives in peace or must kill themselves to avoid capture? Didn't care whether the gallant Mountain Girl, her heart aflame with unselfish love for her king, succeeded in saving him or not? Then what in the world *do* Mr. Johnson and Mr. Jacobs care about in the theater?

This is not to say that *Intolerance* has no faults. As Iris Barry has pointed out before me, the Judean story is undeveloped[33] while the French story gets lost and then, after we have almost forgotten it, surprisingly bobs up again.[34] Moreover, intolerance plays so slight a role in the modern story that the unity of the film is somewhat impaired. When the Boy's (Robert Harron's) enemies plant a wallet upon him, the authorities "intolerate him away for a term." At the allegorical end, cannon and prison bars, "wrought in the fires of intolerance," are destroyed. Griffith's titles keep harping on intolerance as if he knew that it was not sufficiently involved in the action so that the audience would naturally keep it in mind. *Intolerance* is even more splendidly pacifistic than *The Birth of a Nation,* but even here the note is forced. War is "the most potent weapon forged in the flame of intolerance." "Cyrus repeats the world-old prayer, Kill, kill, kill, and to God be the glory, world without end, forever and ever. Amen." And again, apropos of capital punishment, "Universal justice: an eye for an eye, a tooth for a tooth, a murder for a murder."

There are other faults, weaknesses, and improbabilities. Griffith had infinite charity for publicans but none for Pharisees, and he depicts "uplifters" and foundations as one-sidedly in *Intolerance* as he depicts Negroes in *The Birth of a Nation.* It may be true that "when women cease to attract men, they often turn to reform as a second choice"—or the sentiment may be merely a colossal ex-

[33] It covers only the marriage at Cana, the incident of the woman taken in adultery, and the Crucifixion.

[34] Griffith is very careful not to offend modern Catholics in the French story. Catherine de Medici covers her political intolerance of the Huguenots "under the cloak of the great Catholic religion." But the Huguenot leader Coligny is as intolerant as she, and past outrages committed by Huguenots against Catholics are shown in flash back. A priest saves a Huguenot child during the massacre by hiding her under his robe. In the modern story the good priest who is attending the Boy nearly faints on his way to the gallows.

pression of masculine vanity—but it is certainly oddly placed in a scene showing the raiding of a bawdy-house. The uplifters could not have seized the Dear One's baby and put it in the asylum without a hearing at which a judge would have had to consider the evidence and make up his mind whether or not she was a fit mother. With the real murderer and her confession in hand, it might be supposed that the warden would have authority to postpone an execution at least until the governor could be reached. And once the Dear One had come to the governor, he could certainly telephone the prison; it would not be necessary for her to bring the written pardon to the very foot of the gallows. In the Babylonian story, the killings in the hand-to-hand fighting seem too obviously contrived and, for once, not cut fast enough, so that when the warrior's head is struck off, the audience has time to see that he is a dummy and be amused instead of horrified.

The acting in *Intolerance* is a strange combination of the intensely naturalistic and the stylized. The former is seen at its best in Mae Marsh's wonderful courtroom scenes and again in her moving reunion with Robert Harron when he is taken down from the gallows. But even Mae Marsh is sometimes required to prolong her comedy scenes, or to force the note, until the point has been blunted. Constance Talmadge's Mountain Girl is more theatricalized and directed for comic effect, but it is certainly very good of its kind. On the other hand, Belshazzar and the Princess Beloved are images rather than characters, like Lincoln in *The Birth of a Nation*. Josephine Crowell's Catherine de Medici is a caricature, not a character; she acts *at* the audience, not *to* or *with* the other actors, and one need only remember her simple, deeply sincere Mrs. Cameron in *The Birth of a Nation* to be sure that this was not Mrs. Crowell's fault. In what seems to have been intended to indicate a spasm of conscience on St. Bartholomew's morn, she was made to flutter like an adolescent.

Only a very great work of art could triumph in spite of such serious faults, and *Intolerance* is a very great work of art. The

Babylonian scenes stimulate the imagination and quicken the pulses; they thrilled even Oxford's great Assyriologist, Archibald Henry Sayce, and they set a standard toward which other directors aspired for many years. "History," said Iris Barry, "seems to pour like a cataract across the screen," and in truth the marvelous onrushing flood of Cyrus' hordes against the doomed city was so overwhelming that nobody who saw *Intolerance* will ever really believe that he did not with his own eyes see Babylon fall. Technically these scenes were far more advanced than anything in *The Birth of a Nation,* anticipating the devices employed by other directors by many years; dramatically an overwhelming contrast was created by showing the great banquet hall first as used for the festivities celebrating the deliverance of Babylon and, later, as overrun in terror by the Persians when Cyrus returns. The cutting is even more brilliant than in *The Birth of a Nation,* for we are obliged to cut not only within each story but from one story to another. We cut from the Boy's dying father, killed by the troops which have fired on the strikers, to Jenkins the millowner, as alone as Mussolini in a comparably vast private office, and back again. After the Dear One's baby has been seized, we cut to "Suffer little children," and then to the baby being carried into the Jenkins Foundation. From the Boy's condemnation for a crime he did not commit, we cut to Christ carrying His Cross, then back to the Boy, while the Mountain Girl's chariot, outracing Cyrus's armies, is paralleled to the Dear One's auto trying to catch the governor's train. But when the train has been overtaken, other scenes and stories intervene before the Dear One is permitted to stand in the governor's presence, and in all these scenes dramatic time is so skillfully manipulated that the spectator is not troubled by the fact that the preparations for the Boy's execution and the overtaking of the governor's train have covered the whole fall of Babylon and the whole Massacre of St. Bartholomew.[35]

[35] "The original print of *Intolerance* was tinted: blue for the Judean story, sepia for the French, grey-green for the Babylonian, and amber for the

Griffith's next "big" picture after *Intolerance* was *Hearts of the World* (1917), which he visited the trenches to make, at the invitation of the British government. It is the only one of Griffith's leading films which I have been unable to review for the purpose of this book; I can, therefore, only speak of it on the basis of what I remember from many years ago. It is hardly necessary to say that *Hearts of the World* presented World War I in terms of black against white, and if it was not quite so bad as those monuments of American culture *To Hell with the Kaiser* and *The Kaiser, the Beast of Berlin,* it was not far behind. In any case I think it not unfair to say that it did more to advance the careers of both Lillian and Dorothy Gish than it did for Griffith's own. Lillian had, I suppose, done other things before that were as fine as her rustic French girl here, but she had done nothing else quite so elaborate and certainly nothing that had been presented in so effective a showcase as was at her disposal in this film. As for myself, though I had seen her many times, I had not, as it now appeared to me, seen nearly as much of her as I ought to have seen or intended to see in the future, and I had certainly not been fully awake to the depth and power of her art. From *Hearts of the World* on I knew that she started acting where other people left off and that I was hers forevermore. Dorothy, as the black-wigged "Little Disturber" (she learned the walk after many tears by following and imitating a London street girl), furnished vigor and brilliant comedy relief—and entered forthwith upon a new phase of her career. Whether Griffith himself was at all troubled in his mind over the contradiction between what he had said about war in *Intolerance* and *The Birth of a Nation* and what he was saying here I do not know; perhaps, like so many others at the time, he thought the Allies were "fighting for peace."[36]

---

modern. Night scenes were blue, sunny interiors yellow, and night battle scenes red." Fulton, *Motion Pictures*, 109.

[36] Lillian Gish *was* troubled, retrospectively at least, and did public penance when, as a member of the America First Committee, she was doing

From *Hearts of the World,* Griffith went on to a series of less ambitious program pictures released through Paramount-Artcraft. Three of these—*The Great Love* (August, 1918), *The Greatest Thing in Life* (November, 1918), and *The Girl Who Stayed at Home* (March, 1919)—were war pictures; and though the last-named represented a certain shift of emphasis, as its title indicates, there were still so many war scenes in it as to suggest that he had a good deal of material on hand to be used up. *A Romance of Happy Valley* (January, 1919) and *True Heart Susie* (July, 1919) provided a refuge from wartime strains by returning to an earlier, somewhat idealized, bucolic America, while *Scarlet Days* (December, 1919) harked back to a still older and more specialized period, the Bret Harte frontier.

The Great Love (Lillian Gish, Robert Harron, Henry Walthall, George Fawcett, etc.) was made—partly at least—in England, with the idea of showing how English society faced up to the war, a circumstance which perhaps misled Lewis Jacobs into making the erroneous statement that the film was shown only in England. *The Greatest Thing in Life* turned out to be brotherhood, and an aesthetic young snob (Robert Harron) learned it through the fellowship of the trenches. Aside from an abundance of spies, suspense, and melodrama, the film was notable for David Butler's character role as the enormous, garlic-eating Monsieur Baby and for an attempt, not followed up in later films, to turn Lillian Gish toward somewhat boisterous comedy (in one scene she did a beautiful cartwheel). *The Girl Who Stayed at Home* gave us a French girl betrothed to a nobleman but in love with an American for whom she was unwilling to break her troth and an American cabaret dancer in love with an American college boy. Lillian Gish was not in this film; in her place Griffith introduced, as the two

her utmost to keep her country out of World War II. See her "I Made War Propaganda," *Scribner's Commentary* (Nov., 1941). There is a careful modern revaluation of *Hearts of the World* by Roger Manvell in *Sight and Sound,* Vol. XIX (1950), 130–32.

girls mentioned, Carol Dempster and Clarine Seymour. Miss Seymour was a real discovery. A tiny girl with enormous eyes, she was as dark and vivacious as most Griffith heroines had been blonde and wistful, a delightful girl, of excellent character, whom everybody in the studio loved; but she died on April 25, 1920, on the threshold of what would almost certainly have been an important film career. After Lillian Gish's departure in the interest of her own starring engagements, Miss Dempster became Griffith's leading actress, but her cold personality did not attract a great following, and few of Griffith's admirers were willing to accept her at his valuation. Richard Barthelmess, too, made his first appearance for Griffith in *The Girl Who Stayed at Home*.

Lillian Gish played again with Robert Harron in both *A Romance of Happy Valley* and *True Heart Susie*. Clarine Seymour, too, appeared in *True Heart Susie* in a most unsympathetic role; she was the venal little milliner from the city who "vamped" Harron away from Lillian after the latter had secretly sold her cow to provide the means for him to study and become a minister. Late in the picture, the unworthy wife was kind enouh to die, so that true love triumphed in the end. So far as the story goes, *True Heart Susie* was soap opera, but the atmosphere had an attractive authenticity, and Lillian was excellent in the scenes in which she was obliged to behave like a perfect lady toward her rival even though her heart was breaking. The opening sequence, in which she and Harron were shown as children at school, was also very charming. *A Romance of Happy Valley* had a weak story too, but nobody except Griffith could have given such a sympathetic picture of the Locust Grove Sanctificationist Church. "If we smile at these quaint people, let it be through tears of sympathy. We must remember that from similar places have come the very highest ideals. Sometimes they do backslide, but the dream is always upward." You may not care for the preaching, but Griffith's handling showed a knowledge of the rural American temperament which could not have been matched elsewhere in the cinema of his time or, I dare say, today. *Scarlet Days,* which I thought a very exciting picture in its time, had Seymour, Dempster, Ralph Graves, and Barthelmess (as a Spanish bandit), but was chiefly notable for the memorable performance of the veteran screen actress Eugenie Besserer (familiar to a later generation as Jolson's mother in *The Jazz Singer*) as a frontier dance-hall habitué who loved her Eastern-bred, gently reared daughter and nearly broke her heart trying to save the girl from finding out about her mother's way of life. Griffith had stopped filming Browning, but he still held to Browning's faith in "what a man [or woman either] may waste, desecrate, never quite lose."

Meanwhile, in the spring of 1919, Griffith had given us the last of his three supremely great films, *Broken Blossoms,* made from Thomas Burke's story, "The Chink and the Child," in *Limehouse Nights. Broken Blossoms* was as intimate and brooding a film as *Intolerance* and *The Birth of a Nation* had been spectacular, and in it Griffith's capacity for using the camera to probe the hearts of his characters appeared at its best.

There were only three real characters: Lucy, the Child (Lillian Gish), Battling Burrows, her brutal father (Donald Crisp), and Cheng Huan, the Chink (Richard Barthelmess). Lucy, who serves Battling as a kind of punching bag to relieve his feelings when he is disturbed, stumbles out through the streets after one particularly terrible beating and faints in the shop of the Chinaman, who had previously admired her. He dresses her in a rich Oriental robe, surrounds her with Oriental finery, and enthrones her in a kind of private shrine above his shop. When a dirty little rat of his acquaintance discovers her there and tells her father, he is outraged, for "most of all Batttling hated those not born in the same great country as himself." In Cheng Huan's absence he invades and smashes the shrine and drags his daughter home. She locks herself in a closet, from which he hauls her out and beats her to death. Cheng Huan follows, shoots Battling, carries the girl back to his room, and there stabs himself to the heart.

Broken Blossoms is a kind of missionary story in reverse. Cheng Huan comes to the West to carry the message of the gentle Buddha to rough Occidentals, represented to him by brawling American sailors in China. The picture opens with a long Oriental sequence. An atmospheric river scene marks the transition to London, where we see Cheng Huan as a "Chink storekeeper" in Limehouse, his dreams wrecked and he himself become an opium smoker. Scenes in Chinese dives in London follow. These do not carry on the story; they are images, memories which flash across the screen as they pass through Chen Huan's brain; from them we return to the Oriental temple bells which we saw at the beginning and also to the river scene.

Next comes "The home of Lucy and Battling Burrows." A subtitle gives us their past and explains Lucy's origin. We see Burrows drinking; a subtitle describes him as a "gorilla" and an "abysmal brute." We flash back to his last fight, which is shown on the screen as he thinks of it. His manager is present; one of his "chippy" friends comes in. The manager complains of his addiction to wine and women, thus putting him in a rage. Not until now do we first see Lucy, picking her way painfully along the dock; she sits down on a coil of rope. As she thinks, flashbacks show her being warned against marriage by a woman of her acquaintance, bending over the washtub while her husband scolds, and against their profession by two girls of the street. She gets up and goes in for her first encounter with Burrows.

Since he wants cheerful faces about him, and Lucy really has nothing to smile about, she pushes the corners of her mouth upwards with the second and third fingers of her right hand.[37] She prepares food for him, and he wolfs it down while she stands, hungry, and watches him. He threatens to beat her, for nothing in particular, but does not; ordering his tea for five, he goes out,

[37] It has been stated that Lucy's forced smile was suggested to Miss Gish by Mabel Normand. I have Miss Gish's authority for branding this story sheer fabrication.

after which she eats a few scraps alone. Now we go back to Cheng Huan and witness his encounter with a smug English cleric whose brother is setting out as a missionary. He hands Cheng Huan a pamphlet. The title, shown in a close shot, is *HELL*. Cheng says, "I wish him luck." From here we return to Lucy, who is now darning socks. She goes out to buy provisions for her father's supper, taking along with her, in addition to money, a roll of tin foil, for which she hopes to get a flower she craves, but it turns out she does not have quite enough tin foil. When she gets out into the street Cheng Huan watches her through his window and stands guard to protect her if she is troubled; when Evil Eye shows signs of molesting her, Cheng Huan comes out of his shop and, walking between them, pushes Evil Eye out of the way.

The second scene between Lucy and Burrows begins when she returns from shopping. The time is 4:30 P.M., and he is enraged because he has got home before her. She cries, " 'Tain't five! 'Tain't five!" When she spills food on his hand while serving him, he pretends that she did it on purpose and beats her cruelly. She stumbles out, more dead than alive, and moves toward her first real contact with Cheng Huan.

Broken Blossoms is not free of subtitles, and some of them are pretty distressing. "Dying she gives her last little smile to the world that has been so unkind." And again: "As he smiles Goodbye to White Blossom all the tears of the ages rush over his heart." (In Thomas Burke, Griffith discovered, perhaps for the first time, a writer whose prose was almost as purple as his own.) But the subtitles are not needed, and can be ignored, for the real story is told by an intimate, probing camera. Take the scene in which Lucy and Cheng Huan first look at each other—he in his shop, she in the street outside. The audience looks through the eyes of each, seeing the girl as the man looks at her and the objects in the shop window as Lucy's delighted gaze travels over them. Later he remembers the flower she had wanted and been unable to buy and brings it to her in her sanctuary. There is a delightful, subdued humor in these scenes, along with all their lyricism and danger, for the girl is still a child, and the doll Cheng Huan brings her is the climax of all her joys. The sight of the Chinaman brings her as much pleasure as that of her father had formerly awakened terror; once she starts to push up the corners of her mouth with her fingers; then she remembers that this is no longer necessary and smiles naturally. Sex intrudes only once—on his part, not hers—and is expressed only in an enormous close-up of his troubled eyes and in the way she shrinks from him momentarily without understanding what he wants. Then he retreats and remembers himself. "Why are you so good to me, Chinky?" she asks him once.

Lucy's hiding place is discovered when the Spying One comes to Cheng Huan's shop on a perfectly legitimate errand. While Cheng Huan slips out for change, he hears a noise upstairs; whereupon, being of a curious temperament, he tiptoes up the stairs to look. First we are with Lucy in the room above; then we are with the Spying One in the shop; we see him *go* up the stairs from the store; then we watch him *come* up from inside Lucy's room; there is a close shot of his foolish, giggling, delighted face. After the sanctuary has been raided, Evil Eye gladly bears the news to Cheng Huan; Cheng Huan rushes home but arrives too late. Lucy runs out when Battling arrives, but is caught by his henchmen and taken "home" through the cloaking river mist; once there, she locks herself in the closet. When Battling and Cheng Huan finally confront each other the camera moves from one to the other and to whatever feature or whatever part of the body Griffith wishes to emphasize. Cheng Huan's pistol is under his coat; Battling is unarmed but there is a hatchet on the floor next to his foot. A close-up directs our attention to this hatchet, and Battling is shot when, after having brought it closer with his foot, he ventures to try to stoop quickly to pick it up. After Burrows' death has been reported at the police station (the police are mulling over casualty lists and are not greatly interested), the authorities come to the flat; it is not until after this that we see Cheng Huan stab himself; next the police arrive at Cheng Huan's; we see them go into the building, but we are not permitted to watch them invade the sanctuary. The film ends as it began with mist-swathed river scenes and the striking of Oriental temple bells.

The enthusiasm which *Broken Blossoms* awakened in 1919 can hardly be overstated; Griffith was everywhere felt to have opened up new dimensions in the cinema and raised it to the level of great tragic art. The foregoing account of the sensitiveness of his direction may, I hope, have given the reader some idea of why these things should have been felt thus, though of course there is no substitute for seeing the film itself. Fortunately the film is available, notably in the Museum of Modern Art Film Library, and to my eyes it looks as good as it ever did, except that, alas, it must now be seen in a plain black and white print without the music and the subtle coloring that heightened its effect when it was first shown. Those who have seen Donald Crisp only of late years will have some difficulty in recognizing him in Battling Burrows. Some may find Richard Barthelmess' Cheng Huan a little thin in Oriental coloring, but his gentleness and idealism will not, I think, leave them unmoved. But so far as the players are concerned, *Broken Blossoms* is Lillian Gish's film first of all, and the deep sincerity of her terror and passion seem all the more moving and remarkable for always being conceived and projected as the terror and passion of a child. When I first met Miss Gish in 1920, I told her, with the brashness of youth, that I did not see how she could ever equal what she had done in *Broken Blossoms;* she received the statement, fortunately, with youth's resiliency, accepted the compliment implied, and let the rest go by. I have learned since then, and she has helped to teach me, that the simulation of hysteria is not necessarily the highest form of acting, yet for all that Lillian's hysteria in the famous "closet scene" of *Broken Blossoms* still seems to me a marvel to behold—inspired, impassioned, altogether beyond the bounds of normal experience, yet wonderfully infused with beauty. This was the wonder of *Broken Blossoms* all along the line: What might have been merely a subtly lighted, skillfully directed slum melodrama—as God knows most of its imitations have been—was lifted into an ideal world of aesthetic purity and clarity, so that the audience went away from it uplifted as well as terrified. How this was done is again, I suppose, the artist's secret, but *Broken Blossoms* was in this aspect no unique phenomenon. Shakespeare and the Greek dramatists too wrought their miracles out of sordid materials, and few of the thousands who have responded to the lyric cry of *Romeo and Juliet* are greatly moved when they hear of a pair of lunk-headed young modern lovers who have slipped off and made an end of themselves because there are barriers in the way of their marriage.

In 1920, Griffith came out with *Way Down East* and three program pictures—*The Greatest Question, The Idol Dancer,* and *The Love Flower,* all released through First National. A spiritual bond between a mother and a son lost at sea during the war, a child who witnessed a murder in babyhood and was later in danger at the hands of the vaguely recollected murderers, a mother's faith and a father's unbelief, a ghost appearing in a graveyard at midnight in answer to prayer, and a discovery of oil as the provision of the Lord—these were the disparate elements in *The Greatest Question.* Griffith never found more exquisite rural settings than in this film, and Lillian Gish and Robert Harron never struck a truer lyrical note. Eugenie Besserer and George Fawcett played powerfully as the contrasted mother and father, and Josephine Crowell was shown in endless, revolting close-ups as Lillian's persecutor. The story was a hodgepodge, however, and the spiritualistic element seemed dragged in to what was basically a melodrama in order to satisfy the postwar interest which had been awakened by Sir Oliver Lodge and others.

Both *The Love Flower* and *The Idol Dancer* had tropical settings; the exteriors were made in the Bahamas, and Griffith and his company were very nearly lost at sea in the enterprise. *The Love Flower* involves a girl's devotion to a father who has killed his wife's lover and taken refuge in the South Seas; the film has some spectacular photography and underwater swimming scenes; and it catches the ecstasy of young love under tropic skies. Except for what she was to do in 1924 in *Isn't Life Wonderful,* the picture probably contained the best acting Griffith was ever to get out of Carol Dempster. *The Idol Dancer* concerns missionaries and traders in the South Seas and a gin-soaked derelict (Richard Barthelmess) and a sickly, high-minded, anemic youth (Creighton Hale), both in love with the luscious White Almond Flower (Clarine Seymour). His love redeems them both—her from a heathenism and him from his atheism and the curse of drink. Although *The Idol Dancer* carries special interest as Clarine Seymour's last film—she died before its release,[38] and it gave her the only opportunity she ever had to reveal her full capacities—it is the fashion presently to abuse it and even to suggest that Griffith probably did not direct it personally, but I have Richard Barthelmess' word for it that he did. In quality it is certainly at least an average Griffith program picture. It is true that the "orgy of destruction" engineered by the rascally white trader is a pretty forced means of working up an exciting ending, with the opportunity for another Griffith last-minute rescue (this time the rescuers come in paddle boats); but the conflict between Christianity and paganism is a sound dramatic motif, the background and the native customs are colorful, and certainly Clarine's White Almond Blossom is good enough for any picture. Comic relief is furnished by the determination of the only white boy on the island to force his native friend to wear pants. He finally gets them on him but they come down during the

[38] In September, 1920, Griffith lost another important player when Robert Harron died of a bullet wound. Since Homer Croy has seen fit to state categorically that Harron committed suicide, it should be recorded here that his death was officially judged accidental. He was supposedly shot when a loaded pistol fell out of a trunk he was unpacking, and though nobody was able to figure out why Harron should have a pistol in his trunk, his character and his devout Catholicism have always made it difficult for his friends to believe he killed himself.

closing excitement, and it must be admitted that he looks much better without them.

Way Down East was the most passionate of Griffith's many paeans of praise for the Christian home; on this score, at least, he could have satisfied Harriet Beecher Stowe. "The one man for the one woman, between them the sacramental bond, life's cleanest and sweetest." In this case the woman, Anna Moore (Lillian Gish), has, as it happens, already borne a child, having been deceived by a scoundrel (Lowell Sherman) through a mock marriage, which gave Griffith an opportunity to open with an attack on the double standard and a preachment of monogamy in the name of Christ, glorifying woman's constancy against the selfishness of the "man-animal." The Lottie Blair Parker–Joseph R. Grismer play, a perennial visitor in every American city, had long been one of the most valuable pieces of theatrical property in America, and Griffith paid $175,000 for the right to film it. His reputation was at its height when it appeared, and even though it admittedly fell below the level of *The Birth of a Nation, Intolerance,* and *Broken Blossoms,* it was still regarded as a major effort, and first-nighters paid eleven dollars for main-floor seats both in New York and in Chicago. In the latter city after the picture had finished its run of nearly four months at the Woods Theater at regular theater prices, interest was still so keen that it was moved, for two weeks more, to the great Auditorium.

Way Down East was an uneven film; the rural scenes are authentically New England, but the home of the rich relations to which Anna journeys in Boston does not seem at all Bostonian. The rural comedy is hokum to the hilt; Vivia Ogden played the old gossip Martha for points, with superb skill, in the nineteenth-century comic tradition, but most of the men comics were just plain bad. I speak elsewhere in this volume of the wonderful scene (borrowed from *Tess of the D'Urbervilles*) in which Anna baptizes her dying baby, but Miss Gish gave a very rich and varied performance all along the line—from the innocent feminine coquetry of the scenes where she is taken in by the rake, through her agony as a deserted mother and her re-establishment of herself at the Bartlett farm, her pain and distress when she feels that she is not good enough to accept the proffered love of David Bartlett (Richard Barthelmess), to the grand denouement when Squire Bartlett (Burr McIntosh), her past now inaccurately known to him, sends her out into the storm.

Griffith was still in sure possession of his old cutting skill in *Way Down East*: David's proposal to Anna in the Bartlett "parlor" was broken in upon by Martha's telling her story about the girl to the Squire, and these scenes intervene between David's "I want you to be my wife" and Anna's agonized reply, "I can never be any man's wife." But there was less reliance upon technique than in his previous major films; except at the end there was little that was spectacular; this time he staked almost everything upon the players, upon his and their sympathetic setting forth of the characters and upon the spectator's sympathetic response to them. Moreover, the spectacular close of *Way Down East* seems to me the part that has worn least well. Like Danton's oration toward the end of *Orphans of the Storm,* the "big scene" at the table, when Anna, ordered out into the storm by the Squire, reveals the truth about her past and denounces Sanderson as her betrayer, is simply not suitable material for the silent film; it requires dialogue; moreover, Griffith's presentation of it is so broken up that it loses the force of a crescendo steadily rising to a climax. As for the ice scenes, which Miss Gish risked her life and froze her hand to make ("All that winter, whenever Mr. Griffith saw an ice cake, he wasn't satisfied till he had me on it"), although they almost lifted me out of my chair when I first saw the film, they now seem robbed of much of their effectiveness by imperfect co-ordination, though the sequence as a whole still deserves all the praise it has received for its *King Lear*–like use of natural forces to underline and support human emotions. Anna runs out into the river and falls down in the middle of an ice cake; a moment later a close shot shows her lying on the edge of it; still later we see it separate and form the edge upon which she is lying. The handling of dramatic time seems to me much less successful in *Way Down East* than it had been in *Intolerance*. At a comparatively early stage, Anna is shown so close to the falls that David could not possibly reach her in time, yet the scenes go on for a long time afterward, with the camera continually shifting, so that it becomes quite clear that the sequence has been patched together out of shots taken at different times and in different places.[39]

Griffith may well have planned the first of his two 1921 films, *Dream Street,* as a major effort, for he had gone once more to Thomas Burke, who had served him so well in *Broken Blossoms* (this time combining "Gina of the Chinatown" with "The Sign of the Lamp"), and he tried special presentations in American cities, even including in some scenes the use of sound. But the picture, which had Carol Dempster, Ralph Graves, Charles Emmett Mack, the elder Tyrone Power, and W. J. Ferguson, is hardly worth analyzing. The story, unconvincing to begin with, is heavily overlaid with allegory and moralization. There are glimpses of hell while the masked fiddler (temptation) plays in the streets, and we see Christ speaking against a painted drop while the street preacher (conscience) is holding forth. Both are equally ineffective, and the theater fire scene, with Carol Dempster doing a ludicrously bad dance to hold the audience in their seats, is certainly one of the most absurd sequences ever filmed.

At the very end of the year came *Orphans of the Storm,* with Lillian and Dorothy Gish as the two orphans, Lucille La Verne as the hag La Frochard, and young Joseph Schildkraut as the young

[39] See the interesting account of the making of the ice scenes in Paine's *Life and Lillian Gish*. Modern spectators should remember that as the film was first shown the ice scenes were tinted blue. As it is now shown, Squire Bartlett turns Anna out into the night and she emerges from the house into blazing sunshine!

chevalier. This time Griffith ventured to use more hackneyed material than he had yet employed in a feature film, for not only was the play *The Two Orphans* as familiar as *Way Down East* but Selig had made it into what was then regarded as an elaborate film as early as 1911, and since then it had been directed by Herbert Brenon as a vehicle for, of all people, Theda Bara. Griffith created novelty—and fresh power—by fusing a very Dickensian French Revolution into *The Two Orphans,* so that he may be said to have made here his most direct and important use of the writer who had been the major influence upon his artistic life.[40]

Orphans of the Storm was a richly mounted, very beautiful film, full of excitement and excellent acting. It began as abruptly as a Biograph with the antecedent slaying of the father of the "orphans," creating a necessary condition for the story with the least possible expenditure of effort. Griffith surprised many people by casting Lillian Gish as the energetic Henriette and making Dorothy the pathetic blind girl Louise, which she made one of her most sensitive characterizations. The camera played lovingly over the investiture of the old regime, and when we came to the revolution even the workings of the guillotine had to be demonstrated, as the trap in the gallows floor had been tried out in *Intolerance.* When the revolution begins the camera moves in on a wholly empty street. One drum appears at the extreme right; the drummer is invisible. Presently it is played by a pair of hands, but we do not see the body to which they are attached; gradually the whole screen fills up with the incipient revolutionists who have been waiting for this signal. It might be argued, however, that the "meaning" of the film is superimposed upon it rather than rising directly out of it. Like Dickens, Griffith approved of the French Revolution but deplored its excesses, and he could not resist telling us, in long subtitles at the beginning of Part II, that while the French Revo-

[40] De Praille's coach accident is, however, the only incident borrowed directly from *A Tale of Two Cities.*

lution rightly overthrew a bad government, we must exercise care not to exchange our good government for "Bolshevism and license."[41]

After *Orphans of the Storm,* Griffith had ten more silent films to make:

1922: *One Exciting Night* (Carol Dempster, Henry Hull, Porter Strong, Margaret Dale).

1923: *The White Rose* (Mae Marsh, Ivor Novello, Carol Dempster, Lucille La Verne, Neil Hamilton, Porter Strong).

1924: *America* (Carol Dempster, Neil Hamilton, Charles Emmett Mack); *Isn't Life Wonderful* (Carol Dempster, Neil Hamilton, Lupino Lane).

1925: *Sally of the Sawdust* (Carol Dempster, W. C. Fields, Alfred Lunt, Effie Shannon).

1926: *That Royle Girl* (Carol Dempster, W. C. Fields, Harrison Ford, James Kirkwood); *Sorrows of Satan* (Adolphe Menjou, Carol Dempster, Ricardo Cortez, Lya de Putti).

1928: *Drums of Love* (Mary Philbin, Lionel Barrymore); *The Battle of the Sexes* (Phyllis Haver, Sally O'Neil, Jean Hersholt, Don Alvarado).

1929: *Lady of the Pavements* (Lupe Velez, William Boyd).

[41] Griffith's relationship to the Communists is interesting. The influence of his films upon Soviet directors has already been mentioned. Iris Barry says: "Lenin arranged to have *Intolerance* toured throughout the U.S.S.R., where it ran almost continuously for ten years." Watching such scenes as those in which troops shoot down the workers, one realizes that the appeal of the film was not wholly technical, and it may be that without *Intolerance*, Lenin would have been slower to recognize the potentiality of the cinema as an instrument of propaganda. But Griffith's anti-Communist stand in *Orphans of the Storm* left no doubt in anybody's mind where he stood personally, and during later years left-oriented critics have persistently disparaged him; see Seymour Stern, "The Cold War against D. W. Griffith," cited in Note 1 of this chapter.

The last two of these are not worth discussing—*The Battle of the Sexes* was, of course, a remake of his old Mutual—and there is not much more that needs to be said about the mystery melodrama spiked with slapstick comedy which Griffith called *One Exciting Night*. When the frightened Carol Dempster crawls into bed and flutters the covers, Griffith seems to have reduced all his fluttering heroines to absurdity, and the storm, too, looks very much like a burlesque of the storms he had created in the past, but I should be happier if I knew these effects had been secured intentionally and not through ineptitude. *Sally of the Sawdust* was a waif-circus picture, unambitious but very well done, and probably Griffith's most consistent comedy film. *That Royle Girl* was a story of the Chicago underworld, culminating in the Illinois cyclone of 1919, but it seemed to me to have a dramatic vitality worthy of better material; I wish I could see it again. Better than any of these was *The White Rose,* which was a kind of elaboration of the unwedmother portion of *Way Down East,* though with a less innocent heroine. Technically *The White Rose* was interesting for its environmental shots, building up the atmosphere of the Southern town and countryside where the action takes place. Symbolism was used freely too—as when the rose droops to indicate the passing of the night of love which Mae Marsh and Ivor Novello spend by the river and the changes it has wrought. This was Mae's last performance for Griffith, and though she had been afraid she could not play a "flapper," she was never better, and, as was usually the case in her pictures, nothing else greatly mattered.[42]

Drums of Love and *Sorrows of Satan* were more ambitious undertakings, and more was expected from them, but they delivered less. The supernatural scenes at the beginning of *Sorrows of Satan* showed imagination, and the love story of the first part, where the director was working mainly from his own imagination, had a good

[42] Harold Dunham, "Mae Marsh," *Films in Review*, Vol. IX (1958), 306–21, covers her entire career to date, with a list of all the films in which she played an important part.

deal of his old power and lyricism; but once Marie Corelli's trashy story had taken over, there was nothing much that D. W. Griffith or anybody else could do. The failure of *Drums of Love* is less explicable, for here Griffith was redoing the great story of Paolo and Francesca. He had Lionel Barrymore, with whom he must have felt much at home; and in Mary Philbin, who had built up her reputation with Universal, he would seem to have discovered another "natural" as an innocent Griffith heroine. Yet the film was turgid, overweighted, and dull in much the manner of some of the von Sternberg enterprises, and Griffith never succeeded in establishing the emotional importance of his characters nor in causing the spectator to care much what became of them.

America was better than that but not so much so as it ought to have been. The story, which centers around the activities of the loyalist Walter Butler (Lionel Barrymore), here depicted as a deep-dyed villain, was written by Robert W. Chambers, and the resultant production was sponsored by the Daughters of the American Revolution. Photographically *America* is one of the greatest and most beautiful things Griffith ever did. A weeping willow silhouetted against the sky at dusk, a body of redcoats traveling along the brow of a hill under a blood-red sun, the Old North Church with its signal lights gleaming across the moon-swept waters of Charlestown Bay, Bunker Hill seen through the masts and rigging of a British man-of-war in the harbor—the only thing wrong with these shots is that they came and went in an instant; one wanted to catch and preserve them forever and hang them on the wall. In some cases marvelously lighted artificial backgrounds were used, and gave the effect of quaint old prints. We saw Patrick Henry ringing out his defiance before the Virginia burgesses; we stood beside Burke when he argued in Parliament against the employment of savages in the American war; we were present when the Declaration of Independence was signed; we watched General Washington receive the sword of Lord Cornwallis. The reproduction of the battles of Lexington and Concord left nothing to be desired, nor did that of Paul Revere's ride, though this would certainly have interested us more if we had had an opportunity to get acquainted with Paul Revere as an individual beforehand. Here, indeed, was the basic weakness of *America;* Griffith never really gave us an opportunity to get well acquainted with anybody. Indeed he seemed to be under the strange impression that he must not give any close-ups to anyone except Carol Dempster, who, to make up for all the rest, as it were, got about ten times as many as she needed.

Isn't Life Wonderful, which Griffith went to Germany to make, and which is supposed to have influenced Pabst and Pudovkin, was more uniformly successful than *America* within a more limited range. In 1924 it was still rather daring for an American producer to make a picture in Germany; Griffith himself seems to apologize for it; conditions were best there, he tells us in a subtitle, to show the triumph of love over hardship. But though the film documents the conditions of German privation—a well-dressed man in a restaurant wrapping up the food he has not eaten to take it home, or the unforgettable scene in which Carol Dempster, in the queue before the food store, feverishly counts her money every time new prices are posted and is at last forced to drop out—the family whose fortunes we follow, and with whom we are expected to sympathize, are carefully presented as Polish refugees, not Germans, and the grandmother is made to tear up the Kaiser's picture. *Isn't Life Wonderful* is a very slow film—it may even be that Elia Kazan here found the inspiration for his never allowing an actor to take less than twenty-five minutes to turn around—but though it has little of the characteristic Griffith excitement, it does have the Griffith intimacy and sympathy and the interest in common people, poverty, and hardship which runs clear back to Biograph days. When Inga puts cotton in her cheeks so that Paul will see how well nourished she is and eat his potatoes instead of saving them for her, we remember Lucy's smile in *Broken Blossoms*. It is true that "villains" are brought in at last to steal the potatoes which

Paul and Inga have raised, and upon whose sale they depend to make their marriage possible, but even villainy is much modified. The leader almost relents when he learns what the situation is; only the thought of his own starving wife (shown in flashback) hardens his heart. But the loss of the potatoes does not resolve the action; it merely postpones the marriage of Paul and Inga for a year. *Isn't Life Wonderful* was not a great film, but it was the closest approach Griffith was able to make between *Orphans of the Storm* and *Abraham Lincoln*.

Abraham Lincoln (1930) was of course a sound film and therefore, strictly speaking, lies outside my range in this book; but it must surely be in order to point out that for Griffith it represented a new false dawn. For *Abraham Lincoln* was a great film, the greatest the movies had had since the coming of sound, and the clearest indication we had yet been vouchsafed that we were not going to be confined to teacup dramas and "production numbers" forever. Though I assert no complete parallelism, there is even a sense in which Griffith here did for the sound film what he had done for the silent film in *The Birth of a Nation;* it seems amazing that both opportunities should have been given to the same man.[43]

But alas, there were no comparable sequelae. Griffith directed only one more film, *The Struggle* (1931), which was considered such a "dud" that, after being shown briefly, it was withdrawn. In is now difficult to see why. For though *The Struggle* has few "Griffith touches," except for its hurried, unconvincing, happy ending, it is not a bad picture. An attack upon both alcoholism and the pro-

[43] *Abraham Lincoln* was written by Stephen Vincent Benét; for an account of his adventures in Hollywood and his impressions of Griffith, see Charles A. Fenton, *Stephen Vincent Benét* (Yale University Press, 1958). The cast included Walter Huston (Lincoln), Kay Hammond (Mrs. Lincoln), Una Merkel (Ann Rutledge), Ian Keith (John Wilkes Booth), Hobart Bosworth (Lee), Jason Robards (Herndon), Henry Walthall, and Lucille La Verne.

hibition law which Griffith believed accentuated and encouraged it, it is a grim picture descending quite legitimately from *What Drink Did, A Drunkard's Reformation, The Musketeers of Pig Alley,* and much more from an earlier and perhaps better day. It cannot honestly be claimed that the world lost a masterpiece when it failed to see *The Struggle,* but it may well be that it was too honest a film for its time.[44]

I must, I think, have made it clear in the foregoing discussion that I do not regard D. W. Griffith as either a faultless artist or a faultless man; but if the motion picture is of any value to the world, he was an important world artist, for he created the best of it. And when we sigh over what we may regard as the degradation of his last years in Hollywood, it might be well to do him the justice to recall that when his independent company went under and he was forced to give up his studio at Mamaroneck, he did exactly what Sir Walter Scott and Mark Twain had done before him; he refused to take advantage of the bankruptcy laws and went to work as a director for other men until he had paid off his creditors dollar for dollar. They had believed enough in him, he said, and in his ability to make good pictures, to entrust their money to him, and he was not going to see them lose through this faith.

He was a strange combination of the idealist and the showman; sometimes one was on top and sometimes the other, but both were always there. It is easy to be impatient of his moralizing, for he

[44] The story was by John Emerson and Anita Loos; the cast included Hal Skelly, Zita Johann, Helen Mack, Charles Richman, and Evelyn Baldwin. There was a ray of hope that Griffith might be about to resume his interrupted career in 1940 when Hal Roach invited him to direct a picture called *One Million B.C.* and sent the mind of every Griffith fan scampering back to *Man's Genesis.* But there was no meeting of minds, and though there were touches in the film which suggested Griffith's hand, his name did not appear in connection with it. I may also record here that Vivian Duncan once told me that when the film production of *Topsy and Eva* got into difficulties. Griffith was employed to come in and straighten them out. She regarded his contribution to the picture as an important one.

was not content to underscore the morals which really inhered in his materials, as in *Intolerance* and *Way Down East;* he had to find morals whether they were there or not. In *True Heart Susie* he is sighing over how few women ever get the chance to marry more than one man. In *Isn't Life Wonderful* he declares that love makes all things beautiful and life itself a wonder. And in *The Idol Dancer* he is reduced to pointing out that *if* the story has a moral it must be that good example is the best preachment! Yet only a moral nihilist believes that art should not be sound in its values, and, sensationalist and sentimentalist though he was, or was tempted to be, Griffith's always was. As late as 1944 he told a reporter that "in one respect, nearly all pictures are good in that they show the triumph of good over evil."

And therefore he falsifies life? I do not think this necessarily follows. For to perpetrate something of an Irish bull, in Griffith not even the "last-minute rescue" always rescues. David Bartlett does get to the edge of the waterfall in time to carry Anne Moore to safety, and Danton does reach the guillotine in time to prevent Henriette Girard from being decapitated. But the Little Colonel reaches his sister only in time for her to die in his arms; the Mountain Girl warns Belshazzar, but her warning accomplishes nothing either for him or for her; Cheng Huan comes to the hovel of Battling Burrows in time to kill him but too late to save Lucy. Rudolph Messel is absurd when he suggests that the point of *Intolerance* is blurred by having the Boy rescued. To permit one story out of four to end happily is certainly not an unreasonably high percentage; not to do that much would be to create the impression of having loaded the dice against one's characters and blown out the gas to see how dark it is. In *Way Down East,* incidentally, we have a variation of the "last-minute rescue" theme which I do not recall ever having seen pointed out: David Bartlett contends not with human "villains" or the human will but with the elements. On the whole, the percentage of success and failure in Griffith's films seems about what it is in life. Virtue and villany are with us always;

if both tend to be less modified in Griffith's films than they are with us, we must remember that artists have always claimed the privileges of both heightening and simplification, and if Griffith's girls are prettier than those we see every day, and his heroes braver and less corruptible, greater artists than he have dedicated themselves to portraying life "not as it is but as it ought to be."

CHAPTER THREE

"America's Sweetheart"

W H E N Mary Pickford published her autobiography, *Sunshine and Shadow,* through Doubleday in 1955, I reviewed it by writing her an open letter on the front page of the Chicago *Sunday Tribune Magazine of Books:*[1]

> DEAR MARY PICKFORD:
> When I reviewed Mary Garden's autobiography for the *Tribune,* Fanny Butcher accused me of writing a love letter to Miss Garden. I didn't, really; I was saving that for you.
> Much of my writing career has been devoted to trying to capture

[1] May 29, 1955 (reprinted by permission). Miss Pickford's autobiography is, of course, the most important single source of information concerning her, but among the many articles signed with her by-line, see also "My Own Story," *Ladies' Home Journal* (July, Aug., Sept., 1923); "The Greatest Business in the World," *Collier's* (June 10, 1922); "Ambassadors," *Saturday Evening Post* (Aug. 23, 1930). Her religious views were expressed in two little books published by H. C. Kinsey & Company (New York): *Why Not Try God?* (1934) and *My Rendezvous with Life* (1935). Julian Johnson deserves credit for the pioneer attempt to tell Miss Pickford's story in "Mary Pickford: Herself and Her Career," *Photoplay* (Nov., 1915, Jan. and Feb., 1916), supplemented in the same magazine by David Belasco, "When Mary Pickford Came to Me" (Dec., 1915). Margaret Case Hariman had a "profile," "Sweetheart," in *The New Yorker* (Apr. 7, 1934). James Card, "The Films of Mary Pickford," with "An Index to the Films of Mary Pickford," *Image,* Vol. VIII (1959), 172–91, is very important.

in words the people and the ideas by which my youth was molded. But I have always found great difficulty in writing about you. Partly this may be because you have not given me a chance to see you on the screen for twenty years. I have never quite forgiven you for that, and, as I have told you, I much regret that my children have had to grow up without seeing you every week or every month as I did when we were both much younger.

As Mr. deMille says in his introduction to your book, there has been no other career like yours. Alastair Cooke has called Garbo "every man's harmless fantasy mistress." Well, she was never mine. And neither were you, though for a very different reason. I should have felt it blasphemous to think of you thus. You speak of your appreciation of your title "America's Sweetheart," but I am sure you know we always read it with a difference.

We who loved you were, in general, much simpler people than the sophisticates who go to the movies nowadays, and you meant more to us than anybody can mean to them. We accepted you without question or analysis; we adored you in the honest simplicity of our hearts. And, paradoxically, your appeal was the more complicated on that account. Your own personality cast a madonna-like exaltation about you, and the roles you often played made you our mischievous child. Neither Garbo nor any other actress in these latter days has commanded your range.

In giving us this book, Mary, you give us a chance to renew our youth. I know much more of you than most of your fans, but even I have learned much. Do you remember when you told me that you couldn't write your autobiography yet because you could not yet tell the truth about some of the people whose lives had touched yours? Though you did not say so, we both knew that you were thinking of Owen Moore and Douglas Fairbanks. I think you have done it in this book, with perfect charity and perfect candor.

It seems odd that you should have been so little a part of your own public. Did we, perhaps, interpret you to yourself, and is "Our Mary" our creation as well as yours? I agree with you that *Less Than the Dust* (or, as the lady misremembered the title, "Cheaper Than the Dirt") was a terrible film, but *The Pride of the Clan* was much better than you thought it. (Thirty years after it was made at Marblehead, Mass., I found production shots of it still on exhibition there.) I cannot understand why you thought *Pollyanna* goody-goody *as you played it,* nor how not only you but all your advisers thought *A Poor Little Rich Girl* unsuccessful until your public had informed you otherwise. Of all your films, this is the one I should most like to see again.

Good luck with your book, Mary, and all God's best to you.

Yours sincerely, as ever,

EDWARD WAGENKNECHT

Doubleday followed up on this review with a "Dear Mary Pickford" display advertisement in the book-review journals—"We got the idea of sending you a love letter from the unabashed mash note the man wrote on the front page of the Chicago *Tribune Magazine of Books"*—and Miss Pickford herself wrote me that she had read my article "at least ten times."

By the time this book is published, babies born after Mary Pickford made her last film will have reached the age of thirty. Now that motion pictures are no longer very important to American young people, it must be very difficult for any such person to realize what she meant to America when she really was "America's Sweetheart"—not only the undisputed queen of the movies but, by all odds, the most famous woman in America. For though the "America's Sweetheart" tag, invented by "Pop" Grauman, was sedulously cultivated by her press agents, and though her career was intelligently geared and self-directed toward the success which she had deliberately set for herself as a goal (when she went to Belasco in 1907, she told him that she was the father of her family and that she must achieve a substantial success before she was twenty), none of this would have sufficed without an enthusiastic public response, and nobody who lived through the years of her fame can doubt that that response was spontaneous, enthusiastic, and impassioned—the kind that cannot be manufactured or bought.

The Pickford career was not built overnight, and Mary herself never had any real confidence that it would last. In her eyes it was "a temporary and freakish phenomenon," and just as some singers live in perpetual fear of losing their voices, so she braced herself with the thought "that every year might be my last in pictures." When she was told, on one occasion, that she had drawn a larger crowd than the President, she could not help thinking "that a white elephant taking a morning stroll . . . would draw a much larger and more curious throng than either of us."

As early as 1909 a trade-journal review of *To Save Her Soul* remarked that "the young woman of the Biograph stock who takes the leading character plays it with fine expression and charming innocence." In 1912 a reviewer of *Friends* found "exquisite grace and charm . . . displayed by the little woman who essays the heroine of this truly interesting episode of the West during the period of the seventies." Yet Mary won none of the popularity contests which the fan magazines conducted in the early days, and though even then I knew people who loved her and regarded her as a being apart, it was not until after she had gone with Famous Players and made *Hearts Adrift* and *Tess of the Storm Country* that it really became clear that she who had hitherto been one among many charming actresses was destined to soar in public favor until she occupied a crag all her own. In March, 1917, she polled 1,147,550 votes in a popularity contest conducted by *The Ladies' World,* outdistancing her closest competitor, Alice Joyce, by a cool half-million. Vachel Lindsay reviewed *A Romance of the Redwoods* in *The New Republic* under the caption "Queen of My People." "To reject this girl in haste," he wrote, "is high treason to the national heart."[2] *Photoplay* once published her picture without a name-tag; if any reader did not recognize her, he was invited to write in. When she had recovered from a serious bout with influenza in the spring of 1919, the Chicago *Tribune* printed her photograph with this caption:

[2] Vol. XI (1917), 280–81.

THE MOST BELOVED FACE IN THE WORLD—Mary Pickford's thousands of ardent admirers followed the news of her illness as devotedly and sympathetically as if it were a personal sorrow.

The *Tribune* KNEW: their film critic, Mae Tinée, had done nothing but answer the telephone all day, assuring Mary's devotees that she was getting better. In 1926, Dorothy Gish came back from England with the shocking news that a London schoolgirl, asked what "M.P." stood for, had replied "Mary Pickford." More shocking— and more touching—still was the story of the congressman's daughter who came home from Sunday school one day with "Mamma, they asked us today who we wanted to be like." "And?" queried her mother. "Oh," sighed the child, "I told them the Lord, but I meant Mary Pickford."

We all idealized Mary in those days, much as that girl did. Reading Schiller's *Die Jungfrau von Orleans* in school, I came across Dunois' great tribute to Joan of Arc:

> *Wenn die Wahrheit*
> *Verkörpern will in sichtbarer Gestalt,*
> *So muss sie ihre Züge an sich tragen!*
> *Wenn Unschuld, Treue, Herzensreinigkeit,*
> *Auf Erden irgend wohnt—auf ihren Lippen,*
> *In ihren klaren Augen muss sie wohnen!*

I am willing to give the reader three guesses whom I was immediately reminded of! Nor was this a wholly idiosyncratic reaction. "There is a radiance about her," wrote Gerald D. McDonald of Miss Pickford in his review of *Sunshine and Shadow,* "and audiences never doubted that even without the make-believe she was kind, noble and true."[3] And James Card added that "there is something heavenly about Mary Pickford. It is a quality, we must admit, most uncommon in motion pictures."

This of course is why she caused such agonizing throughout

[3] *Films in Review*, Vol. VI (1955), 295–97.

the length and breadth of America when, in March, 1920, she divorced Owen Moore and married Douglas Fairbanks. We knew that she had lived miserably with—and apart from—Moore for many years; we knew, too, that Fairbanks' former wife had already remarried after their divorce. No matter! We could not bear the thought that "Our Mary" could, in any way, have even put herself in the way of being suspected of doing wrong. And the Reverend J. Whitcomb Brougher, pastor of the Temple Baptist Church in Los Angeles, had to come out with a long statement, which was solemnly syndicated throughout America, and in which he assured us that the Pickford-Fairbanks marriage was "Scriptural," and that he had agreed to perform the ceremony only after he had investigated all the circumstances and satisfied himself that there was no Christian or Biblical impediment.

For all this, Miss Pickford has been much neglected, both by film historians and by modern film *aficionados.* Her films were, for the most part, long unavailable for rescreening, and even now most of those which have survived can be seen only at the George Eastman House in Rochester, which, unlike the Museum of Modern Art, does not circulate its films. But I think the basic reason is that, more than any other great star, Mary Pickford really did belong to the Age of Innocence. Her films encourage, and submit to, little analysis. Thus while it is quite as easy to be enthralled by Mary's antics in, say, *Rebecca of Sunnybrook Farm* as by Griffith's heroics in, say, *The Birth of a Nation,* it is more difficult to write about them.

Mary Pickford was born Gladys Smith in Toronto, on April 8, 1893. Her family was Irish Catholic on her mother's side, English and Methodist on her father's—a situation which led, absurdly, to her being baptized twice, once by a Catholic priest and once by a Protestant minister. Pickford was her Irish great-grandmother's maiden name. Her Grandmother Faely was an excellent storyteller and mimic. The story of Mary's own poverty-stricken, hardship-filled childhood, as she tells it in her autobiography, is as moving as the story of Chaplin's boyhood, except that in her case the sordidness of the surroundings was always redeemed by her mother's heroism and high-mindedness. As a small child she used to worry about God and the devil and sin—and how she had got here—and how she could get back to the place she had come from, which was much nicer. She was also greatly interested in money— so that on one occasion she was narrowly restrained from breaking the keys of the piano to retrieve a five-cent piece that had been dropped between them—and in beauty, since she not only bought rosebuds from the florist but also begged wilted roses of him, which she carefully ate to possess herself of their desirable properties.

She made her stage debut as a small child in a stock company production of *The Silver King,* from which she went on to *Uncle Tom's Cabin, East Lynne, The Little Red Schoolhouse,* and *The Fatal Wedding.* ("Baby Gladys Is a Wonder," said the playbills.) It was a great day when she, her mother, her sister Lottie, and her brother Jack all got jobs with Chauncey Olcott in *Edmund Burke;* not only were they now all together but they got out of the flea-bitten theaters in which they generally played. She assumed the name Mary Pickford at David Belasco's suggestion in 1907, when she played for him in *The Warrens of Virginia.*

The first motion pictures she ever saw were "Hale's Tours" in Chicago, while she was playing there in *The Warrens.* She was violently carsick. In the spring of 1909, at her mother's suggestion, and against her own better judgment, she made a second, and this time successful, try to get work with Biograph. (She had also flirted vainly with both Kalem and Essanay.) Her first impression of D. W. Griffith was that he was "a pompous and insufferable creature," and the word "studio" frightened her and made her think of Stanford White and Evelyn Nesbit. The first film in which she worked was *What Drink Did,* but her scene was cut out. She appeared briefly in *Her First Biscuits;* but her earliest real part was in *The Violin Maker of Cremona.* She was a member of the first Biograph company which went to California, producing *Ramona* and other films.

In 1911, Laemmle lured her from Biograph to Imp by offering her $175 per week, but she found the Imp standards of production distressingly low, was unhappy, and left after nine months. Much briefer was her stay, that same year, with Majestic. Most of her Imp and all of her Majestic films seem to have perished. The Imps which I remember best are *In the Sultan's Garden* and *Science;* the only Majestic that I can recall is *Little Red Riding Hood,* in which she dreamed the whole fairy-tale experience. *In the Sultan's Garden* seemed wonderfully romantic to me at the time; I thought of it years later when I saw the lovely Ali Baba insert in *A Little Princess. Science,* with King Baggott, was a very brief, unacknowledged adaptation from *A Dog's Tale,* by Mark Twain.

In 1912, Miss Pickford returned to Griffith and Biograph and stayed there until Belasco offered her the leading role in his production of Madame Rostand's play *A Good Little Devil* in 1913, when she left the screen, as she believed, forever. Zukor brought her back by making a screen version of *A Good Little Devil* while the play was still running. Edwin S. Porter directed, and Belasco supervised, but the actors were required to go through their lines just as if they had been on stage. Apparently Zukor at once realized both that *A Good Little Devil* was a very bad picture and that Mary Pickford was a star who gave much richer promise of establishing his new Famous Players Film Company on a firm foundation than any of the cinematically inexperienced great personages whom he was bringing in from the stage. Although it was made in May, 1913, the picture was not released until March, 1914, after three other Pickford Famous Players features had been shown. The first was Porter's and J. Searle Dawley's production of Miriam Nicholson's novel *In the Bishop's Carriage,* released in September, 1913. In November, Dawley followed with *Caprice,* the play in which Mrs. Fiske made one of her early successes, and in which the song "In the Gloaming" was first sung. If these pictures left any questions in anybody's mind about Mary's success, all doubts were removed when Porter's *Hearts Adrift,* from Cyrus Townsend Brady's story, "As the Sparks Fly Upward," was released in February, 1914. In this innocent but touching little romance, Mary played a Spanish girl shipwrecked on a deserted island, and later joined by a man (Harold Lockwood), also the survivor of a wreck. They marry each other and have a child, after which, of course, the man's family arrives with a rescue party, and Nina throws herself and her baby into a volcano.[4]

Encouraged by the success of *Hearts Adrift,* Famous Players ventured unloading *A Good Little Devil;* hard on its heels (March, 1914), they released Porter's production of Grace Miller White's story **Tess of the Storm Country.*[5] If any one film can be said to have "made" Mary Pickford, it was *Tess*—I can still remember how stock companies used to advertise their stage productions of it as "MARY PICKFORD'S Great Success"—and this may now seem a little hard to explain, for though Mary works hard in *Tess,* she gets little help from anybody, and none whatever from Porter, whose direction quite lacks emphasis or definition of any kind. Moreover, there is not a single close-up in the film. But it did present her as a violent, warm-hearted squatter girl in a variety of appealing situations. When she gets religion from her high-toned, Divinity School-student lover, she "cribs" a Bible from the mission and devotes herself industriously to learning—and practicing—its teachings, and when her lover's sister bears a child out of wedlock to his best friend, she not only takes both mother and child into her

---

[4] *Hearts Adrift* was the first Pickford feature film ever made in California. In his book, written with Dale Kramer, *The Public Is Never Wrong* (Putnam, 1953), Adolph Zukor reports, amazingly, that it "flopped," thus proving that, as historians, producers may be quite unreliable.

[5] In the following paragraphs, films which have survived, and of which there is a copy at George Eastman House, are marked with an asterisk the first time they are mentioned. The Eastman House print of *The Taming of the Shrew* is the silent version, and they have also a *negative* of *The Hoodlum* as prepared for exhibition in England. The Museum of Modern Art Film Library has a very brief excerpt from *A Good Little Devil.*

To Mr. Edward Wagenknecht, with sincere good wishes. Cordially—

April 2nd, 1919.

Mary Pickford.

Mary Pickford

Mary Pickford, with H
old Lockwood (Picture
above), in *Hearts Ad*
(1914) and (Picture 35, *le*
in *Tess of the Storm Co*
try (1914); Mary Pickf
again (Picture 36, *below*)
Rags (1915).

PICTURES 34, 35, 36

ry Pickford in three
es: (Picture 37, *above*)
Hulda from Holland
16); and as Unity Blake
cture 38, *right*) and Stel-
Maris (Picture 39, *below*),
Stella Maris (1917).

PICTURES 37, 38, 39

Miss Pickford in her little-girl aspect. A publicity photograph of c.1917.

Mary Pickford in *A Poor Little Rich Girl* (1917

PICTURE 40

PICTURES 41, 42

Mary Pickford (Picture 43, *above*), with Matt Moore, in *The Pride of the Clan* (1917), and (Picture 44, *below*), with Theodore Roberts, in *M'liss* (1918).

Picture 45 *(above)*, Mary Pickford, with Katherine Griffith, Helen Jerome Eddy, Herbert Prior, and William Courtleigh, in *Pollyanna* (1920); Picture 46 *(below)*, Mary Pickford in *Through the Back Door* (1921).

Mary Pickford as Lord Fauntleroy (Picture 47, *above left*) and as "Dearest," his mother (Picture 48, *above right*), in *Little Lord Fauntleroy* (1921); (Picture 49, *below left*) in *The Love Light* (1921); and (Picture 50, *below right*) in *Dorothy Vernon of Haddon Hall* (1924).

shack but protects the girl by telling her brother that she herself is the child's mother. When she is punished for stealing milk for the child from its own grandfather's icebox, she says, "I have been beaten. Now am I to have the milk?" When the baby is dying, she marches into the church with it and herself baptizes it before the congregation after the clergyman has refused to do so. And when, at last, all confusions are ironed out, and she gets her proposal of marriage, she replies, "I air Daddy's brat, but [after the proper interval] I air your squatter." The materials were there all right, and if Porter would not sort them out for us, we were quite intelligent enough to do it ourselves. I remembered *Tess* affectionately for years, and it was not until I saw it again for this book that I realized how much superior the 1922 remake, directed by John S. Robertson, was. (*Tess,* of course, was the only film Miss Pickford ever remade.)

The year 1914 was filled out with four lesser films: *The Eagle's Mate,* a Southern mountain story, from the novel by Anna Alice Chapin (July); *Such a Little Queen,* from the play by Channing Pollock in which Elsie Ferguson had starred (September); *Behind the Scenes,* which opposed a career to domesticity and in which domesticity won (October); and finally *Cinderella* (December), which I remember most fondly as a radiant, springlike thing, but of which unfortunately I cannot renew my impressions.[6]

In 1915 there was a heavy reliance on screen adaptations of stage successes: *Mistress Nell* in February (the most innocent of all conceptions of Nell Gwyn, from the George C. Hazelton play which had been acted by Henrietta Crosman); *Fanchon the Cricket* in May (which goes back ultimately to George Sand, and which as acted for so many years by Maggie Mitchell had been one of the great successes of the American theater); two Frances Hodgson Burnett pieces—*The Dawn of a Tomorrow* in June and *Esmeralda* in September, and, in November, a **Madame Butterfly,*

---

[6] All of Miss Pickford's films between *The Eagle's Mate* and *Esmeralda* (both inclusive) were directed by James Kirkwood, except *Such a Little Queen,* which was directed by Hugh Ford.

directed by Sidney Olcott, but announced as having been adapted from the John Luther Long story rather than from either the Puccini opera or the Long-Belasco play. I loved both *Mistress Nell* and *Fanchon,* and *The Dawn of a Tomorrow* gave Mary Pickford an excellent opportunity to express the religious feeling of which at her best she was capable. Since Geraldine Farrar was now a Lasky star, it seems odd that *Butterfly* should have been assigned to Mary. When it was released the *Dramatic Mirror* found it a triumph "photographically and technically" but thought that the tragedy had been "so softened that it is practically eliminated" and Cio-Cio-San's emotions "so rigorously suppressed that it was hard to realize that they existed." With this Miss Pickford must have agreed, since Samuel Goldwyn quotes her as having complained that the picture had no action whatever and ought to have been called "Madame Snail." It seems to me much better, however, than what I remember of *Little Pal* (July), an original story for the screen, in which she played a half-blood Alaska Indian girl who seldom had even an opportunity to smile. *A Girl of Yesterday* (October), directed by Allan Dwan, was a very light comedy about an old-fashioned girl brought up to date, from a story by Miss Pickford herself.[7] But probably the most successful Pickford film of 1915 was a lively and entertaining waif story called *Rags (August), from the pen of Edith Barnard Delano.

At the beginning of 1916 it was announced that Miss Pickford would receive half a million dollars during 1916 and that she would also have a larger voice in the selection and production of her films. The first four pictures released in 1916 were still under the Fa-

[7] Although Miss Pickford turned out many scenarios in the Biograph days, this was apparently the only feature film for which she ever wrote the story. According to her cameraman Charles Rosher, she had a very important share in the direction of all the films on which he worked with her except *Rosita,* which was wholly in charge of Ernst Lubitsch. She calls *Rosita* "the worst picture I ever made, bar none," thus usurping a distinction which, I think, clearly belongs to *Less Than the Dust.*

mous Players trade-mark: *The Foundling* (January); *Poor Little Peppina,* a Kate Jordan story (March); *The Eternal Grind* (April); and *Hulda from Holland* (July). *Peppina* was directed by Sidney Olcott, the others by John B. O'Brien. The first two are both waif stories, though the child is not an orphan but merely one who has become separated from her parents. Reviewing *Peppina* in 1961, I did not think it nearly as good a picture as I had considered it in 1916, and it may be that if I could review *Hulda,* I should have the same experience with it; on the other hand, since it was another Edith Barnard Delano story, it might very well hold up as successfully as *Rags* does. *The Eternal Grind* was a somewhat depressing sweatshop yarn, with Mary as the high-minded girl, contrasted to her sister, who goes astray. There is (literally) a shotgun wedding for the sister, with Mary holding the gun behind a curtain. The Chicago censor board "pink-slipped" *The Eternal Grind,* which meant that it could be shown only to adults. The Oak Park Theater did not run it, and I had to go in to Austin to see it at the Plaisance.

There was no Pickford film between July and November; then came the first Artcraft, *Less Than the Dust,* a story of India, directed by John Emerson, in which Miss Pickford played a girl of the bazaars. The trade journals had announced with great fanfare that from now on Miss Pickford would produce her own pictures; Artcraft exchanges were opened in various cities to handle them; and the general public did not know until later that Zukor was behind the whole enterprise. Miss Pickford was promised a larger measure of control than ever materialized—this was the basic reason why she finally left Zukor for First National in 1918 —and when, after the production of *A Poor Little Rich Girl,* everybody inexplicably thought they had a "dud" on their hands, the imagined failure was used to discipline her and bring her into line. In May, 1917, it was announced that the Famous Players–Lasky Corporation, as it had now become, had "acquired" Artcraft, and afterward for a few years this organization used both the Paramount and Artcraft trade-marks and even issued "A Paramount–Artcraft Special" at quite regular intervals.

The year 1917 was possibly the greatest in Mary's career; if we stretch it to include January, 1918, when *Stella Maris* (which was, of course, produced during 1917) came out, I think there can be no doubt of this. She worked all the year with top-notch directors. First came *The Pride of the Clan* (January) and *A Poor Little Rich Girl* (March), both directed by Maurice Tourneur. There followed two Cecil B. deMille films: *A Romance of the Redwoods* (May) and *The Little American* (July). *A Poor Little Rich Girl* was the last film Miss Pickford was ever to make in the East; with *A Romance of the Redwoods* she transferred her producing activities permanently to California. In September, with *Rebecca of Sunnybrook Farm,* she found one of her best directors in Marshall Neilan, who directed all her pictures from *Rebecca* through *M'liss* in 1918, and returned to her for *Daddy Long Legs* in 1919 and *Dorothy Vernon of Haddon Hall* in 1924. They closed the year together with *A Little Princess* (November), and, as I have already said, they opened 1918 with William J. Locke's *Stella Maris.* There is not a poor picture in the series.

I have not, I must confess, quite had the courage to review *The Little American.* This is Mary's "patriotic" wartime picture, and wartime hysteria is still sufficiently repulsive to me so that I am not sure I could evaluate it fairly. The story of an American girl with a German lover who, by some pretext, was got into the war zone (being torpedoed on the way), only to find her lover transformed into a "Hun" who first threatens to rape her, then, upon discovering her identity, is so quickly redeemed that he defies the whole German high command for her sake—I doubt that I need say more to explain why I shrink from seeing it again, or why it was one of the greatest successes of its time.[8]

[8] But compare the tribute Harvey O'Higgins pays to her acting in *The Little American* in his article "To What Green Altar?" *New Republic,* Vol. XVIII (1919), 80–81. He is speaking of the scene in which a wounded

For the others, no reservations need be taken. *A Poor Little Rich Girl,* made from the Eleanor Gates novel and play, has always been one of my favorite films: a rich, yet somehow not inharmonious, combination of Mary's gift for mischief with Tourneur's fine pictorial sense, which is seen at its best in the dream sequences in which the delirious child relives all the joys and sorrows of her life in fresh nightmare patterns. I have been told that Kate Douglas Wiggin did not care much for Mary's *Rebecca,* and I can understand why this might be the case, for the book is a minor masterpiece, unsurpassed in its kind in American literature, and the film makes changes in the story and adds many irrelevant pranks; yet, for all that, I think its spirit has been miraculously preserved. Certainly Mary never made a happier picture, nor one that sparkles more brightly or offers a faster succession of entertaining situations. *A Little Princess* was more somber and wistful, and therefore less popular, but audiences of imagination did not love it less.

Stella Maris is often called Miss Pickford's greatest film. I should hate to have to choose between it and two or three others, but there can be no doubt that it is the most unusual thing she ever did. She was very lovely as the crippled rich girl Stella Maris, protected from all the evil and sorrow of the world by her enforced isolation and painfully shocked into awareness by the contacts

French soldier, carried past her, salutes. "There came over her face the look of a mother who sees a dying child reach for a toy from her hands. Pitiful and apologetic, with a halting, awkward, painful gesture, she returned his salute . . . and her face was all purely human maternal tenderness; and she tried even to smile encouragingly, but with a certain heart-broken blindness as if she could not quite see him for the mist of tears in her eyes; and then the struggling smile achieved complete expression in a conflict of emotion that mirrored the most subtle aspects of reality as only a great imagination could conceive them.

"There was nothing theatrical about it. There was nothing stereotyped . . . . But you might go a long way and see a great deal of famous acting without meeting the expression of an emotion so true, so poignant, and so beautiful."

which follow her recovery after an operation; and she was more than startling as the twisted slavey Unity Blake, who adored Stella and the man who adored her, and finally committed murder and suicide that they might be happy together. *Stella Maris* had, too, a quite extraordinary performance by Marcia Manon as the sadistic, drunken wife of John Risca, whom Unity finally liquidated.

It was her last really first-rate Artcraft. There followed *Amarilly of Clothes-Line Alley* (March, 1918), a Belle K. Maniates story about a girl of the lower class who learns that "you can't mix pickles and ice cream"; Bret Harte's *M'liss* (May, 1918); and then three quite trifling comedies—*How Could You, Jean?* (June, 1918); *Johanna Enlists* (September, 1918), and *Captain Kidd, Jr.* (April, 1919), all expertly directed by the ill-starred William Desmond Taylor.

During 1919, First National released three Pickford films. The first, Jean Webster's *Daddy Long Legs* (May,) is one of her most famous and successful pictures. Both of the others were directed by Sidney Franklin. *The Hoodlum* (September) is a somewhat inconsequential slum comedy. *Heart o' the Hills* (December) is a John Fox, Jr., story, very good of its kind. In the spring of 1919, Miss Pickford joined with D. W. Griffith, Charles Chaplin, and Douglas Fairbanks to form the United Artists Corporation, through which all the rest of her films were released.[9]

Her United Artist offerings began auspiciously in January, 1920, with Eleanor H. Porter's *Pollyanna,* directed by Paul Powell. Her only other 1920 film was *Suds* (June), directed by Jack Dillon, a screen version of the play *'Op o' Me Thumb,* by Frederick Fenn and Richard Pryce, in which Maude Adams had starred. For this startling departure Miss Pickford was perhaps fortified by the success of *Stella Maris;* but *Suds* was more daring, not only because it lacked the carrying emotional force of the earlier story, but because *Stella Maris* had permitted Mary to act her head off as the

[9] See Arthur L. Mayer, "The Origins of United Artists," *Films in Review*, Vol. X (1959), 390–99.

ugly little drudge and at the same time give the audience a chance to enjoy "America's Sweetheart" with her golden curls in a more conventional kind of role. Here the little slavey who worked in a London laundry had to carry the whole picture, and we never saw the golden curls at all except in the brief interlude in which she told of her life not as it was but as it ought to be, an excellent burlesque of popular chivalric literature. (They used Gothic type for the subtitles of this portion of the film, but the fine ladies and gentlemen all talked cockney dialect. They also had Pickford curls on Lavender, the broken-down horse!) Why have the people who cherish Chaplin, Keaton, and the Sennett films overlooked *Suds?* Perhaps the only adequate answer is Dr. Johnson's to the lady who asked him why he had defined "pastern" as "the knee of a horse." "Ignorance, Madame," said the doctor, "pure ignorance."

The year 1921 saw three films; it was the last in which she was to give us so much. *The Love Light* (January) and *Through the Back Door* (May) were comparatively unimportant, though *The Love Light,* in which Mary played an Italian girl who is married, unknowingly, to a German spy, was an interesting attempt to experiment with grown-up roles. The year ended on one of the high points of her career with her final return to Mrs. Burnett for one of her most elaborate films, *Little Lord Fauntleroy* (September), in which she played both the boy and Dearest, his mother. Frances Marion, who had done so many of Miss Pickford's scenarios, directed *The Love Light,* in which her husband Fred Thomson was the leading man. This is the only time Mary was ever directed by a woman. The other two films were credited jointly to Jack Pickford and Alfred E. Green.

In 1922 came the remake of *Tess of the Storm Country,* already mentioned. In 1923 and 1924, with *Rosita,* directed by Ernst Lubitsch, and *Dorothy Vernon of Haddon Hall,* Miss Pickford made two more attempts to break away, in different directions, from the child roles with which she had so long been associated. *Rosita* was one of a number of screen versions which have been

153

made of the old play *Don Caesar de Bazan,* and *Dorothy Vernon,* of course, was a Tudor costume picture, gorgeously mounted, of another novel by Charles Major, who wrote *When Knighthood Was in Flower.* Clare Eames, incidentally, did a highly competent but rather unpleasantly ribald Queen Elizabeth.

Both of these films had their merits, *Dorothy Vernon* being, for my taste, the better of the two; but her own, or her public's, lack of enthusiasm for them, or a combination of both, left Miss Pickford with the feeling that she should return to child roles. She did so with *Little Annie Rooney* (1925), directed by William Beaudine, a good deal of which was given over to kid gang-fighting and the solution of a murder mystery. To my way of thinking, it was the poorest film she had made in some time, but it proved popular. Beaudine also directed its successor *Sparrows* (1926), a somewhat Dickensian piece about greed and loyalty on a baby farm in the swamps. *Sparrows* is Dickensian in its preoccupation with children, in its background of crime and mystery, and above all in the Squeers-like creature of murderous instincts (Gustav von Seyffertitz) who runs the farm. It was beautifully photographed— some of the scenes looked almost like paintings—but I do not see how anyone could speak of it as a great story of intense dramatic vitality. About half of it was devoted to tracing Mary's escape through the swamps with her ten little protégés, sometimes in close proximity to huge, vicious crocodiles, who would have liked nothing better than to devour them all.

Sparrows was followed in November, 1927, by an entertaining love story, *My Best Girl,* in which she played with Charles B. ("Buddy") Rogers, and which turned out to be her last silent film.[10] With it, too, Miss Pickford acquired Sam Taylor, who directed

[10] The last years of Miss Pickford's once very happy marriage to Douglas Fairbanks were clouded by his infidelity. She received her final decree of divorce from him on January 10, 1935. On June 26, 1937, she made her third, very fortunate and happy, marriage to "Buddy" Rogers.

all the rest of her pictures except the last, *Secrets,* which was directed by Frank Borzage. She received an Oscar for *Coquette* (March, 1929), the play by Ann Bridges and George Abbott in which Helen Hayes had been so successful on the stage. It was her first talking picture and the first (except for *Kiki* it was also the last) in which she was to capitalize on the screen on her newly bobbed hair. Her Katherine in *The Taming of the Shrew* (October, 1929), the only film she ever made with Douglas Fairbanks (she says he was so difficult during its production that he permanently destroyed her faith in her ability to make pictures), lacked the physical stamina traditionally associated with the role; but it was a thoroughly knowledgeable and intelligent interpretation nevertheless, assuming (non-Shakespeareanly), as Sothern and Marlowe used to do, that Katherine "caught on" to what Petruchio was doing and "played along" with him. (In the film this was conveyed by having Petruchio speak the "Thus have I politely begun my reign" soliloquy to his dog, and be overheard by Katherine from a balcony.) If the Pickford-Fairbanks *Taming of the Shrew,* "with additional dialogue by Sam Taylor"—there was not much—was a less successful screen adaptation of Shakespeare than those which Laurence Olivier was later to achieve, it was surely the best that had been accomplished up to its time, and it has never received the credit it deserved. The picture which followed, the French farce *Kiki,* which David Belasco had adapted for Lenore Ulric, and in which she had given such a blockbuster of a performance,[11] was not a bad picture, but Mary seemed out of place in it. I regretted her decision to retire from the screen with *Secrets* (1933), but she could hardly have ended her career with a finer film. Her scenes with Leslie Howard, when their baby dies with-

[11] It seems odd that Norma Talmadge had anticipated Miss Pickford's production of both of her last films—*Kiki* and *Secrets.* As a matter of fact, Miss Pickford filmed *Secrets* twice but disliked the first production and decided not to release it.

out his being aware of what is happening, while he is defending their cabin against an Indian attack, were surely among the finest sequences she ever played.

Nobody has ever questioned Miss Pickford's great skill and knowledge in all matters relating to motion-picture technique, but there is a tendency among those who do not know her films well to identify her exclusively with the portrayal of children and young girls

> *Standing with reluctant feet,*
> *Where the brook and river meet.*

If this were true, I should not think it necessary to apologize for it in any terms of abjectness. Most actors specialize in one thing or another; to all intents and purposes, Mr. Chaplin has played only one character, but those who disparage Miss Pickford have not, therefore, thought it necessary to remain blind to his great achievements. If you are going to specialize, it seems to me that children and young girls afford a very good field. I can think of highly regarded actresses who have specialized in prostitutes, and I do not believe that prostitutes are more important than young girls or that they are more varied in their motivations or more difficult to portray. "A woman of moral depravity," said Julia Marlowe, "offers the modern playwright greater scope than a good woman because her life is full of incidents that are dramatic." But, she added, rightly, that "it takes a greater artist to make a good woman interesting than to make a base woman sympathetic and thrilling."

As a matter of fact, however, it was not until after the beginning of the feature era that Miss Pickford became definitely associated with ingénue roles, and it was not until *A Poor Little Rich Girl* that she appeared all through a feature film as a child. As we have already seen, the public preference for seeing her in youthful roles became an ever-increasing problem to her as she grew older, and she made a number of attempts to break away. "Through my professional creations," she says, "I became, in a sense, my own baby," and I think there can be no doubt that her cutting her curls (an act which she now questions her right to have performed, and says she would not do again), was an attempt to destroy the persona standing in the way of her future development.[12] Nevertheless, Mary's children and girls were not undifferentiated; of course there was a family relationship between them, but is not this also true of the types favored by certain other actresses? Gwen in *A Poor Little Rich Girl,* for example, is a very different girl from either Rebecca or Pollyanna—more helpless and less resourceful and considerably more wistful. She also gives the impression of being considerably younger. Her movements, her reactions are all those of a *small* child; so too is her fright when she is told by a lazy servant that she cannot be taken to her father's office because the place is full of bears. When she asks another girl, "Are you scared of BEARS?" she reads the line like a small child, and it is no exaggeration to speak of her "reading" such lines, though the film is silent, and we cannot hear what she says except in the mind's ear. Her

[12] In her autobiography she writes of being overwhelmed by the avalanche of public criticism which followed her act. "You would have thought I had murdered someone, and perhaps I had, but only to give her successor a chance to live." In 1929 bobbed hair was still a moral issue in America; it marked the difference between the old-fashioned "womanly" woman and her "emancipated" successor, between the Victorian maiden and the "flapper." When Mary Pickford, who had been the symbol par excellence of all the cherished old values, cut her hair, it seemed to many as though the citadel had been betrayed from within. When, as late as 1925, Miss Pickford had appealed through *Photoplay* for letters telling her what she should play, the 25,000 people who responded were overwhelmingly in favor of the youthful roles, the gist of the argument being that other actresses could portray emotional maturity but that what Mary was doing could be done by her alone. The stories most frequently asked for were "Cinderella" (which she had already done), *Anne of Green Gables* (which Mary Miles Minter had done), *Alice in Wonderland, Heidi, The Little Colonel,* and *Sara Crewe* (which she had done as *A Little Princess*). Disney is said once to have considered a production of *Alice* with Mary as the human child and cartoons for the fairyland characters.

tantrums are a small child's tantrums too, entirely lacking the elements of calculation and self-satisfaction of which Rebecca is capable or the sense of compulsion which sometimes possesses Pollyanna.

What I am saying of course is that the composite Pickford character was considerably less simple than she is generally supposed to have been. As I have already said, if she was "America's Sweetheart," she was also America's—and the world's—darling child, sometimes even problem child. But she was also the Madonna in *The Foundling* and again, briefly, in Douglas Fairbanks' production of *The Gaucho* in 1927.

She was, to be sure, in general, "good," and if you do not like good women in art—or if you subscribe to the juvenile and idiotic nonsense that bad women are more "interesting"—then she is not for you; but if you reject her on this ground, I fear you will have to reject most of Shakespeare's heroines with her. What you will have to learn, however, before you can approach her intelligently, is that "good" and "saccharine" are not synonymous terms.[13] I have

[13] Miss Pickford, as I have already remarked, was not one of her own fans. In her autobiography she declares that she never made a film which she liked in its entirety, and in her 1923 articles in the *Ladies' Home Journal* she went even further: "Of all the films that I have made I do not believe that there is one that is even half-way right or one that I would care to have brought out twenty years from now except as a curiosity, as a family album might be brought out." Once—horrible thought!—she even planned to buy up her films and destroy them. I am sure, therefore, that she will not mind my saying that while it never troubled me greatly, I do know what people mean when they object to a certain stock "cuteness" at times in her characterizations of children and young people, though I should prefer to describe this as a tendency to apply, at times, just a shade too much pressure. This seems to me her only fault as an actress within her range (I speak here of faults, not limitations), and I must take care not to overstress it, for she was, in general, an extremely restrained actress. Look at any of her early films— look, especially, if you can find it, at the Imp, *Going Straight*—and you will find Mary getting her effects by understatement while everybody else is acting all over the place. This was the source of her early squabbles with Grif-

already spoken of Mary's high jinks. Her repertoire in this kind was as rich and varied as that of the slapstick artists who did nothing else, and sometimes, as when, in *Through the Back Door,* she tied scrubbing brushes on her feet and turned the kitchen into a skating rink, she achieved a ballet-like ecstasy.

In *Rags, Tess of the Storm Country,* and several other films, she was a captivating and innocent young virago, with what you would have called outrageous conduct in anybody else accepted as endearing in her because of the disarming air of innocence that went along with it; and in *Daddy Long Legs* she was a devil toward all who were in authority over her at the orphan asylum but a tower of strength to every abused younger child. In *Rags* she made her first appearance riding on a goat. Overalls-clad, she charged head-on into a gang of boys who were abusing a dog, disciplined her drunken father in a saloon, and compelled him to return the money he had stolen; then she went into a temper tantrum, culminating in free-swinging a chair about her head after one of the habitués of the place had ventured to rumple her hair. In *The Pride of the Clan* she used equally violent methods to get the fisherman into church. In *The Foundling* she fed Mrs. Grimes's birthday cakes to the puppies, and when the dogcatcher tried to seize her own dog, she not only resisted him but unlocked the back of his wagon and set every animal imprisoned in it loose in the streets. She also made a statuette of the cruel Mrs. Grimes and then punished it; probably she did not know that she was practicing witchcraft, but the impulse was there. In *Poor Little Peppina* she and her brother Beppo (Jack Pickford) attacked a servant and kicked him in the shin in order to get in to see the duchess when Peppina needed her help to avoid an unwelcome marriage, and from there went on to more violence, culminating in an escape

fith: "I will not exaggerate, Mr. Griffith. I think it's an insult to the audience." She once told George Pratt of Eastman House, "Mr. Griffith always wanted to have me running around trees and pointing at rabbits, and I wouldn't do it."

for Peppina in Beppo's clothes. But perhaps she was more vigorous in *Tess* than anywhere else. She jumped on Dan Jordan's back when he tried to put out the squatters' fire, made impudent faces at Elias Graves and did a mocking dance step to tease him, and rushed into a tug of war when the warden was taking a net from a fisherwoman so that she got pulled along the ground on her bottom.

In *Rags,* Mary prepares to entertain an admirer (Marshall Neilan) at a miserable little lunch in her poor hut. She gets everything arranged to her satisfaction, but when she steps out for a moment, her drunken father and his companions come in and wolf the food. Mary, returning, arranges the few remaining scraps on Neilan's plate and greets him with a disarming "I was so hungry I jes' couldn't wait for you." James Card has rightly compared this with the famous scene in *The Gold Rush* in which Chaplin waits for the girl who never comes, and Iris Barry long ago pointed out the Chaplinesque elements in her arrangement of her hat and gloves before she sets out for church in *The New York Hat.* These are no isolated instances, and since Mary was doing this kind of thing before Chaplin came to the movies, there can be no question of indebtedness on her part. Unity Blake's pantomime with John Risca's coat in *Stella Maris,* which culminates when she makes him put his arm about her—perhaps the best thing about Mary's characterization of Unity is that she holds our sympathy for the girl even when she quite fails to keep her "place"—is Chaplin to the life. And *Rebecca* is full of this kind of thing: consider the dance-step movement Rebecca performs backward during her embarrassment while selling soap to Mr. Aladdin, or her recitations at school; consider her battle with the divided door when she arrives at the brick house (so like Keaton's never-ending war with gadgets). In closing the upper half she knocks the bottom half open again, and when she stoops back under to remedy this, the upper half knocks her hat off. Finally, consider the wonderful running and jumping from one piece of oilcloth to another, trying not to step on Aunt

Miranda's carpets, culminating in a run down the final strip close to the camera, ending in a dead stop and jerk which brings her hat down over her eyes and inspires her to remark that she is sure she is going to like it here. In *Hulda from Holland* she falls through a skylight onto a young man's bed. In the way of gadgetry again, she has regular Rube Goldberg contraptions on her bed curtains and fishing tackle in *Tess,* and when she arrives in England in *Less Than the Dust,* she makes a floral offering to a suit of armor.

It must not be supposed that even in her feature pictures, made when she had become such a valuable theatrical property that she could do virtually nothing without considering its probable effect upon millions of admirers, did she ever give the impression of having wrapped herself in cotton wool or of not understanding the world she lived in. In *Madame Butterfly* she killed herself for love (not by the traditional hara-kiri method, to be sure, but more genteelly by wading out into the water). In *Hearts Adrift* she cast herself and her child into a volcano. In *Stella Maris* she committed both murder and suicide. She was a girl thief in both *Less Than the Dust* and *In the Bishop's Carriage.* As a messenger boy in *Poor Little Peppina* she choked on a cigar; in *M'liss* she picked up a five-foot snake. In *A Romance of the Redwoods* she saved Elliott Dexter, as a reformed road agent to whom she was not married, by pretending that she was pregnant by him, using doll clothes as garments which she had prepared for the expected baby. The sheriff married them on the spot, and not until after they had got away did he understand that she had tricked him. *The Moving Picture World* thought this situation very daring and speculated on how the public would take it, though stipulating that "it is hardly necessary to add that the acting and personality of Mary Pickford make the situation without actual offence."

If the reviewer had remembered his Biographs, he might have been less shocked. Miss Pickford has denied that she got good parts at Biograph from the beginning. "I got what no one else wanted, and I took anything that came my way because I early decided that if I could get into as many pictures as possible, I'd become known and there would be a demand for my work." It is certainly true that in many of the Biographs I have seen she is shown briefly and ineffectively. Nevertheless, Griffith gave her a wider range of roles at Biograph than she was ever to have again, and if she could have continued on this basis, the misunderstandings concerning her which I have been opposing here would never have arisen.[14] Look at the scene in which she "vamps" the British sentry in the otherwise comparatively ineffective *1776; or, The Hessian Renegades* (1909) if you want to see how early the fetching manners so eagerly exploited in her later films were beginning to develop. On the other hand, there is hardly a trace of them in the many pictures in which she was cast as an Indian, and, as she says, she played mother to people who were only a few years younger than herself. When she acted Glory Quayle in *To Save Her Soul*, Griffith's one-reel adaptation of Hall Caine's *The Christian*, she could not give Griffith what he wanted from her because she was too young to understand the emotions she was supposed to express.

To understand Griffith's art, or Mary's, or that of any of a number of other fine Biograph players, there is a crying need to have all the surviving Biographs printed up and exhibited in chronological order. I have not, of course, been able to do this. Of the Pickford Biographs that I have seen, the best are *The New York Hat, The Informer,* and *A Feud in the Kentucky Hills.* (I suspect that *Lena and the Geese,* which Mary herself wrote, is about the most Pickfordish of all the Biographs, but I have not seen it since childhood.) *The Informer* is a Civil War picture, with *The Birth of a Nation* just around the corner. The lover's (Walter Miller's) return to Mary on the porch at the close of *The Informer* even partly

---

[14] I know of no complete list of Miss Pickford's Biograph, Imp, and Majestic films. Mr. Card's list in his *Image* article (see Note 1 of this chapter) includes only those in the Eastman House collection. It should be noted, however, that his list of the feature films is complete, and that he gives considerably more data concerning them than I have been able to crowd in here.

anticipates the Little Colonel's return in *The Birth of a Nation* (Walthall, this time, is not hero but villain). And in *A Feud in the Kentucky Hills* the fighting is directed with the same skill as that in *The Informer*. But there are other Biographs in which I can find better support for my argument.

In *Fate's Interception* (1912), with Mary as a Mexican Indian girl, we have the *Madame Butterfly* situation *without* a mock marriage and without any imputation of innocence to the woman in the case. Not only has she been living with her American lover without benefit of clergy, but after she has been jilted, she sends her Mexican admirer to kill him; through a fluke, the Mexican is killed instead, and she goes back to the American! "Who shall blame?" asks a subtitle. One might expect there would be a good many takers.

A much better—and better known—picture of the same year, *Friends,* goes in for more ambivalence, ending with the question "Which shall she choose?"—Walthall or Lionel Barrymore. But the amazing thing is that the girl, elegantly dressed in an 1890's gown with balloon sleeves (it had belonged to Mrs. Pickford), lives alone and receives her admirers in a room over the village tavern, where much of the action takes place. How much we are intended to read into this is doubtful, but it is safe to say that if the director and the players were conscious of all the implications, many of their 1912 customers must have missed them (I am very well acquainted with one who did).

Finally, what shall be said of yet another 1912 film, *The Female of the Species?* Oddly enough, Griffith called it "A Psychological Tragedy," yet it has a happy ending. Claire McDowell, her husband Charles West, her sister Mary, and a lone girl played by Dorothy Bernard wander through a wind-swept desert as the sole survivors of a massacre. The husband makes up to Bernard—what a man to function thus under such circumstances!—and shortly thereafter dies. Although the girl is entirely innocent, the wife suspects her and treats her cruelly, and the climax comes when, for what seemed in 1912 an interminable time, she stands over her sleeping form with a hatchet, "half mad with brooding," trying to make up her mind whether to kill her or not. The girl is saved when the woman is distracted by the cry of an abandoned Indian baby nearby, and reconciliation ensues. The psychological motivation here is none too clear; otherwise *The Female of the Species* is a stark and powerful film, with a grim natural background much like that Sjöström was later to use in *The Wind*. But the interesting thing is that Griffith did not cast Miss Pickford as the wronged girl and proceed to exploit a sentimental, Little Nell kind of helplessness, as almost any later director would have done. Instead he gave this role to Dorothy Bernard, who did not play it in anything approaching a sentimental manner, and he made Mary the wife's bitter and abetting sister, who went through the whole film with a frown between her eyes and a sneer on her lips, encouraging Claire McDowell's murderous desires and exuding venom toward her potential victim.

The Female of the Species was an interesting film, and I am glad to have seen Mary in this aspect, yet I doubt very much that anybody would really have preferred to have her career develop along *The Female of the Species* lines rather than *Tess of the Storm Country* lines. I well remember myself, aged twelve, coming home from *The Female of the Species* at the Victoria and announcing that I had seen a perfectly horrible picture! I even told the manager so afterward, and he agreed with me, or said he did, despite his general enthusiasm for Biograph films. All our naïveté notwithstanding, I cannot help believing that in the larger view the Age of Innocence did pretty well by Mary Pickford—and by us.

Benjamin Hampton points out that Mary "is the only member of her sex who ever became the focal point of an entire industry." Her rivalry with Chaplin changed the salary pattern for the whole film business, so that Zukor actually tried to keep her from going to his competitors by offering to pay her a large salary every week for a number of years *not* to make motion pictures—there is devotion to the film medium for you, and to Mary, too. Make whatever qualifications and reservations you like, for us Mary was sweetness and light, and this was more important to us than any possible characterization. If we made her up, this was all the more credit to ourselves. If there are no girls in the world like those she portrayed, then, since life imitates art quite as much as art imitates life, it was all the more important that such girls should appear on the screen, where their influence would extend farther and among more susceptible people than in any other medium. Whatever history makes of her, and whichever of her films may survive, no other generation will ever have her as we had her. If you say that you do not understand how we were able to read such ineffable meanings into her, I can only remind you of the painter and the lady who could not see the effects of which he had spoken in the great painting. ("Don't you wish you could, Madame?" he asked her. "Don't you wish you could?") But none of that is very important. The important thing is that we did it. And because we did it, we shall cherish her in our hearts as long as we live, along with the memories of our own youth, and be grateful in troubled times for the joy she brought us.

CHAPTER FOUR

"*Famous Players in Famous Plays*"

Surveying the films of the feature era must be quite as selective an enterprise as that undertaken in Chapter I.[1] I have taken as my title the old slogan of the Famous Players Film Company because though both Zukor and Lasky soon learned that a great stage star is not necessarily great on the screen, the screen actors themselves soon became more famous than those of the stage had ever been.[2]

[1] Since, as was shown in Chapter I, some feature-length films were produced in America before 1910, the beginnings of the feature era cannot be precisely dated. Similarly, though the death knell of the silent film was sounded in 1927, when Al Jolson appeared in *The Jazz Singer*, silent films continued to be produced into 1930. In 1929, Richard Watts, Jr., reviewed *The Passion of Joan of Arc* in the New York *Herald-Tribune* under the caption "A Dying Art Offers a Masterpiece." Chaplin, lone holdout for the silents, offered *City Lights* in 1931 and *Modern Times* in 1936.

[2] There were times, though, during the twenties and thirties, when stars and films alike were in danger of being buried in the great movie "palaces" or "cathedrals" where both plays and players became items in an elaborate "show," and where a luxurious "Shangri-la" was created in which any American who had a quarter could escape for an hour or two from the cares of life. This whole aspect of American culture has been fittingly memorialized by Ben M. Hall in an extremely entertaining (and luxurious!) book, *The Best Remaining Seats: The Story of the Golden Age of the Movie Palace* (Clarkson N. Potter, 1961).

This is not the place to tell the complicated story of the rise of Adolph Zukor and Jesse L. Lasky.[3] They began independently, joined to distribute their films, along with those of Morosco and Pallas (Hobart Bosworth), through Paramount, which was at first controlled by W. W. Hodkinson but later acquired by them, and ultimately their interests were merged in the Famous Players–Lasky Corporation.[4]

Having imported *Queen Elizabeth*,[5] Zukor began production with James O'Neill in *The Count of Monte Cristo* and James K. Hackett in *The Prisoner of Zenda*. Because *Monte Cristo* would have had to play against a rival production, *Zenda* was released first. Mrs. Fiske (in *Tess of the D'Urbervilles*), Lily Langtry, and

[3] See Zukor and Kramer, *The Public Is Never Wrong*; Will Irwin, *The House That Shadows Built* (Doubleday, 1928); Jesse L. Lasky and Don Weldon, *I Blow My Own Horn* (Doubleday, 1957); William C. deMille, *Hollywood Saga;* Donald Hayne, ed., *The Autobiography of Cecil B. De-Mille* (Prentice-Hall, 1959).

[4] Zukor also bought a controlling interest in Select and for a time established a subsidiary company, Realart, for his second-string stars and program pictures. To be sure that he would have an outlet for his pictures, and to meet competition from First National and United Artists, he began buying up theaters; by 1922 he had between four and five hundred but was later required by the government to dispose of them. The best account of these matters is in Benjamin B. Hampton, *A History of the Movies.*

[5] Much the best analysis of *Queen Elizabeth* is that of A. R. Fulton, *Motion Pictures*, 62–73, where it is clearly shown that though Mercanton designed it as a photographed play, it does have some cinematic qualities. When Nottingham discovers his wife with Essex, we see him first in the corridor from which he looks in upon the guilty couple, and then we look at him from inside the room itself. On the stage we would have had to see him from one room or the other. Modern viewers of *Queen Elizabeth* in Museum of Modern Art Film Library prints sometimes fail to appreciate Sarah Bernhardt because they assume that she is trying without success to achieve the kind of naturalistic acting they are accustomed to. She is of course striving for nothing of the kind. She is doing a highly stylized kind of acting which was in vogue on the French stage in her time, and doing it superbly.

Carlotta Nilsson followed, all in 1913; then, in 1914, May Irwin, Henrietta Crosman, H. B. Warner, and Hazel Dawn; in 1915, Gaby Deslys, William H. Crane, Maclyn Arbuckle, and others. Lasky began in 1913 with a production of *The Squaw Man,* starring Dustin Farnum, and codirected by Cecil B. deMille and Oscar Apfel in a barn near Hollywood and Vine. Dustin Farnum also did *The Virginian* for Lasky (this was deMille's first solo film), and his brother William Farnum appeared in *The Sign of the Cross.* Edward Abeles acted in *Brewster's Millions,* Charlotte Walker in *Kindling,* Ina Claire in *The Wild Goose Chase,* etc. "We were naïvely assuming," confessed Lasky, "that any play would make a good movie." But with Mary Pickford running away with Famous Players, Lasky still found it judicious, in 1915, to sign, along with the stage celebrities, such established screen favorites as Blanche Sweet[6] and Carlyle Blackwell.

Zukor and Lasky have often been blamed for trying to make the screen over into an imitation stage, and in a measure these complaints are justified.[7] The movies were becoming much more genteel at the beginning of the feature period, moving out of the store-

[6] Miss Sweet's first six Laskys were *The Warrens of Virginia, The Captive, Stolen Goods, The Clue, The Secret Orchard,* and *The Case of Becky.* After her Lasky period she had a varied career. She was excellent in a Bret Harte story, *Fighting Cressy,* in 1919, and she was much praised for her energetic comedy in *Object Matrimony* in 1920. In 1923 she gave a fine performance in the screen's first *Anna Christie.* The next year she appeared in *Tess of the D'Urbervilles,* directed by her husband Marshall Neilan.

[7] As has already been made clear, this tendency did not begin with Zukor and Lasky, though they greatly stimulated it, and after their success other producers were quick to take it up. In 1916, Vitagraph even captured E. H. Sothern, though his wife Julia Marlowe refused to capitulate. On the other hand, not even Famous Players was completely committed to the star system. On February 20, 1914, they released *The Pride of Jennico,* "Enacted by the Famous Players Stock Company," and on May 10, *A Woman's Triumph,* a screen version of Sir Walter Scott's *The Heart of Midlothian,* likewise without stars, which played in competition with a Hepworth importation under the author's title.

show rank, losing the somewhat working-class outlook they had had at the beginning, and appealing more and more to the people who read *Harper's* and the *Century* and patronized plays produced by the Frohmans and Belasco. Yet it is not correct to assume that none of the stage stars whom Zukor and Lasky brought into pictures were to be really successful there or that they contributed nothing to screen progress. Marguerite Clark (Famous Players, 1914 ff.)[8] and Pauline Frederick (Famous Players, 1915 ff.)[9] became great screen stars; so, a little later, did Elsie Ferguson (Artcraft, 1917 ff.).[10] John Barrymore, whose greatest success with Paramount was to be made in 1920, in John Robertson's production of *Dr. Jekyll and Mr. Hyde,* virtually deserted the stage for the screen; H. B. Warner and Theodore Roberts quite did so. Both the Farnums, William particularly,[11] had important screen careers. Marie Doro made a number of successful films for Lasky, including *Oliver Twist* (1916), which she had already done on the stage; and Fannie Ward had at least one great triumph in Hector Turnbull's story *The Cheat,* directed by Cecil B. deMille, in which she shared honors with the Japanese actor Sessue Hayakawa, himself

[8] See Chapter V, 225–29, in this volume.

[9] Her first films were *The Eternal City* (made in Rome), *Sold, Zaza, Bella Donna, Lydia Gilmore, The Spider.* Later she appeared in, among other things, screen versions of both *Resurrection* and *La Tosca.* See Muriel Elwood, *Pauline Frederick, On and Off the Stage* (Chicago, A. Kroch, 1940).

[10] This beautiful and patrician actress made her screen debut in 1917 in *Barbary Sheep* under Maurice Tourneur. There followed *The Rise of Jenny Cushing, The Song of Songs, The Rose of the World, Under the Greenwood Tree, A Doll's House,* and others. In 1921 she appeared with Wallace Reid in *Forever,* an elaborate production of *Peter Ibbetson,* directed by George Fitzmaurice. Miss Ferguson once stated that she made sixteen films during her first two years and nine months in pictures, working every day from nine to six. She died in 1961.

[11] Although William Farnum was primarily a Western or "he-man" star, he sometimes did other things. He was very successful in Fox's productions of *A Tale of Two Cities* (1917), in which he played both Carton and Darnay, and *Les Miserables* (1918).

destined to a whole series of film successes, including Stevenson's story *The Bottle Imp,* who, after many years' absence from the American screen, was at last to return to us in *The Bridge over the River Kwai.*[12]

It is true that none of these people, firmly established in the theater though many of them were, had achieved such celebrity there as belonged to a number of those who failed to impress in the new medium. But this certainly cannot be said of the most illustrious artist Paramount brought to the screen, Geraldine Farrar, who was bagged by Lasky in 1915 in what was regarded as the most sensational coup in motion-picture history. No prima donna had ever appeared in pictures before, and Miss Farrar was one of the greatest prima donnas in the world—from the American point of view, *the* greatest. When her private car arrived at the Santa Fe station, the mayor of Los Angeles was on hand to greet her. All six of her Lasky films were directed by Cecil B. deMille, with whom she hit it off perfectly, being as much adored by her fellow workers, down to the very prop boys, as she had always been by the stage-hands at the Metropolitan Opera House.

Maria Rosa was the first Farrar film made, but *Carmen* was released first. It was presented with great fanfare, within the sacred precincts of Symphony Hall in Miss Farrar's own Boston, on October 1, 1915, and Lasky took a four-page advertisement in *The Moving Picture World,* October 30, specially set up in script, with quotations from the reviewers.[13] In 1917, Miss Farrar appeared as

[12] *The Cheat* is probably the only motion picture which, reversing the usual process, has been both dramatized and turned into an opera. It was famous for the sensational scene in which the Oriental branded the white woman who had neglected to pay her debt to him. For the French enthusiasm for *The Cheat,* see Bardèche and Brasillach, *The History of Motion Pictures,* 106–108.

[13] Miss Farrar's screen debut seems to have been marred only by a flurry in Canada after she had made a statement which was interpreted as pro-German. Although Miss Farrar was completely an American, she had made her first success in Germany, was on terms of personal friendship with

her very favorite heroine, Joan of Arc, in the only one of her films she ranks among her first achievements, *Joan the Woman,* though many objected to the nonhistorical elements added to Joan's history and to the frame story in which Wallace Reid, who was Miss Farrar's leading man in all but one of her Lasky films, appeared as the reincarnation of an Englishman who had helped deliver Joan to the English and must now atone by giving his life for France in World War I.[14] Among other things, *Joan the Woman* was deMille's first great spectacle, but he almost equaled it in this aspect with *The Woman God Forgot,* an Aztec story in which Miss Farrar appeared in the fall of 1917.

After leaving Lasky, Miss Farrar made seven pictures for Samuel Goldwyn, who had come a dreadful cropper trying to establish Mary Garden as a film favorite in Miss Farrar's wake. Eloquent as Miss Garden's acting always was in the opera, her style proved ill adapted to the screen, and she got no help from scenario writers or directors. Her first picture, *Thaïs* (1917), directed by Frank Crane, was dull and stagy in the extreme, and its successor, *The Splendid Sinner,* written for her by Kate Jordan and directed by Edwin Carewe, was "patriotic," pseudo-uplifting nonsense.

In his autobiography, *Behind the Screen* (Doran, 1923), Goldwyn is somewhat naïvely wistful over the fact that Miss Farrar, always agreeable while she was with Lasky, began to make difficulties as soon as she worked for him, but he neglects to mention the fact that Lasky gave her generally very good material while

the German imperial family, and did not think it necessary to join in the crusade of hate then raging. Lasky gravely assured his Canadian customers that she had been paid outright for her work in *Carmen* and would receive no further profits from the sale of the film, after which, one may hope, they were able to enjoy it with a clear conscience, if there is such a thing in wartime.

[14] See Cecil B. deMille's account of the making of *Joan the Woman* in his *Autobiography,* 169–76, and Miss Farrar's own account in her *Such Sweet Compulsion* (Greystone Press, 1938), 171–76.

he for the most part gave her trash. Her best Goldwyn pictures were *The Stronger Vow*, a Spanish melodrama; *The World and Its Woman*, a story of the Russian revolution; and *The Woman and the Puppet*, a story by Pierre Louÿs which has since served the needs of both Marlene Dietrich (*The Devil Is a Woman*) and Brigitte Bardot (*A Woman Like Satan*).[15] Miss Farrar was as great a screen star for five years as if she had had no other career to rely on, and how many Americans she won for the opera and the concert hall nobody will ever know.

If the screen may be seen reaching out toward gentility with the Paramount companies, the same was true, only more so, when D. W. Griffith, Thomas H. Ince, and Mack Sennett were drawn into the new Triangle company which, in 1915, grew out of the old Mutual personnel. By September 23, Triangle were ready to put on their first program, at regular theater prices, at the Knicker-bocker Theater in New York, and thereafter in other leading cities. The Griffith (Fine Arts) offering was *The Lamb*, with Douglas Fairbanks and Seena Owen, directed by Christy Cabanne; Ince (Kay-Bee) offered *The Iron Strain*, with Dustin Farnum and Enid Markey; Sennett (Keystone) had two comedies: *My Valet*, with Raymond Hitchcock, and *A Game Old Knight*, with Charles Murray.

[15] Goldwyn, then Samuel Goldfish, broke off from the Lasky group in 1917 to form Goldwyn Pictures in association with Edgar Selwyn; after the latter's withdrawal he adopted the firm name as his own. The first Goldwyn pictures, in the fall of 1917, were Mae Marsh in *Polly of the Circus*; Madge Kennedy in *Baby Mine*; Maxine Elliott in *Fighting Odds*; and Jane Cowl in *The Spreading Dawn*. Mary Garden and Mabel Normand soon followed. Goldwyn also brought many well-known popular writers to Hollywood; they were, in general, less successful in mastering the new medium than the stage players had been. For the most part the early Goldwyn films were not well received, and Goldwyn did not really show what he had as a producer until later when he began to produce independently, doing one picture at a time and giving it his full attention. See Alva Johnston, *The Great Goldwyn* (Random House, 1937), and Richard Griffith, *Samuel Goldwyn: The Producer and His Films* (Simon and Schuster, 1956).

Next week came *Old Heidelberg* (Fine Arts), with Wallace Reid and Dorothy Gish, in which the familiar old play, later to be set to music as *The Student Prince,* was transformed into rousing peace propaganda in accord with Mr. Griffith's own ideas; *The Coward* (Kay-Bee), with Charles Ray and Frank Keenan; and the Keystones—*A Favorite Fool,* with Eddie Foy, and *Fickle Fatty's Fall,* with Roscoe ("Fatty") Arbuckle. The third week was devoted to *Martyrs of the Alamo* (Fine Arts); *The Disciple* (Kay-Bee), with William S. Hart; and, in Mr. Sennett's department, *Saved by Wireless* and *Her Painted Hero.*

Since Griffith, Ince, and Sennett were all film men, the reliance upon stage talent seems excessive in these programs—Triangle also brought in De Wolf Hopper to do a *Don Quixote* and Sir Herbert Beerbohm Tree and Constance Collier for a *Macbeth*[16] —but this shows how earnestly the movies were flirting with their elderly relative at this time.

In the long run Triangle turned out something of a disappointment, and it may even be that at the time we took their pictures more seriously than they deserved because we had been told that we were expected to do so.[17] By the summer of 1917, Griffith, Ince, and Sennett had all withdrawn from the organization, and by 1919 it was trying to keep alive, as Biograph had done in its final phase, by reissuing old successes. Yet while those first three weeks of the company's activity in 1915 had brought forth no

[16] According to Rupert Hughes, Triangle wanted to cancel Tree's contract after *Macbeth* but he refused. They considered trying to force his hand by putting him into blackface but compromised by casting him as an American farmer in Hughes's *Old Folks at Home,* which Hughes says he played magnificently. See Hughes, "Early Days in the Movies," *Saturday Evening Post,* (Apr. 6 and 13, 1935).

[17] The Oak Park Theater, I recall, being already pretty well tied up with the Paramount program, finally put in Triangle pictures—one feature and one Keystone at each throw—on Wednesdays and Saturdays, raising the tariff to twenty-five cents. (Motion-picture theaters were not allowed to operate on Sundays in Oak Park until a good many years later.)

masterpiece, they had held out some interesting pointers. *The Lamb* was Douglas Fairbanks' first picture. Charles Ray established himself in *The Coward*.[18] And though *The Disciple* was neither Hart's first picture nor even his first feature, it did mark an important stage in his stride to glory as the greatest of Western stars.

About the work of Thomas H. Ince in general between 1911, when he moved from Biograph to Imp, until his death in 1924, I can say much less than his position and influence in pictures deserve. Jean Cocteau and other French critics have been very enthusiastic about Ince, tending to rank him ahead of Griffith. I have

---

[18] Ray's acting in *The Coward* still seems beautiful and sensitive, but Frank Keenan's mugging at his father is now merely repulsive. The film, directed by Reginald Barker, takes up a very different attitude toward war than Ince's *Civilization*, which appeared the next year. The father drives the boy to enlist at the point of a gun; when he deserts, the old man takes his place in the ranks; his behavior is outrageously self-righteous throughout, yet the audience is evidently expected to sympathize with him. The son finally redeems himself by stealing the battle plans of the Union soldiers who have taken possession of his home, thus making a Confederate victory possible; he is shot while dashing through the Confederate lines to report to his commanding officer, and dies in his father's arms. In view of the large number of girls who have functioned successfully as ingénues, it is interesting that Ray was the only male who ever had an important career as whatever it is that corresponds among men to an ingénue, though it is possible that both Robert Harron and Richard Barthelmess might have companioned him if Griffith had not rescued them by casting them in more varied roles. Barthelmess' superb *Tol'able David* (1921) was, in a way, a kind of Charles Ray film. Jack Pickford was very charming in his early series of Paramounts with Louise Huff; this was interrupted by the war; his best later opportunity in kind was in *The Little Shepherd of Kingdom Come* (1920), which was very fine. As it was, however, Ray became the screen's barefoot boy par excellence. Among his films were *The Clodhopper, String Beans, Hayfoot Strawfoot, The Busher, The Girl I Love, The Old Swimmin' Hole*. He ruined himself financially with an elaborate but inept production of *The Courtship of Miles Standish* in 1923, which had Indians running about naked in the heart of a Massachusetts winter; thereafter he appeared in somewhat more varied and sophisticated roles until his early death in 1943.

never seen anything of his that could justify such an evaluation, and I suspect it to be due primarily to the curious enthusiasm of the French intellectuals for Westerns and to Ince's own freedom from sentimentality and his gift for a taut, straightforward line of development. I suspect, too, that his admirers have given him credit for a good deal of work which was actually done by Hart. It may be, however, that Ince's films were more impressive in the early days, when he directed personally, than they were after 1914, when, as the Lord of "Inceville," he presided over a film factory, sending out detailed scripts to his subordinate directors and marking them "Shoot as written." But so little of his best work is available for inspection that I cannot be dogmatic about these things.

The most famous Ince film, *Civilization* (1916), directed by Raymond B. West, has been credited with an important part in re-electing Woodrow Wilson on the campaign slogan "He Kept Us Out of War." This would have been a greater service if he had not taken us in immediately afterward. But whoever was responsible for that, it was certainly not Ince, and his intention must be respected even if one cannot consider *Civilization* a great film.[19]

[19] Let it be recorded by the gods of irony, however, that in May, 1917, it was announced that *Civilization* had now been "rearranged with new titles and inserts of the American flag, etc., as well as President Wilson's great message to Congress." In the theaters *Civilization* contended against J. Stuart Blackton's ripsnorter *The Battle Cry of Peace*, which was based on Hudson Maxim's book *Defenceless America*. As Henry Ford pointed out in full-page newspaper advertisements attacking both the book and the film, the fact that Maxim's munitions stock was on the market was not purely coincidental. *The Battle Cry of Peace* was much inferior to *Civilization*. The first part, with Norma Talmadge, Charles Richman, Rogers Lytton, and many members of the Vitagraph stock, showed an unnamed foe invading America; the last part was purely argumentative, with a number of distinguished Americans haranguing the audience in lengthy subtitles. The proportion of printed matter to picture probably reached an all-time high in this film.

The fullest account of Ince is by George Mitchell, "Thomas H. Ince," *Films in Review,* Vol. XI (1960), 464–84. An article, "The Early Days at Kay-Bee," appeared over Ince's by-line in *Photoplay* (Mar., 1919). See also

The crowd scenes and battle scenes in *Civilization* are in themselves masterly. Their weakness, compared to similar scenes in *Intolerance* and *The Birth of a Nation,* is that they do not add up to an overall design. In *The Birth of a Nation* we witness a battle; in *Civilization* we see some detached shots of fighting, each splendid in itself. But the story is rather silly—or in any case incapable of supporting so large a design—and the encounters between individuals are dull and slow-moving; it is never possible to care very deeply about the individuals involved.

The crisis in *Civilization* is precipitated when the hero-inventor refuses to fire a torpedo against a passenger ship; his crew rebels, and he goes back home to preach peace and to be imprisoned. In jail the Spirit of Christ takes possession of his body and calls forth the soul of the king to view the carnage he has wrought, as a result of which the monarch is converted and the war comes to an end.

In the picture the women of the country too have formed a great peace organization; they move upon the palace and kneel before it to demand the cessation of hostilities. In fact, the hero has been won to the pacifist point of view through his fiancée (Enid Markey), who belongs to this organization. But even she does not have enough to do in the film to become a real person to us.

Ince's refusal to tell us what the war is about is helpful in that it helps drive home his central thesis that it is war itself which is evil, not some particular war, but it also adds a certain element of unreality and evades some aspects of the problem. The uniforms and accouterments of the troops suggested imperial Germany. It may be that *Graustark* and *The Prisoner of Zenda* have made it difficult for us to take seriously political crises which occur in imaginary kingdoms.

It will already have appeared from my comments upon various personalities that innocence, real or simulated, was still the most highly rewarded quality in the feminine film star during at least

the references to him in the Sennett-Shipp *King of Comedy* and in William S. Hart's autobiography, *My Life East and West* (Houghton Mifflin, 1929).

the early part of the period now under consideration. But we are now getting some films in which rather more mature actresses appear, involved in more or less realistic situations, though it is also true that the point of view in such films is still inclined to be almost painfully moral; indeed the more unpleasant the material, the more proper the interpretation of the material seems bound to be.

There were also a number of actresses like Norma Talmadge and Ethel Clayton who, without making worldliness or sophistication a special stock in trade, were certainly not ingénues. I do not know that I ever saw either give a poor performance, and in view of the absurd statements by both Paul Rotha and Iris Barry that Norma Talmadge could not act at all, I should like to say this with considerable emphasis. Even *Du Barry* (1931), which is supposed to have finished her career, was not at all a bad film. The difficulty was simply that the kind of material presented in it was out of fashion in a very bad period; if it had appeared a few years earlier, it would have been warmly received. Miss Clayton appeared with Lubin, World, and Paramount. Lasky is said greatly to have admired her work and to have promised himself that sooner or later he must have her in his employ; but having secured her, he was not much more successful in finding material worthy of her than World had been, and I cannot think of a single memorable picture in which she appeared.

This was not true of Norma Talmadge, much of whose career was skillfully managed by her husband Joseph M. Schenck, who gave her the best material available, well chosen to suit her needs. Half-Jewish, half-Irish, which is a very good combination for an actress, Miss Talmadge began, as we have seen, with Vitagraph. As early as 1915 she was being billed as "The International Darling" in Henry Sydnor Harrison's story *Captivating Mary Carstairs,* and she was very fetching in such Triangles as *The Social Secretary;* but perhaps the first pictures in which she really showed her full capacity were *Panthea* and *Poppy,* both in 1917. Here, as Julian

Johnson declared, were the performances of a young virtuoso, "ringing true in every tone." Her later films included *The Passion Flower, The Sign on the Door, Smilin' Through, Ashes of Vengeance, Within the Law, The Dove,* and many more.[20]

Another prominent star was Miss Talmadge's fellow Vitagrapher, Clara Kimball Young. Mrs. Young had now lost the girlish beauty of her Vitagraph days and become a handsome, considerably more substantial-looking woman than the other actresses I have named. She appeared in a series of films based upon such works as *The Common Law, The Easiest Way, The Price She Paid, Magda,* and *Mid-Channel.* It was pretty sophisticated fare for the period, and I should say most of it was tailored to appeal especially to her women admirers, who were legion. Mrs. Young, however, was less intelligent than Norma Talmadge, and bad judgment forced her into retirement much earlier than would have been necessary.[21]

The real exotic among the stars of the time was the Russian actress Nazimova, who, having already appeared with the young Richard Barthelmess in Herbert Brenon's antiwar film *War Brides* (1916), created a sensation in 1918 in a religious film called *Revelation,* made by George D. Baker from Mabel Wagnalls' story "The Rosebush of a Thousand Years," and who went on to become, for a few years, Metro's most brilliant star. There can be no question about Nazimova's ability, but she herself put her finger on the weakness that finally destroyed her when she told an interviewer that her devilish ambition "makes the most unsuitable role the part I love best." She was well suited in such films as *The Red Lantern* and *Out of the Fog.* But trying to be Sarah Bernhardt did not satisfy her; she had to be Mary Pickford and Mabel Normand too, and

[20] In addition to Miss Talmadge's own reminiscences (cited in Chapter I, note 14), see the book by her mother Margaret L. Talmadge, *The Talmadge Sisters: Norma, Constance, Natalie* (Lippincott, 1924).

[21] See Henry R. Davis, Jr., "Clara Kimball Young," *Films in Review,* Vol. XII (1961), 419–25.

Picture 51, Maurice Tourneur   Picture 52, Cecil B. deMille

Two Directors Who Helped Bring Stage Technique to the Screen

Sarah Bernhardt taking a bow at the close of Louis Mercanton's production of *Queen Elizabeth* (1912). An example of direct imitation of the stage by the screen.

ture 54 *(right)*, Geraldine Farrar in
n the Woman (1917), directed by
cil B. deMille; Picture 55 *(below)*,
ss Farrar, with Theodore Roberts and
lly Marshall, in the trial scene.

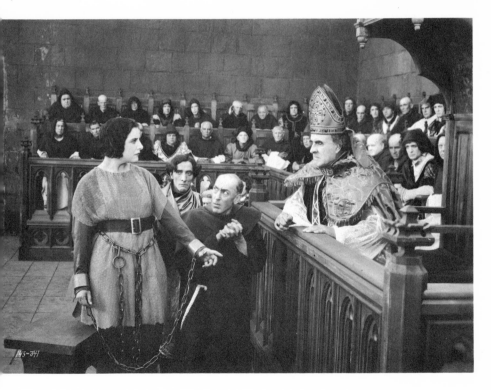

Charles Chaplin

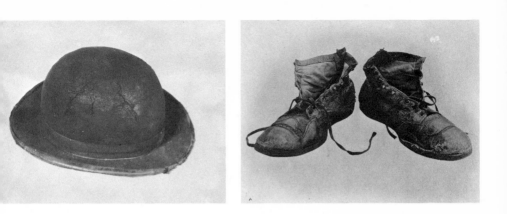

Picture 57 *(above left)*, Chaplin's hat; Picture 58 *(above right)*, Chaplin's shoes; Picture 59 *(below)*, Chaplin, with Mack Swain, in *The Gold Rush* (1925).

icture 60 *(above)*, *The Cabinet of Dr. Caligari* (1921); Picture 61 *(center)*, he body of the dead Siegfried is brought back to the castle in Fritz Lang's *Die Jibelungen* (1923–24); Picture 62 *(below)*, *The Golem* (1921).

Picture 63 *(above left)*, Lilian Harvey in *Congress Dances* (1931); Picture 64 *(above right)*, Emil Jannings in *The Last Laugh* (1925).

Great German Films Admired and Imitated in America

Douglas Fairbanks (Picture 65, *above*), as the laughing philosopher of his early screen years and (Picture 66, *below*) in *The Black Pirate* (1926). Picture 67 *(right)*, a portion of the castle set for *Robin Hood* (1922), a film in which Fairbanks starred.

such films as *The Brat* and *The Heart of a Child* proved that she was not able to be either. Later she achieved highly stylized and somewhat freakish productions of *Camille*, *A Doll's House*, and *Salome*, the last named designed by Valentino's wife, who liked to call herself Natacha Rambova. *Photoplay* listed *Salome* as one of the best six pictures of the month in which it was released but described Nazimova's conception of her role as "a petulant little princess with a Freudian complex and a headdress of glass bubbles." In private life Nazimova was a trusting, sincere woman who was an easy prey for charlatans.

But the prime dweller in the tents of wickedness was Theda Bara, who, in her way, was as much an institution during World War I days as Pearl White. She was the glory of the Fox Film Corporation, then characteristically given to somewhat lurid films, often, it must be confessed, rather more cinematic than the competing products of their more staid contemporaries.

Not, of course, that Miss Bara was really sophisticated. Hers was a comic-strip conception of wickedness, designed mainly to impress the hinterland. Her name was Theodosia Goodman; her father was a Cincinnati tailor; before, during, and after her years of fame she led a quite blameless life. But the Fox publicity department manufactured a past for her which was as colorful as the name they gave her—an anagram for "Arab Death"—and posed her with skeletons and other Gothic properties.[22]

[22] This specimen of the press agent's literary genius is too precious to be allowed to perish. The souvenir program issued with *Cleopatra* contained an article "Is Theda Bara a Reincarnation of Cleopatra?" The following arguments in favor of the proposition were advanced: (1) that "the character of Theda Bara and the character of Cleopatra are similar in many respects"; (2) that "in appearance, so far as can definitely be ascertained, Miss Bara and the 'Siren of the Nile' were similar"; (3) that "Miss Bara's last name is similar to an Egyptian word meaning 'Soul of the Sun'"; (4) that "the prophecy of Rhadames fits Cleopatra as easily as Miss Bara." And the lady herself was quoted as having declared that she "felt the blood of the Ptolemies coursing through . . . [her] veins" while making the film. Was

Her first film was *A Fool There Was* (1915), directed by Frank Powell, who had been trained under Griffith, from the play by Porter Emerson Browne in which Robert Hilliard had starred, and which in turn had been suggested by Rudyard Kipling's poem "The Vampire." Overnight the word "vamp" as a noun and a verb became part of the American language.

The review of *A Fool There Was* in *The Moving Picture World,* January 30, 1915, took the film very seriously indeed, identifying the star as "leading woman at the Theatre Antoine, Paris," which would certainly have been news to the innocent French. As Miss Bara's career progressed the notices became less respectful, although when she appeared as Cigarette in *Under Two Flags* in 1916, Julian Johnson was kind enough to say that she was as charming as Marguerite Clark, and two years later Randolph Bartlett paid her a kind of left-handed compliment by remarking that he preferred her Camille to that of many stage stars because he didn't have to listen to the coughing and "because Miss Bara makes Camille the brazen hussy we believe she was." But I doubt anybody could have given Miss Bara's career a more cruel *coup de grâce* than Miss Bara herself gave it when in 1919 she appeared on the stage in *The Blue Flame,* under the direction of Al H. Woods, and spoke the immortal first line, "Have you brought the cocaine?"

It will be seen that Miss Bara did sometimes use standard materials—she was Carmen, Cleopatra, Salome, and Du Barry as well as Camille—and that she was not invariably wicked. There was nothing or nobody that she feared to take on; her *Carmen* was made

---

Miss Bara taken in by her own publicity? During her film career it seemed that this must certainly be so. In two retrospective articles which appeared over her by-line in *The Forum* in 1919—"How I Became a Film Vampire," Vol. LXI, 715–27, and "The Curse on the Moving-Picture Actress," Vol. LXXII, 83–93—she lamented her reputation as a vampire-woman and proclaimed her dislike of motion pictures; but she was still absurdly pretentious about her "art," even comparing herself to Duse and Bernhardt. See also Agnes Smith, "The Confessions of Theda Bara," *Photoplay* (June, 1920).

to run competition to Geraldine Farrar's, her *Romeo and Juliet,* to the sumptuous Metro production with Francis X. Bushman and Beverly Bayne. The *Cleopatra* and the *Salome* have now lost the shock-value they once owned through what was then considered Miss Bara's very daring nakedness, but it may perhaps be in order to record that J. Gordon Edwards directed them with quite tasteless splendor, and that Fritz Leiber, a good actor, trained under Robert Mantell, was quite overwhelmed as the Antony. (He came back for more punishment in Edwards' production of *The Queen of Sheba* in 1921, by which time Betty Blythe had succeeded Miss Bara as Mr. Fox's prime embodiment of sinful lure.) Miss Bara was in *Kathleen Mavourneen, The Two Orphans, The Darling of Paris* (which was Victor Hugo's *Notre Dame de Paris*), *Heart and Soul* (Rider Haggard's *Jess*), *East Lynne,* and *Her Greatest Love* (Ouida's *Moths*); in 1916 she did not enact a single "vamp" between May and December, though she had four pictures during that period. Most of the time, however, she was *The Vixen* or *The Serpent* or *The She-Devil* in synthetic trash concocted especially for her, in which she had no function save to lure some helpless and completely "dumb" male to his ruin.

I have as yet said nothing except in passing of the three great male stars of the early feature era—Douglas Fairbanks, William S. Hart, and Charles Chaplin. Fairbanks, as already observed, was brought to Hollywood in the Triangle package; his greatest stage success had been in light comedies which allowed scope to his climbing, jumping, and athletic prowess. One critic called one of his early pictures, *Manhattan Madness,* "really nothing more than St. Vitus' dance set to ragtime," and though he was in the Fine Arts division of Triangle, Griffith himself at first shared this reaction, feeling that if Fairbanks had a future in pictures it must lie with Keystone. It was Harry Aitken and Frank Woods who, on the managerial side, saw Fairbanks' screen capacities, and it was the scenario writer Anita Loos and her director-husband John Emerson who furnished him with the materials that put him over.

The films were called *Double Trouble, His Picture in the Papers, Reggie Mixes In, The Americano,* etc.; later, when he moved to Artcraft, *In Again Out Again, Wild and Woolly, Down to Earth, Say Young Fellow, He Comes up Smiling,* and others did much to create happiness and relieve the strain of troubled days. One of them was called *His Majesty the American;* Fairbanks was always that. Another was *When the Clouds Roll By;* he never waited; he pushed them.

Fairbanks was not really a good actor; in the proper sense of the term he was hardly an actor at all. Even in his most ambitious days—in *Robin Hood,* for example—he would cleverly turn away from the camera or cover his face with his hands as a substitute for expressing emotion. On the other hand, his feeling for rhythm and movement was flawless, and he was ideally adapted to the film medium. National idols either express an ideal or else they provide an outlet for emotions which must otherwise be stifled; Fairbanks was emphatically in the first class. He was the Yankee Doodle Boy whom George M. Cohan had put on the stage when the eagle screamed more lightheartedly than he does today, but he performed on a larger stage than was ever available to Cohan; there was a touch of Theodore Roosevelt about him, especially in his enthusiasm for clean living and athletic prowess. He deliberately dared to set himself up as an ideal for youth, and his thin little pocket philosophies—*Laugh and Live* (1917) and its many successors[23]—may be said to have anticipated the "peace of mind" and "power" books that have made life so much more trying than it would need to be during these latter days. But it is only fair to Douglas to point out that, unlike the solemn latter-day purveyors of such junk, he was always able to "kid" pretension. Take *Reaching for the Moon,* for example, whose hero is a daydreaming young businessman who

---

[23] *Making Life Worth While, Initiative and Self-Reliance, Taking Stock of Ourselves, Whistle and Hoe—Sing as We Go, Assuming Responsibilities, Profiting by Experience, Wedlock in Time,* all published by the Britton Publishing Company.

aspires to walk among the kings of the earth. What is the moral of *Reaching for the Moon?* This: "If you wish for something, make a mental picture of it and concentrate [so far the "power" people have got forty years later], but [and here Fairbanks moves out beyond them] be careful what you wish for—you may get it." In the picture the young man gets it in a dream and doesn't like it, and when he has lost his job and nearly lost his girl, he wants to throw the concentration book away, but she will not have it, for she has been using it rightly. The picture ends on a note of comfortable acquiescence which goes far toward explaining why the great conservative body of the American people accepted Fairbanks as they did. He is doing his tricks to amuse his little son in the family living room; he has had enough of reaching for the moon.

There was a brashness about the early Fairbanks which at first I found it hard to like. "I was disappointed in the Grand Canyon," he was once reported to have said; "I couldn't jump it." He never opened the door of an automobile; he jumped over it. In one picture he jumped onto a moving bus and climbed up over the side; one shudders to think how many broken arms and legs he must have been responsible for among the children of America during the years of his vogue. All this suggested an element of strain in the Fairbanks optimism, and we know now that there was a moroseness in his make-up alongside the bounce, and that one element was probably a reaction against the other. One of his films, *Bound in Morocco,* had a trick ending. After the heroine had finally tumbled into the hero's arms at the proper moment, instead of the expected "The End," we encountered a subtitle "One hundred years later," which was followed by a brief shot of an ancient graveyard. Men whose cheerfulness is eight or ten times the size of life are likely to have this difficulty, and one thinks of G. Lowes Dickinson's saying that "the Red-Blood is happiest if he dies in the prime of life; otherwise he may easily end with suicide." Fairbanks did not do that—thank God—yet the absurd and undignified restlessness of his later years and his inability to adjust himself to the thought that he had passed his physical prime had a suicidal element in them. They destroyed his marriage with Mary Pickford and finally committed him to a way of life which, at his age, he could not have expected to continue long. But few of these sober thoughts intruded into the war years, when he and Chaplin and Miss Pickford performed as eagerly and spectacularly on their Liberty Bond selling trips as they did on the screen, nor later, after his marriage to Mary in 1920, when they toured Europe together and received such a welcome as has rarely been given kings.

Fairbanks' most important contributions to the screen came after 1920, when he turned away from his farces of contemporary life to produce *The Three Musketeers* and usher in a grand revival of costume pictures. He had felt his audience out for it as early as 1918 when he included a D'Artagnan sequence in *A Modern Musketeer,* and in December, 1920, he had ventured, with some misgivings, a kind of semihistorical comedy-drama called *The Mark of Zorro.* Although he appeared in other lesser films of the same kind later, his three masterpieces were *The Three Musketeers* (1921), directed by Fred Niblo; *Robin Hood* (1922), directed by Allan Dwan; and *The Thief of Bagdad* (1924), directed by Raoul Walsh. Probably the first of these was the most straightforwardly direct and entertaining and the second the most emotionally satisfying, but the third was unquestionably the most brilliant technical achievement. Who could ever have supposed that in our time life would give him a chance to go on pilgrimage with an Eastern vagabond, to pass through the Valley of Fire and the Mountain of Dread Adventure, to sail on the Sea of Midnight and invade the Crystal Realm beneath where all the monsters of fable abide, to climb the thousand steps which lead to the Citadel of the Moon, to wear the Cloak of Invisibility, to travel through space on the Winged Horse and the Magic Carpet?

The Thief of Bagdad showed the influence of the great contemporary German "studio" films and especially that of Fritz

Lang's *Destiny,* which it directly imitates in some aspects; some have even said that Fairbanks picked up a little of the German heaviness along with the wonder and imagination. However that may be, the wonder and imagination are there, and they are there because they had been deliberately planned for and created.

First of all [says the souvenir program], there was the fact that when a thing is photographed, it is given substance and reality. This was overcome by building acres of glazed floor, which reflected the buildings, gave gleaming high lights along the base lines, destroyed the reality of solid foundations. This imparted the illusion of floating so that the magnificent structures, with their shadows growing darker as they ascend, seem to have the fantastic quality of hanging from the clouds rather than of being set firmly upon the earth.

To further the illusion, the environment of the characters was designed out of proportion to human fact. Flowers, vases, stairs, windows and decorative effects were given a bizarre quality suggestive of the unreal.

It must not be assumed that in creating such films as *Robin Hood* and *The Thief of Bagdad,* Fairbanks was breaking altogether with his cinematic past. His spectacular slide down the huge curtain in the vast castle hall scene of *Robin Hood* is the one thing in the picture that nobody ever forgets. Incidentally, it was performed quite simply with a concealed slide, quite like that which every child in America uses in the school playground. But this too was suitable for Fairbanks, whose whole conception of Robin Hood seemed at times to have got crossed with Peter Pan. Although always properly susceptible to feminine charm, Fairbanks had never been much of a lover in his American films; it was quite suitable therefore that the Earl of Huntington should exercise the appeal of inexperienced awkwardness in such matters after his victory in the tournament, fleeing from the girls who flock about him begging him to wear their favors. He even jumps into a moat to escape them, and when he comes up in the vicinity of a woman washing clothes in the river, he resubmerges before she can see him. Later the king ties him to a pillar, where he manages to look properly sheepish with a bevy of girls about him until he sees Maid Marian menaced in the distance, when he promptly and heroically bursts his bonds and swings into action. In *The Thief of Bagdad* he jumps in glee like a little boy after killing a monster, much as Theodore Roosevelt is said to have done while hunting in the American West. Fairbanks put the Griffith last-minute rescue into *The Thief of Bagdad* also, but he burlesqued it as he used it. There was a touch of insolence in the way he rode the Winged Horse through the heavens, and there was humor as well as splendor in his method of raising his armies by magic spells. Their numbers staggered the imagination, but there was dramatic justification for this, for surely a million men would have been needed to take Bagdad on the scale to which he had constructed it.

Personally I do not see why the Winged Horse and the Flying Carpet of *The Thief of Bagdad* (or the wonderful flying coach in Herbert Brenon's production of *A Kiss for Cinderella*) are not quite as authentic cinematic material as the doings in the street to whose focusing some film aestheticians seem inclined to limit the camera. (In what other medium could they appear?) The great Fairbanks films came in a bad period. The old, specious wartime idealism had sagged, imagination had sagged with it, and producers were showing a sad tendency to confine themselves not only to the contemporary but even to the duller aspects of the contemporary. Fairbanks was not alone in resisting this tendency; the month of October, 1922, in which *Robin Hood* was first shown in Chicago also unreeled *The Prisoner of Zenda, The Old Homestead, Under Two Flags, When Knighthood Was in Flower, Oliver Twist,* and *To Have and To Hold.* But the influence of his example was great, and none of the others came within hailing distance of his work. At the beginning of *Robin Hood* a drawbridge comes down toward the camera. Over it the audience marches into the

Middle Ages, and there it stays until the film is over. I have said that Fairbanks was not a very good actor. But in these films he did prove himself a high-minded and idealistic producer, and if he had done nothing else he would still deserve to be kept warmly and gratefully in remembrance.[24]

I have less to say about William S. Hart, but this does not mean that I think him less important. If "Broncho Billy" was the first Western star, Hart was the greatest. Tom Mix may sometimes have been more entertaining; certainly he deserves high praise for his determination to guard his example and keep his pictures scrupulously clean. But he did not achieve, or even strive for, Hart's authenticity.[25]

Hart had come by it honestly, and it was bred in the bone to such an extent that he denounced even *The Covered Wagon* (1923) as a falsification. The son of a miller, he learned the West and the Middle West at first hand during his childhood, as he learned to talk Sioux from those to whom it was their native tongue. (Thus early, too, he decided that all claims of racial superiority were "arrant drivel.") The Hart family, which was of English and Irish ancestry, was poor, but they had standards. On the stage Hart supported distinguished stars; Modjeska called him the best Armand Duval she had ever had, and Alan Dale described him as "a sort of masculine Julia Marlowe," which sounds like a very silly statement even for a dramatic critic. He almost got a chance to produce *Cyrano de Bergerac* before either Mansfield or Arnold Daly got hold of it. He was the first Messala in the stage *Ben Hur,* and he he began to find the character which would thereafter be associated

[24] Ralph Hancock and Letitia Fairbanks wrote Fairbanks' biography in *Douglas Fairbanks: The Fourth Musketeer* (Holt, 1935); see also Alastair Cooke, *Douglas Fairbanks: The Making of a Screen Character* (Museum of Modern Art, 1940), and the many references to him in Mary Pickford's autobiography.

[25] See Olive Stokes Mix and Eric Heath, *The Fabulous Tom Mix* (Prentice-Hall, 1957).

with him in the stage productions of *The Squaw Man, The Virginian,* and *The Trail of the Lonesome Pine.*

Hart lived from 1870 to 1946. His screen career extended from 1914 to 1925—with Kay-Bee, Triangle, Paramount, and United Artists. He probably made the mistake of his life when he did not accept the invitation which Griffith, Chaplin, Fairbanks, and Mary Pickford extended to him in 1919 to join them in establishing United Artists. According to his autobiography,[26] he was not treated fairly either by Paramount or by Ince, and his screen career seems to have been forcibly terminated while his drawing power was still very great.

If Fairbanks was not a very good actor, what shall be said of Hart? I have no doubt that most of his films would seem much more old-fashioned today than those of Fairbanks and that his "emoting" would be much easier to laugh at. In a way they were already old-fashioned when he made them, for he harked back to a West that was already passing away. That West he carried in his heart along with the memory of his youth, and he went into pictures because he saw it being outraged and misrepresented in contemporary films: "Here were reproductions of the Old West being seriously presented to the public—in almost a burlesque manner—and they were successful. It made me tremble to think of it."

Such intensity was characteristic of Hart. It showed in his good men, his bad men, and his Indians; it showed in his reverential attitude toward women. He seems to have fallen romantically and idealistically in love with nearly all his leading ladies, but nobody said "yes" and meant it until Winifred Westover came along in 1921, and the resultant marriage, which produced one son, was not successful and did not endure. Hart's code, which carried the insignia of the frontier he loved upon it, was not everyman's,

[26] Hart's *My Life East and West* is the fullest account of his career. He also wrote a number of books for boys. See George Mitchell, "William S. Hart," *Films in Review,* Vol. VI (1955), 145–54.

but nobody has ever suggested that he did not live up to it. It seems to me that much the same thing must be said of his acting. He was a figure of great dignity; within his range, and granting his presuppositions concerning human character and values, he achieved what he set out to achieve. Louis Delluc called him "the first real figure established by the cinema" and his subject matter "the first really cinematic theme . . . the adventures of an adventurer in search of fortune in Nevada or the Rocky Mountains, who holds up the mail coach, robs the mails, burns the rancher's house, and marries the sheriff's daughter." But Hart was not always so lawless as this summary would suggest. As George Mitchell has observed, his pictures are documents on the old West, along with the paintings of Frederic Remington and Charles M. Russell. Among the most famous are *The Aryan, The Dawn Maker, The Narrow Trail, Wagon Tracks, The Toll Gate, Wild Bill Hickok,* and *Tumbleweeds.* Contrary to popular opinion, Ince never directed a Hart film; all he did was give Hart a chance to break into pictures and refuse to share with him the enormous earnings his pictures made. Outside of the films he directed himself, Hart's best director was Lambert Hillyer.

It may seem odd that at the very time when short films were being superseded by features, the greatest of all motion-picture careers should have been in process of being built up in short films. Gilbert Seldes has called Charles Spencer Chaplin "the one universal man of modern times." No doubt it can be argued that up to *The Great Dictator* he had created only one character, but that character is so rich that to describe it adequately you must compare it with such creations as Falstaff and Don Quixote. Chaplin's "Charlot," as the French call him, is one of the great comic characters of world art. As Chaplin himself later remarked, looking back upon his early career, "Even then, I realized I would have to spend the rest of my life finding out more about the creature. For me he was fixed, complete, the moment I looked in the mirror and saw him for the first time, yet even now I don't know all the things there are to be known about him."[27]

Chaplin came to Keystone in December, 1913, from an English pantomime company which was touring America. He remained with Sennett only until the end of the year, yet thirty-five titles are listed in Theodore Huff's book about him.[28] One is the six-reel *Tillie's Punctured Romance,* with Marie Dressler and Mabel Normand, which is still being shown commercially; most of the others were single-reelers.

Popular acclaim was immediate; nothing like it had ever been seen before, nor have we had anything like it since. Chaplin swept first America, then the world. This was not anything that had been expected or planned for by the motion-picture industry or by Chaplin himself; both indeed were greatly surprised by it. From the beginning he was somewhat at odds with his Keystone environment; from May, 1914, on he was generally permitted to write and direct his own pictures. Yet crude as Chaplin's Keystones now seem in comparison with his later work, his association with Sennett and the Keystone comedians was of great value to him in laying the foundations of his style. He built upon that foundation in later

[27] The Dickensian influence—or affinity—in Chaplin is obviously very important; the most elaborate discussion of this is in Robert Payne, *The Great Charlie* (London, Andre Deutsch, 1952); see also Edward Wagenknecht, *Cavalcade of the English Novel* (Holt, 1943), 229–30. As a filmmaker Chaplin was of course influenced by Griffith; according to Theodore Huff, he saw *The Birth of a Nation* nearly every week during its long Los Angeles first run. In view of Griffith's own indebtedness to Dickens, described in Chapter II, this is very interesting.

[28] So much has been written about Chaplin in so many languages that it is difficult to single out any one work as the best. Huff's *Charlie Chaplin* (New York, Henry Schuman, 1951) is indispensable for the information it contains and because it describes what takes place in the films with some fullness. Thomas Burke's penetrating essay in *City of Encounters* (Constable, 1932) is not to be missed. Harry A. Grace, "Charlie Chaplin's Films and American Culture Patterns," *Journal of Aesthetics and Art Criticism*, Vol. X (1952), 353–63, is over-formalized and humorless.

years; he altered, deepened, and vastly improved it, but he never discarded it.

The next year he spent with Essanay, for whom he made fourteen films, mostly two-reelers, including *The Champion, The Tramp, A Woman, The Bank, Shanghaied,* and a burlesque of *Carmen.*[29] These films seemed wonderful in their time. *The Tramp* was the first striking expression of Chaplin's gift for pathos, and *The Bank* is certainly a very funny film by any standard. Compared to his later work, however, the Essanays still seem very definitely early Chaplin.

At the outset his admirers were children and outcasts, hewers of wood and drawers of water, the poor and simple souls of the world; and most of her genteel admirers regarded Mrs. Fiske as slightly mad when, in a brave article published in the very last number of *Harper's Weekly,*[30] she hailed him as "a great comic artist, possessing inspirational powers and a technique as unfaltering as Réjane's." During 1914 he had no "story" of any kind in *The Moving Picture World* and rated only passing mention in reviews of Keystone films up to October 24, when his picture ap-

[29] Chaplin designed *Carmen* in two reels but after he had left them Essanay outrageously padded it with discarded scenes and issued it in four, which was not the last disservice they did him by sending scraps and fragments into the market. Chaplin sought an injunction to prevent the film's being shown but lost. Meanwhile, the Juvenile Film Corporation burlesqued the burlesque in *Chip's Burlesque on Carmen.* While we are concentrating on this exalted branch of the motion-picture business, let us not overlook the two-reel travesty of *War Brides,* "as played by Mme. Alley Noximova, and then some!" which Flora Finch perpetrated in 1917. "Miss Finch appears in a number of gowns imported for her by Woolworth (5 and 10)." When Lewis J. Selznick threatened legal action on the ground of holding screen rights to *War Brides,* Miss Finch's company changed their title to *War Prides!* Chaplin was also imitated as to make-up, costume, etc., by a number of comedians who had best now be left undisturbed in the oblivion they so dearly earned.

[30] Minnie Maddern Fiske, "The Art of Charles Chaplin," *Harper's Weekly,* Vol. LXII (1916), 494.

peared in an advertisement for *Dough and Dynamite*. Both this film and its successor, *His Trysting Place,* got display reviews. Yet on November 7, Sydney Chaplin was identified in a write-up as "brother of Charlie Chaplin (the funny drunk) of Keystone fame."

When Chaplin signed with Essanay, *The Moving Picture World* declared that "Mr. Chaplin in a remarkably short time has created for himself a unique position in the film world." But they still knew so little about him that they speculated about "the name of the director under whom he will work." On January 23, 1915, Essanay announced in a display advertisement that they were "now offering exhibitors three of the greatest stars the photoplay world has ever seen—the 'A.B.C.' of drama and comedy—Mr. G. M. Anderson, Mr. Francis X. Bushman, and Mr. Charles Chaplin." This was arranged so that Anderson still got the top of the page and Chaplin the bottom—"the most wonderful comedian ever seen on the screen . . . in himself a guarantee of ESSANAY QUALITY." And even on August 7, with Bushman lost to Metro, Walthall got the top half of a page advertisement in *The Woman Hater,* directed by Charles Brabin, while Chaplin in *The Bank* made out with the lower half.

The *Dramatic Mirror* made an even worse showing at a later date. Reviewing Mary Pickford in *Less Than the Dust* on November 11, 1916, the reviewer declared that there were "comedy moments, bordering on the Chaplinesque, which might have been eliminated." When Chaplin's marriage to Mildred Harris was reported on November 23, 1918, he was identified as "Charles S. Chaplin, reputed to be the funniest of all film comedians." As late as 1919, the *Dramatic Mirror* gave *Sunnyside* a bad review, indulging in asinine conjectures that Chaplin might be slipping because his brother Sydney was no longer on hand to guide him. But the booby prize goes to the distinguished *Theater Magazine,* where, in October, 1919, one Harcourt Farmer pulled out all the stops in an article titled "Is the Charlie Chaplin Vogue Passing?" According to Mr. Farmer, Chaplin's appeal was "an extremely unintellectual one," directed toward "the lowest of human instincts."

It is difficult to be patient with such nonsense, but it is important to understand it. Surely Griffith and Mayer are just when they find "a smile of . . . angelic innocence" in the youthful Chaplin, "coupled with a surprising streak of meanness, violence, and a certain deliberate vulgarity." Sennett himself, who was certainly not finicky about such matters, has remarked that it was a long time before Chaplin "abandoned cruelty, venality, treachery, larcency, and lechery as the main characteristic of the tramp." Charlot, says Buster Keaton, "was a bum with a bum's philosophy. Lovable as he was he would steal if he got the chance. My little fellow was a workingman and honest." Brooding over *Monsieur Verdoux,* Robert Payne found that "Charlie had never been a sentimental figure. He was the murderer, the pimp, the panderer, the seducer, the criminal, the artist and *l'homme moyen sensuel* from the beginning, just as we have been all these things ourselves."

As an aesthetic creation, Charlot was no less impressive for the presence of these elements; indeed Chaplin was far bolder in putting the natural man on the screen than pre-Hemingway writers were in describing him on the printed page. But so long as these elements remained, one could not justly blame parents for not feeling that they had no right to object to the example he was setting their children simply because he was dressing it up with wonderful art. The truth is that there were already elements in his pictures that were destined to cause Chaplin considerable trouble during his later life. A commentator who, like the present writer, can approve neither of many of the statements Chaplin has made during recent years nor of the way he has been treated for having made them must tread very warily at this point; he feels himself surrounded by enemies, and he does not wish to give aid and comfort to any of them. Nevertheless there was a subversive element in Chaplin from the beginning, and this not only, nor even mainly, in the political sense. In 1924 he declared that the accusation of vulgarity might just as well be applied to Shakespeare as to him. "Why can't we face facts and admit that we are all human beings?" So far as vulgarity is concerned, this is not far off the mark. Mrs. Fiske had admitted Chaplin's vulgarity but insisted upon pointing out that he shared it with other comic geniuses from Aristophanes through Shakespeare to Swift. "Vulgarity and distinguished art can exist together." But what are "human beings"? Hitler was a human being, and so was St. Francis of Assisi. If we are going to accept conduct merely because it is "human," then we can rule nothing out.

Chaplin's mind is that of an artist rather than a philosopher, to be respected for its brilliant perceptions rather than for any systematic formulations which may result. Yet it is disquieting to hear him hold forth upon his lack of respect for humanity. "The human race I prefer to think of as an underworld of the gods. When the gods go slumming they visit the earth." More personally, he tells us that "often when I am hardest at work a sense of utter futility comes over me. I make my characters the pawns of Fate because I believe them to be so." I raise no question here as to whether Chaplin is "right" or "wrong" about these matters. I do raise the far more relevant question: Can such views serve as an adequate ideational background for an important work of art?

In any event, *Monsieur Verdoux* was not the first film in which Chaplin threw down the gauntlet. I love *The Pilgrim*, though I do not think that the David and Goliath pantomime sermon, which once seemed to me about the most brilliant thing I had ever seen, has worn anything like so well as the inimitable roll dance in *The Gold Rush*. Yet the caricature of churchgoing people which Chaplin perpetrated in *The Pilgrim,* with the whisky bottle sticking out of the deacon's pocket, is merely rude and mean; it would not be tolerated on the screen today. You may reply that it is good fun, but you are not very sensitive to overtones if you find no malice in it. And the beginning of *The Kid* is not fun at all. Edna Purviance leaves the asylum with her illegitimate child, and we are told in a subtitle that motherhood is her "only crime." From here we cut to a shot of a drawing of Christ carrying His cross, and surely the implied comparison is one of the most outrageously sentimental things in films. Next she passes a church from which is emerging a sad-faced bride who has just been married to a man much older than herself.[31] Fortunately this is not the whole story about either Chaplin or Chaplin's films. Like some of the rest of us, he has often transcended his "philosophy," creating on the screen so sensitive and touching a character that at times it becomes a faintly satiric image of humanity itself, and in such moments *l'homme moyen sensuel*—or even, if Robert Payne will have it so, the seducer, the panderer, the criminal—becomes the voice of all the regimented, persecuted, dispossessed ones, the scapegoat, the innocent, the nonresistant, "the sacrificial hero, the redeeming martyr," the terrible meek who at last must inherit the earth.[32]

In 1916, Chaplin went to Mutual at a salary of $670,000 a year. Between May 15, 1916, and October 23, 1917, Mutual released twelve films, each in two reels, of which almost every one was a masterpiece: *The Floorwalker, The Fireman, The Vagabond, One A.M.* (this is the film in which he shows Max Linder's influence most clearly and also comes closest to Buster Keaton), *The Count, The Pawnshop, Behind the Screen* (the least of the series), *The Rink, Easy Street* (perhaps the greatest short comedy ever made), *The Cure, The Immigrant,* and *The Adventurer.* Even the titles were inspired. The improvement in style which Chaplin revealed in these films was almost miraculous; here, too, he proved that he was a master of pathos as well as humor. This, indeed, was

[31] For more examples of this kind of thing, see Arthur Knight's comments on *A Woman of Paris* in his *The Liveliest Art,* 131–33.

[32] There is a brilliant commentary on Chaplin in this aspect in Edgar Morin, *The Stars,* translated from the French by Richard Howard (Grove Press, 1960), 109–19.

Chaplin's *annus mirabilis*. He was to achieve greater single films later on, but never again would be live through a year and a half in which he accomplished so much.

In 1918, First National captured him. His first film for them, *A Dog's Life,* was a three-reel masterpiece; this was followed by *Shoulder Arms,* possibly the only film in which the poor doughboy ever really saw himself. Two short films followed in 1919—*Sunnyside* and *A Day's Pleasure,* in three and two reels respectively. The ballet sequence in *Sunnyside* is Exhibit A to show the close resemblance which exists between Chaplin films and music and ballet. They resemble music too in their ability to submit to any number of reviewings and their reluctance to submit to being described. As has been well said, you never see everything Chaplin does even while you are watching him.

In 1921, Chaplin took the longest single forward step of his career: he made his first feature, *The Kid*. In some quarters it is no longer fashionable to admire this film. It probably does not seem so extraordinary today as it did when it first appeared; taken as a whole, it is probably less of an achievement than some of Chaplin's later pictures. Yet there are wonderful things in it and passages of quite unsurpassable tenderness. In *The Kid,* Chaplin was generous enough to introduce another player who almost matched the sensation which he himself created—the diminutive Jackie Coogan, who offered the finest and most sensitive child-acting any of us had ever seen, or ever would see until Margaret O'Brien should come along in 1943 and prove that from here on the only admissible standards should be those which she would set. After *The Kid,* Chaplin made two more two-reelers—the last he was ever to make —*The Idle Class* and *Pay Day,* and one of moderate length (four reels), *The Pilgrim*. This finished his First National contract in 1923. He had helped form United Artists in 1919, but it had not yet got a picture from him.

It did not get one in which he starred until 1925, but meanwhile, in 1923, he had directed Edna Purviance in a somewhat Continental yet in some aspects sentimental film called *A Woman of Paris*. His own first film for United Artists was the immortal *Gold Rush* in nine reels. He was now doing only full-length films with long, long waits between them: *The Circus* (1928), *City Lights* (1931), *Modern Times* (1936), *The Great Dictator* (1940), *Monsieur Verdoux* (1947), *Limelight* (1952), *A King in New York* (1957).

Although he had burlesqued the sound film by using gibberish in some passages of *Modern Times,* Chaplin did not make a "talking picture" until *The Great Dictator,* in which he did his devastating burlesque of Hitler (Hynkel) while Charlot was more or less transmogrified into a hapless little Jewish barber under Nazi tyranny (thus, as critics were quick to point out, sacrificing the universality he had owned until this time, but perhaps Chaplin meant that in such a persecution everyman was involved), and which culminated in the denunciation of tyranny and the plea for love and freedom which was certainly the most moving thing of its kind that has ever emanated from the screen. There are few things I regret more than the fact that I have never had a chance to see *Monsieur Verdoux,* which Chaplin seems to have intended as an indictment of the basis of violence upon which all civilization rests, but which his American admirers either did not understand or did not wish to understand; and he has not permitted *A King in New York* to be shown in this country. *Limelight* did not bring Charlot back, though the superannuated, drunken, English music-hall star whom Chaplin played, who loved a girl much younger than himself and who died at the end of the picture, did have something in common with him. In *Limelight,* Chaplin shared honors with Buster Keaton; he had already given Chester Conklin a place in *Modern Times.* Claire Bloom was very important in *Limelight* too, as Paulette Goddard had been in both *Modern Times* and *The Great Dictator.* These pictures are all so good that choosing between them becomes largely a matter of individual taste. *The Gold Rush* and *City Lights* are the general favorites; my own favorites are *The Circus* and *Modern Times*.

After 1921 there was another world figure in pictures, a young man called Rodolpho Alfonzo Rafaelo Pierre Filibert Guglielmi di Valentina d'Antonguolla who finally decided that he wished to be known as Rudolph Valentino. He had been around Hollywood for some time—Geraldine Farrar, in her Goldwyn days, had wondered whether he might not have something, and Dorothy Gish is said to have told D. W. Griffith that he was losing good money by not putting him on—but he did not get his real chance until June Mathis got him into Rex Ingram's big production of *The Four Horsemen of the Apocalypse* (Mack Sennett says he couldn't pronounce the word).

I cannot say much about Valentino, for I walked out on *The Sheik,* and though I did see him later in *Blood and Sand* and *Monsieur Beaucaire* and *The Eagle,* I never saw his last (and many people think his best) film, *The Son of the Sheik,* until recently. He made "sheik" in its slang sense as popular in America as Theda Bara had made "vamp," but I did not happen to be the right sex for sheiks to work on; and at the time I am afraid I more or less agreed with the outrageous Chicago *Tribune* "Pink Powder Puff" editorial, in which they urged that, in the interest of the public welfare, "the beautiful gardener's boy" be taken out and drowned. I had no prejudice against Latins; I greatly enjoyed Ramon Novarro; but that sensible and earnest young man did not "smoulder" in the Valentino fashion, and though he was far handsomer than Valentino ever dreamed of being, he probably would have been very much embarrassed if anybody had exploited or interpreted him in Valentino terms.

Paramount found Valentino hard to handle, especially when he was under the domination of his second wife Natacha Rambova, and some of his short years in films were wasted in litigation—according to Lasky, his box-office rating was already slipping at the time of his death—but those who worked with him seem generally to have liked him, and it now seems to me that I was not fair to him: if he gave American women their most exciting experience of love-making by remote control, he was certainly much less of a fool about it than they were. Considering his background and his provocations, Valentino behaved himself very well indeed; he did not have a happy life, and it was bitter irony that the man for whom so many women would cheerfully have died never found anything for himself except a hopeless mismating. As everybody knows, he himself died at thirty-one, after an operation for appendicitis during a trip to New York in the summer of 1926. He died at the same time as President Eliot of Harvard and the distinguished littérateur Stuart P. Sherman, and the newspapers gave him all their space, so that it was some time before most people knew that the other two less important Americans had also been taken. But that was not Valentino's fault either, nor the fantastic celebration (as I am tempted to call it) of his funeral, nor yet the nauseating exercises in which heaven only knows how many empty-headed women have participated down through the years at his grave.[33]

Valentino's unabashed screen sexuality (he seems to have been decorous enough in his private life) was a symptom of the time; the big heartthrob just preceding him had been Wallace Reid, who had always impressed his followers as a fine, upstanding young American man—a kind of animated Arrow collar advertisement—not an innocent like Charles Ray, but gallant, well-behaved (he had but one wife), and certainly not oversexed. Reid, too, died at thirty, in 1922, and after his death the public was shocked to

[33] See Alan Arnold, *Valentino* (Library Publishers, 1954), and cf. H. L. Mencken's touching account of his meeting with Valentino, just before his death, in *Prejudices, Sixth Series* (Knopf, 1927). "He was essentially a highly respectable young man, which is the sort that never metamorphoses into an artist." His agony was "the agony of a man of relatively civilized feelings thrown into a situation of intolerable vulgarity."

learn that he had been using narcotics. This was one of a series of scandals which led to the setting-up of the Motion Picture Producers and Distributors of America, with Will Hays at the head of it, to "clean house," [34] but the hysterical public reaction did not create any more favorable atmosphere than it usually does in which to achieve a sensible view of the problems involved. It might reasonably be argued that Reid died less of drug addiction than of a heroic attempt to break off drug addiction,[35] and though "Fatty" Arbuckle probably did give a disgusting party at the St. Francis Hotel in San Francisco, there was never any reasonable ground for supposing that he had misused the girl who died afterward or contributed to her death; neither did anybody who knew him ever believe that it was in his character to do the things he was accused of having done.[36]

Miss Pola Negri contributed importantly to the increasing sophistication of American films during this period; in a measure she and Emil Jannings and Ernst Lubitsch too may be said to have been brought over to sophisticate them. As we have seen, French, Italian, and Scandinavian films had been much at home on the American screen before World War I, but when foreign films began coming in again after the bloodletting had ceased, none of these countries loomed up as primarily important; instead the pictures which really roused enthusiasm came first from Germany and then from Russia. The German film industry, which itself de-

[34] See Hays's *Memoirs* (Doubleday, 1955).

[35] See *The Autobiography of Cecil B. DeMille*, 143. After Reid's death, his mother, Bertha Westbrook Reid, published a very sentimental little book about him: *Wallace Reid: His Life Story* (New York, Sorg, 1923).

[36] Contrary to popular belief, Arbuckle was not tried for murder but for involuntary manslaughter. The first two juries disagreed; the third not only cleared him but criticized the state for having brought him to trial. The mischief was done, however, and his career was ruined. See Buster Keaton and Charles Samuels, *My Wonderful World of Slapstick*, 156–61, for an impassioned apologia for Arbuckle.

rived much inspiration and personnel from Denmark,[37] had been put on its feet with the aid of government subsidies in 1917, when the Ufa (Universum-Film-Aktiengesellschaft) was formed; this was to remain the magic symbol in the eyes of world cinema *aficionados* for a number of years.

Lubitsch had directed Pola Negri in *The Eyes of the Mummy* and in *Carmen* (*Gypsy Blood*) before the end of the war, but the German film which began the conquest of America was *Madame Du Barry,* a Lubitsch production with Negri as the heroine and Emil Jannings as Louis XV, which opened Berlin's Ufa-Palast am Zoo on September 18, 1919, and as *Passion* was imported into the United States the next year. First National paid $30,000 for the American rights; the picture cleared $1,000,000. Among the films which followed were *Gypsy Blood* and *Anna Boleyn*, or as we called it, *Deception,* with Jannings still in royal aspect as Henry VIII, but with Henny Porten, not Negri, in the feminine lead.

Deception was the finest of this group of films to be brought over, but *Passion* proved the most popular. To those accustomed only to operatic incarnations of the heroine, Negri's Carmen seemed very earthy; this in itself may well have been on the credit side, but her overacting was not. Her Du Barry too was a very active siren with none of the langours of vice about her; she vaulted out of a box to greet her lover at a public ball as quickly and surely as Douglas Fairbanks could have done it. *Passion* and *Deception* were said to have been made to show the Germans how degenerate the French and English could be. I doubt this; in view of the conduct attributed to Germans themselves in their own great films, it seems unlikely that they could have been shocked, or that they

---

[37] The importance of the Danish film in early days is now too seldom remembered. Ole Olson, founder of the Nordisk Film Company, left the nation an art collection valued between five and six million pounds. See Joseph Somlo. "The First Generation of the Cinema," *Penguin Film Review,* Vol. VII (1948), 55–60; cf. James Card, "Influences of the Danish Film," *Image,* Vol. V (1956), 51–57.

could have been expected to be. What Lubitsch did do was to go in for a kind of backstairs view of history, in line with the "debunking" tendencies then so popular in biography. Du Barry takes the initiative by giving Louis a quick kiss at their first meeting, and the affairs of state must wait, as a caption moralizes, while he attends on the whims of a courtesan. He does her nails for her while his minister waits to see him, and when he accidentally cuts her, she slaps him in the face. But all the pageantry and color which movie audiences were accustomed to in historical films was retained— Lubitsch was always distinguished for his handling of crowds— and a good deal of familiar romantic motiving survived with it. The heroine's real love is the young Armand de Foix, whom she had loved before the king found her, and he is so shocked when he discovers who Du Barry is that he becomes a revolutionist. Later he presides over the court which condemns her. To help her escape he comes to her cell disguised as a monk, but they are apprehended by the watch; Armand is shot, and Du Barry goes to the guillotine.

On the heels of *Passion* and *Deception* there came in 1921 the great expressionistic film *The Cabinet of Dr. Caligari,* closely followed by *The Golem. Caligari* is surely one of the half-dozen most famous films ever made, but there has been a surprising amount of controversy over it, involving both sociological and aesthetic considerations.[38] When it was first shown in Chicago, Carl Sandburg declared, as film critic of the *Daily News,* that here at last was a motion picture which Shakespeare would have enjoyed! Why

[38] See Siegfried Kracauer's discussion in *From Caligari to Hitler: A Psychological History of the German Film* (Princeton University Press, 1947) and that of C. Dennis Legge, *"Caligari*: Its Innovations in Editing," *Quarterly of Film, Radio, and Television,* Vol. XI (1956), 136–48. Perhaps the most passionate eulogy of *Caligari* is Paul Rotha's in *The Film till Now,* 43–47. H. H. Wollenberg, *Fifty Years of German Film* (London, The Falcon Press, 1948), is a considerably less brilliant and detailed history than Kracauer's but it is also much less opinionated. See also the autobiography of Emil Jannings, *Theater-Film: Das Leben und ich* (Berchtesgaden, Verlag Zimmer & Herzog, 1951).

Shakespeare, I have no idea; I cannot think of any film which is less like his plays. Yet personally I never tire of watching *Caligari,* and the off-center settings are justified by the assumption that the story proceeds from a madman's brain. The same justification cannot be entered for the use of similar settings in Paul Wegener's *Golem,* but this is a beautiful film about the rabbi of Prague who saved his people from a pogrom by creating an artificial man to deliver them. There is more individual characterization than one generally expects in a film of this kind. The rabbi's daughter falls in love with the Gentile knight Florian, and it is the jealousy of her Jewish lover which brings the Golem to life again after the rabbi has learned that, having served his purpose, he is now a danger to the Jews themselves. Characterization enters also with the Golem's own desire to live and his consequent resisting the rabbi's attempt to pluck from his bosom the star in which the life principle resides. There is a lovely imaginative touch at the close of this film; when the Golem emerges from the city gate, all the children who have been playing there outside the walls run from him in fear—all save one little girl, who stretches out her arms to him. He picks her up to fondle her; instinctively she reaches for the pretty star; accidently she destroys him and saves the city, after which the other children return and gather about his recumbent figure with their daisy chains.

The Golem represents the German "studio film," of which other examples were such masterpieces as F. W. Murnau's *Tartuffe, Nosferatu (Dracula),* and *Faust,* and Fritz Lang's *Destiny,* and *Die Nibelungen* (shown in two parts in this country as *Siegfried* and *Kriemhild's Revenge*). It is difficult to conceive of beauty of *décor* and depth and sureness in characterization being carried much further on the screen than they were taken in *Die Nibelungen,* nor do I see how anybody could ever use the camera more daringly and imaginatively than Murnau did in *Faust.* This great director's mastery of his medium was attested by the fact that dazzling as his achievements were, one never thought of them for themselves: the supernatural scenes really seemed supernatural and not the effect of camera magic. In the more realistic portions of the film it seemed as though the camera never occupied the normal position except when Murnau could find no other place to put it. Yet he was never guilty of exploiting it for its own sake; every shot, every position involved its own revelation.

No other directors have ever created such Gothic splendor as the Germans under the Republic. But German films were not all Gothic.[39] G. W. Pabst's *The Joyless Street* (1925), with Asta Nielsen and a more natural and attractive Greta Garbo than we ever saw in American films, was a far cry from Gothicism; and the camera angles of Murnau's *The Last Laugh* (1925), with Jannings as the demoted hotel doorman, had more influence upon American film-makers than all the Gothic films together. By the time Jannings appeared in E. A. Dupont's *Variety* (1926), in which the audience swung on the trapeze with him, naturalism and contemporaneity seemed to have gone far toward taking over; and the last German films which enjoyed a great vogue in this country, after the coming of sound and before the shadow of Hitler fell upon everything German, were Josef von Sternberg's *The Blue Angel* (1930), with Jannings and Marlene Dietrich, *Mädchen in Uniform* (1931), and a whole series of light musicals, several of which starred the English actress and singer Lillian Harvey, and of which at least one, *Congress Dances* (1931), was an unquestioned masterpiece.

In the course of time nearly all the great German stars and directors were brought to Hollywood, generally to be hastily evacuated with the coming of sound. This draining of the German studios of their best blood necessarily had its effect upon European production. Worse still, the sacrifice was in vain, for none of

[39] For Paul Wegener's great service in creating films of wonder, see Wollenberg, *Fifty Years of German Film*, 21–22. For Lubitsch, see the same writer's "Ernst Lubitsch," *Penguin Film Review*, Vol. VII (1948), 61–67.

the artists involved equaled their European achievements in Hollywood. Lubitsch, to be sure, became a great power in the American film, and Miss Negri enjoyed a successful Paramount career and did much creditable work, but those who had admired her European films found themselves begging for another *Passion* to the end of the chapter. Only when he cast him as the mad Czar Paul I in *The Patriot* (1928) did Lubitsch ever give Jannings a chance to duplicate in kind what he had done in Germany, and this film was thrown subtly off balance by the fact that the star played a subordinate role; the center of dramatic interest lay inevitably in the name character, who was portrayed by Lewis Stone. Jannings had brought a great talent to America nevertheless, and in such pictures as *The Way of All Flesh* (which was not Samuel Butler's novel), *The Last Command,* and *The Sins of the Fathers* he gave compelling performances. It is not fair to leave the impression that Lubitsch devoted his Hollywood years wholly to sophisticated sex comedies like *The Marriage Circle* (1924) and, after the coming of sound, musicals like *Monte Carlo* (1930.)[40] He did a wide variety of things: the silent *Student Prince* in 1927, for example, with Ramon Novarro and Norma Shearer, and in 1932 (in sound) *The Man I Killed* (also known as *Broken Lullaby*), one of the most powerful of all antiwar films. He also directed Greta Garbo in *Ninotchka.* Taken as a whole, however, his American years were certainly not a climax, except perhaps in a commercial sense, to his years in Europe, and it seems to me that the same thing would have to be said, in different accents, for practically everybody who came over. Perhaps, all things considered, the great Swedish di-

---

[40] Wollenberg points out that Lubitsch himself had begun with comedy before turning to historical spectacles, also that light comedies, films intended merely to entertain, and pictures based on musical comedies had been made all through the "golden age" of the German film. He complains that German films were misunderstood in America because the whole product was not shown here.

rector Victor Sjöström (or Seastrom as they called him here) made the best showing,[41] especially in his two films with Lillian Gish, *The Scarlet Letter,* and *The Wind.* Like Miss Gish herself, Sjöström was a great human being as well as a great artist; each instantly perceived kinship in the other and drew upon their own and each other's deepest resources, and they remained close friends to the end of Sjöström's life.

It may be that the German films had more influence upon Hollywood production than the Russian films were to have because the latter were themselves derivatives of D. W. Griffith, and we had our Griffith at first hand.[42] But I am not sure that even the German influence was salutary, though I do not mean to suggest that if it was not, the Germans are in any sense to blame for it. We soon learned that we could reproduce all the German camera angles, but finding out why the Germans had used them was something else again, and one reviewer was prompted to remark of a certain Hollywood production that it was a very sophisticated achievement, offering an incomparable view of the heroine's nostrils. Fritz Lang's *Fury* (1936) was much admired over here, and F. W. Murnau might perhaps have accomplished more if he had lived, but he was killed in an automobile accident soon after finishing the work he did with Robert Flaherty on *Tabu* (1931). If not as good as the best of his European films, *Sunrise* (1927), with Janet Gaynor, was certainly still a film of which any director had a right to be proud.[43]

[41] See Charles L. Turner, "Victor Seastrom," *Films in Review,* Vol. XI (1960), 266–77, 343–55.

[42] For Eisenstein's own adventures in America, see Marie Seton's biography, *Sergei M. Eisenstein* (A. A. Wyn, n.d.).

[43] Dorothy E. Jones, "*Sunrise*: A Murnau Masterpiece," *Quarterly of Film, Radio, and Television,* Vol. IX (1954–55), 238–62, reprinted in Lewis Jacobs, ed., *Introduction to the Art of the Movies* (Noonday Press, 1960), is one of the best and most detailed analyses we have of any film. Flaherty's pictures, beginning with *Nanook of the North* (1922), were as much documentaries as anything, and hardly belong to the subject-matter of this book,

Of course American films would have grown more sophisticated after the war with no help from Europe. Among others, Cecil B. deMille was taking care of that.[44] Up to 1918, deMille, though always one of the best-known directors, had established no definite "line." *The Cheat* and the films starring Geraldine Farrar and Mary Pickford were probably his most famous pictures, but he had also made a variety of other "stylish," elegantly mounted, and well-lighted films which it would have been difficult to classify. Now came, in not quite unbroken succession, *Old Wives for New, We Can't Have Everything, Don't Change Your Husband, For Better For Worse, Something to Think About, Forbidden Fruit,* etc., to say nothing of Barrie's *The Admirable Crichton,* renamed *Male and Female.* These were the films that caused deMille to be forever tagged as the glorifier of the bathtub; their subject matter was domestic turmoil, infidelity, and readjustment; all in all, they seemed an odd preparation for the big religious epics upon which he embarked in 1923 with the first *Ten Commandments.*[45] In his *Autobiography,* deMille points out that he made these pictures under pressure, but it is hard to take this at face value. It is true

but they stand among the glories of the cinema nevertheless. Fortunately they have been fully and excellently described by Richard Griffith in *The World of Robert Flaherty* (Little, Brown, 1953).

[44] Besides deMille's *Autobiography,* already cited, see Phil A. Koury, *Yes, Mr. DeMille* (Putnam, 1959). Perhaps deMille's most fervent admirer is Alfred Gordon Bennett; see his tribute to *King of Kings* in particular in *Cinemania* (London, Jarrolds, 1937), 202–207.

[45] Like George Loane Tucker's *The Miracle Man* (1919), the *Old Wives for New* series helped to break down the star system by showing that pictures without "names" could succeed commercially. Lewis Jacobs (*The Rise of the American Film,* 399–400), is absurd on *The Miracle Man;* redemption, religion, and supernaturalism do not add up to a new materialism; neither is it possible to make a film about redemption without having sinners in it to be redeemed. It may be that Mr. Jacobs was somewhat misled by the fact that Tucker had also made the screen's first great sex film, *Traffic in Souls* (1913); see Ramsaye, *A Million and One Nights,* Chap. 61.

that the idea of *Old Wives for New* originated with the New York office and that deMille was reluctant to give up his period settings, but he himself admits that "when New York saw it, it was such strong stuff that they were scared"—Zukor so much so that he seriously considered not releasing it at all.

Yet in July, 1920, the *Motion Picture Magazine* hailed Mr. de-Mille as "the apostle of domesticity. Surely no married couple would come to grief who heeded his lessons." Another of his admirers wondered why the bathroom shouldn't express "as much art and beauty as the drawing room"? Why not indeed? It may be that such questions are less foolish than they sound. Certainly there are plenty of wives about who need somebody to teach them that if they are too lazy to keep themselves up, there is a very good chance of losing their husbands to other women who are not, and if there are fewer of these now than there were in 1920, it may even be that some of the credit belongs to deMille. From Tweeny's eating habits in *Male and Female* it is just possible that some of the comfortable gum-chewers in our movie "palaces" may have learned that it is not good form to leave your spoon standing in your cup or to cover a whole slice of bread with jelly and then bite into it; and if you are so unfortunate that your mother did not teach you these things, and you will not or cannot read Emily Post, why was it not pure charity on deMille's part to take you on? And if in the same film spoiled luxury was elegantly depicted by Gloria Swanson—well, did not Mr. deMille himself give you fair warning that she had been spoiled?

Gloria Swanson, Bebe Daniels, Wanda Hawley, Sylvia Ashton, Elliott Dexter, Thomas Meighan, Theodore Kosloff—these were some of the leading professors in deMille's manners-morality school. Bebe, who had hitherto been known as a very luscious leading lady in Harold Lloyd comedies, was just about ready to embark upon a starring career of her own. She blazed out with considerable force in brother William's production of Rachel Crothers' play *Nice People* in 1922, and ran along merrily for a number of years, generally in program pictures of little or no importance but considerable entertainment value, though *The Glimpses of the Moon* (1923), from Edith Wharton's novel, was an admirably close-knit and intelligent piece of direction by Allan Dwan. When sound came, she discovered, or at least we discovered, in *Rio Rita* (1929), that she had a beautiful voice; later she and her husband Ben Lyon made such a hit in English radio that they were lost to us for good. But Gloria Swanson was the deMille star par excellence, and nobody else ever took to the role of film diva off screen and on quite as she did. She herself put all the pieces together in her remorseless portrait of the aging movie queen in Billy Wilder's production *Sunset Boulevard* (1950), in which both deMille and Eric von Stroheim appeared, and which is said to have drawn from Mae Murray the scornful comment, "None of us floozies were *that* nuts!" La Swanson's war with Pola Negri over the studio cats hit every newspaper in America; Pola wanted them destroyed and Gloria protected them, which must be accounted unto her for righteousness even if it was not pure benevolence on her part but also an attempt to prove, once and for all, that she, not Pola, was the queen of the Paramount lot. And it may be that movie diva splendor reached an all-time high when Gloria returned from Europe after making *Madame Sans-Gene* in 1925, with her third husband, the Marquis de la Falaise de la Coudray, and having made an Elizabethan progress across the land after a big party at the Ritz, turned down a cold eighteen thousand a week from Zukor—"I was prepared to go somewhat higher," he says wistfully, "perhaps to a flat million dollars a year"—because she wished to make her own pictures. To be perfectly frank, I never cared much for Gloria, never thought her a beauty nor, except in *Sunset Boulevard,* much of an actress; neither did her eccentric costumes and coiffures attract me, but I have come to feel somewhat more sympathetic toward her with the passing of time. Many of Robert Flaherty's friends must have been surprised when it was revealed that he admired her. The explanation was simple, and Flaherty himself gave it." "Gloria has courage," he said. It requires courage, and character too, to play any role as long as Gloria has played the glamour queen through good fortune and bad.[46]

I feel much the same way, only more so, about deMille. I cannot honestly say that I thought him a great director, though he was certainly a very competent one. Overcrowding and tasteless splendor made up his Achilles heel. Nevertheless, he was a man of character far over and beyond that possessed by many of those who made a business of sneering at him. He proved that when he gave up a lucrative radio contract rather than allow a union to levy a one-dollar assessment which he could not grant their right to claim. His private life was a credit to himself and to the motion-picture business; if all great Hollywood figures had been like him, the image of Hollywood in the public mind would be very different from what it is. I confess that I was surprised by his autobiography; it is the work of a shrewd, earnest, and sincere man; I had not expected it to be so good. DeMille was a poseur and a showman *à la outrance*. It would be absurd to call him a devout man, but it would be even more absurd to regard his religious films as the work of a hypocrite. I am sure that the satisfaction he took in the fact that his *King of Kings* (1927) was shown for years and years at the ends of the earth, and in places where no other motion picture had ever been exhibited, was perfectly genuine.[47]

Another important influence in American films during and after World War I was that of the French director Maurice Tourneur. Born in Paris in 1876, he had probably the richest aesthetic

[46] See Helena Huntington Smith, "Ugly Duckling," *The New Yorker* (Jan. 18, 1930).

[47] DeMille's own profits from both *King of Kings* and the 1956 *Ten Commandments* went to charity. He was very proud of the fact that a university press published the results of the research undertaken for *The Ten Commandments*; see Henry S. Noerdlinger, *Moses and Egypt* (University of Southern California Press, 1956).

background of any film director. Not only did he work with Antoine and manage the Odeon but he illustrated books and magazines, designed posters and fabrics, and served as assistant to both Rodin and Puvis de Chavannes. Having directed for Eclair in France, he came to America in 1914 as a substitute for Émile Chautard and worked for Peerless, Paragon, and World before becoming best known for his Paramount films. He became an American citizen in 1921 but returned to France in 1926 after having walked out on a production of *The Mysterious Island* at M-G-M because he would not accept the new system which required him to work under a "producer." Thereafter he directed both in France and in Germany; the best known of his later films was the *Volpone* which he made with Harry Baur and Louis Jouvet in 1939–40, just before the fall of France, but which was not shown in this country until 1947. In 1933 he did another *Two Orphans,* with one of the greatest artists in the world, Yvette Guilbert, as his La Frochard. His last picture was *L'Impasse* (1948), with Simone Signoret and Danielle Delorme. In 1950 he lost a leg in an automobile accident. He died in Paris on August 4, 1961.

Tourneur's greatest limitation as a film director was his tendency to think in terms of the theater. "The idea of sending a company to Central America to film a Central American story is, to my way of thinking, valueless from the standpoint of art," he once declared. "What we really need is an artist to produce the story so that we will get an artist's impression of tropical America." On general aesthetic principles I have considerable sympathy with this point of view, but it does make for a rather specialized kind of cinematography. Although I have never seen any lovelier outdoor composition on the screen than Tourneur achieved in his most ambitious independent production *Woman,* he did not greatly enjoy directing exteriors and when possible turned them over to Clarence Brown. In its way Tourneur's influence was similar to that of the German "studio" technicians, but he was as Gallic as they were Gothic and temperamentally he was far more of an idealist. He opposed using the theater for moralistic or other propaganda purposes, and he disbelieved in the star system because he thought there were no stars in life and considered real people neither very good nor very bad; but he wanted lovely things on the screen, not "cowboys loitering around bars and vampires smoking cigarettes," and, especially when Ben Carré was designing his sets, he pretty consistently got them.

Woman was another of the screen's episodic "masterpieces," clearly influenced by *Intolerance* but without the *Intolerance* integration, and with no continuing theme or interest to take the place of a unifying single story. (The idea of illustrating different types of women was too general to take hold and did not make for a unified film.) *Trilby,* which he made with Clara Kimball Young and Wilton Lackaye for World in 1915, was probably the most successful of Tourneur's early films. The best of all, probably, was *Prunella,* with Marguerite Clark, of which I shall speak in the last chapter. I have already expressed my admiration for *A Poor Little Rich Girl,* and, passing to more realistic yet still very colorful, materials, he certainly got from Elsie Ferguson the very best she had to give. Perhaps he was more unfettered in *The Blue Bird* (1918), and this richly tinted film was very beautiful, though it might legitimately be objected that at times it seemed more like a series of surpassingly lovely illustrations for a book that a complete motion picture. Another fine achievement was *The Brass Bottle* (1923), an *Arabian Nights* fantasy, largely in modern dress, in which it was clearly shown that genies do not take kindly to modern social conditions. After the war Tourneur was used on almost every conceivable type of film: the melodrama *Sporting Life,* Conrad's *Victory, Lorna Doone,* and Hall Caine's *The Christian,* which was filmed partly on the Isle of Man and caused him to begin to see some value in foreign locations. The *Treasure Island* sets were very beautiful, but attractive as Shirley Mason was as Jim, it was probably a mistake to cast a girl in this role and to take the liberties which Tourneur took with so well known a story. Lon Chaney was an impressive Pew. Chaney was also in *Victory,* along with Jack Holt, Seena Owen, Wallace Beery, and Bull Montana, and this, as I recall it, was a much better film. Tourneur was injured early in the filming of *The Last of the Mohicans* (1922), and this picture, though generally credited to him, was largely directed by Clarence Brown. I myself was so much impressed by *The White Circle* (1920), which was adapted from one of Stevenson's less popular stories, "The Pavilion on the Links," that I wrote Tourneur of my enthusiasm, adding rashly that I had enjoyed it all the more because I had been disappointed in several of his recent films. This brought a charming letter. "I do not blame you for having been disappointed," he said. "So was I. Unfortunately, in this complex and fascinating business, there are so many elements to be considered that you don't always do what you want, but most of the time what you can." He added that he was "always so doubtful myself about what I am doing" that he was glad to hear from those who thought he had succeeded. Whatever Tourneur's limitations as a director may have been, he was a sincere and accomplished artist, and he not only created beauty on the screen himself but his example caused other directors to be far more concerned for it than they would otherwise have been. It is interesting to know that even though she had worked with Griffith, Mary Alden rated Tourneur the greatest of directors and the one most capable of inspiring great acting.[48]

[48] It would be interesting to try to trace Tourneur's influence, but the task would be a difficult one at this date. There was a time in the early twenties when the public was so hostile not only to fantasy but to imagination that such things had to be smuggled into "prologues," etc. I feel sure that the screen was lastingly impoverished by the fact that the directorial activity of the artist Penrhyn Stanlaws fell in this period. Twice at least Stanlaws proved himself a master of screen fantasy, but so far as any evidence that has ever reached me goes, no eyes but mine ever noticed it. The first instance was in *The Green Temptation* (1922), with Betty Compson and Theodore Kosloff. The second was in *Singed Wings* (1923), with Bebe Daniels, where he worked out a little parable about gossamer fairies, the witch's broomstick,

The Continentalism that Tourneur brought us was his French sense of beauty; his pictures never contained anything to affront American—or any other—moral standards. If you want a director who was, in the popular sense, "Continental" in his morality, as we have come to savor Continentalism in countless European sound films, you must go to Austria and Erich von Stroheim.

It is difficult to evaluate von Stroheim fairly, for few of his pictures reached the screen as he designed them; Irving Thalberg "fired" him three times—from *The Merry-Go-Round* (1923), *Greed* (1923), and *The Merry Widow* (1925). *Greed* (Frank Norris' novel *McTeague,* which von Stroheim tried to film page by page and paragraph by paragraph, and to make a monument of American naturalism, with as little "truckling" as Norris himself had done), emerged as a monster of some forty reels; under protest von Stroheim cut it down to twenty but that was as far as he would go, so that it was taken away from him, reduced to ten reels, and released in a form which he disowned. All this is supposed to serve as Exhibit A in the Drama of the Endless Struggle between

and the lovely queen who must be slain by the jester in the hour she gave herself to love; I have never seen anything quite like it on the screen. One of the few brave attempts of the period to rely upon fantasy for a whole film was *Puritan Passions* (1923), an adaptation of Percy MacKaye's play *The Scarecrow*, with Glenn Hunter, directed by Frank Tuttle. I remember, too, a short called *Frogland*, produced by the Russian Art Society of Paris, and distributed by Pathé. This was La Fontaine's fable of the frogs who prayed to Jupiter for a king and received a stork which gobbled them up. (James Card tells me this was Ladislas Starevich's *The Frogs Who Wanted a King*.) The frogs were charming, and the wicked, dissolute caricature of Jupiter was irresistibly funny.

The most important article about Tourneur is George Geltzer, "Maurice Tourneur," *Films in Review*, Vol. XII (1961), 193–213; Tourneur was interviewed in the *Dramatic Mirror* (June 30, 1915) and contributed an article on "Stylization in Motion Picture Directing" to *Motion Picture Magazine* (Sept., 1918); see further the articles about him by Dorothy Nutting, *Photoplay* (July, 1918), and Truman B. Handy, *Motion Picture Magazine* (Nov., 1920).

the Artist and the Harsh, Conscienceless, Commercial Monster known as Hollywood. I am not sensitive about Hollywood, but I can only regard this as poppycock. Commercialism actually had very little to do with the case. Adaptation of means to end had everything. It is part of every artist's problem to create within the limitations of the medium in which he is working and under workable conditions, and if he fails to achieve these things then he fails as an artist. "In der Beschränkung," said Goethe, "zeigt such erst der Meister."

Von Stroheim came to America before World War I and served his apprenticeship under Griffith. He was a Pharisee in *Intolerance* and a "Hun" in *Hearts of the World.* (By World War II he had become a Nazi "monster"; this was von Stroheim in his most familiar aspect as "The Man You Love to Hate.") I am no judge of how close his Prussian officers came to nature; on the screen they gave the effect of fantastic caricature, and I would say the same thing about much more in von Stroheim's films—Trina's famous line in *Greed,* for example, when she and McTeague are courting: "Let's go over and sit on the sewer." I am not denying that this might be said—and done—in life, but life is not art, and it admits exaggerations which art cannot afford.

As a director von Stroheim arrived with *Blind Husbands* (1918), a picture about mountain-climbing and womanizing, with Sam de Grasse as the complacent husband, Francelia Billington as the wife, and von Stroheim himself as the eternal army-officer seducer. The indictment which this film enters of husbands who neglect their wives and leave them as prey to more attentive men was more like deMille than Griffith, but it was announced in Griffith-like sermonizing subtitles with footnotes to them, like those in *The Birth of a Nation* and *Intolerance,* proclaiming that in the mountains "man is little and God is great" and much more to the same effect—some of it strikingly at variance with the searching sexuality of the film, and even more with the director's later taste for staging orgies and deliberately searching out all the nastiness of

215

the old regime. The general tone of von Stroheim's work was as unlike Griffith's as possible, but except for his indifference to cross-cutting and his preference for securing his effects within the individual scene, he shows the Griffith influence plainly not only in his early films but even in the omnipresent symbolism he used in *Greed*.[49] His last important directorial work was on the uncompleted *Queen Kelly,* upon which Gloria Swanson finally stopped production in the conviction that "a madman is in charge."[50] After the end of his directorial career von Stroheim returned to acting; the most notable film in which he appeared was probably Jean Renoir's antiwar film *Grand Illusion,* made in France in 1937. In this country he did *The Great Gabbo* for James Cruze, supported Garbo in *As You Desire Me,* and played Field Marshal Rommel in *Five Graves to Cairo* in 1943. Seven years later he worked under the same director Billy Wilder in *Sunset Boulevard.* He died in 1957.

The film upon which von Stroheim's admirers stake their special claims for him is *Greed,* which many consider, even in its mutilated state, one of the greatest of motion pictures. I am not trying to disparage von Stroheim. Despite all the ugliness and brutality in which he reveled, there is an undeniable vitality in his films; I only protest against entering inadmissible claims. The gods of the heathen become as a matter of course the demons of Chris-

[49] A number of examples are pointed out by A. R. Fulton in his *Motion Pictures.* Chapter VII of this work is the best general brief account of von Stroheim. For a fuller account see Peter Noble, *Hollywood Scapegoat.* Bob Bergit, *Erich von Stroheim* (Paris, Le Terrain Vague; distributed in England by Rodney Book Service), is said to be much better, but I have not seen this work. It was reviewed in *Sight and Sound,* Vol. XXX (1961), 98–99. See also Herman Weinberg, *Index to the Creative Work of Erich von Stroheim* (British Film Institute, 1943), and Gavin Lambert, "Stroheim Revisited: The Missing Third in the American Cinema," *Sight and Sound,* Vol. XXII (1953), 165–71, 204.

[50] Miss Swanson's own print of *Queen Kelly,* edited by herself, is in the Museum of Modern Art Film Library.

tianity, and there has never been any halfway house so far as this man is concerned. Enthusiasts regard him as the greatest of all directors, while those who disliked his films will not stop with pointing out their faults; they must hate them with a consuming hatred. Neither extreme proved in the long run serviceable to a director who though he often showed poor judgment, and was certainly one of the most difficult men who ever lived, never lacked integrity nor the courage to follow his star even when it led him to his destruction. Though von Stroheim had his problems, there were no resemblances between his own personality and the hateful image he characteristically presented on the screen, and those who worked under him generally trusted and admired him. Certainly he knew how to inspire fine acting. The high regard in which ZaSu Pitts has always been held is largely due to what she did for him, and though he and Mae Murray hated each other, the performance which he got from her in *The Merry Widow* was worth everything else she ever did put together.

I have tried in this chapter to achieve a kind of selective description of some of the important films of the feature era and of the men and women who made them, but the reader must understand that there was a great deal which does not now seem important and which still loomed large in the lives of the millions (yes, millions) of men and women and boys and girls who, night after night and week after week, "went to the movies," in the great "palaces," in the neighborhood theaters large and small (there were several of these, not one, within easy walking distance of every city address), and in humble little halls and theaters at the crossroads where there was nothing much but a screen and a projection booth and so many rows of seats. One reason why no book about the movies can ever be entirely satisfying is that each reader will discover that the author has omitted some of the plays and players which meant most to him. Indeed, space limitations, coupled with the fact that he may have nothing in particular to say about them, must cause the writer to leave out even many of the people who were important to him. I have no idea what has become of Vera Reynolds, for example, but I liked her much in deMille's *The Road to Yesterday* in 1925 and again in support of H. B. Warner in Rupert Julian's *Silence* the next year. Last summer I saw again William C. deMille's production of *Miss Lulu Bett* (1921), with Lois Wilson, Milton Sills, Theodore Roberts, and others. Without being in any way an outstanding piece of work, it exemplified a type of "family picture," very popular in its day, which has practically disappeared from the contemporary film theater. I wonder if this may not be one of the reasons why the "family" audience has largely disappeared also. And since the bill of fare now generally consists of sex for the entree with sadism for the dessert, I have been reluctantly driven to the conclusion that it is fortunate that this is the case.

During the last years of the silent features, Metro-Goldwyn-Mayer replaced Paramount as the dominant film company,[51] and a great many new personalities emerged, many of whom had part—often the more significant part—of their careers in the sound film. These included Greta Garbo, Janet Gaynor, Joan Crawford, Norma Shearer, Dolores Costello, Ronald Colman, Vilma Banky, and Gary Cooper. These and many others might well be considered here if space were available. Garbo and Gaynor are the two who interest me most for their exemplification of opposed tendencies. If anybody inherited the Pickford public, it was Janet Gaynor, followed by little Margaret O'Brien in the sound period. Jeanne Crain might have had more of it if her career had been better managed; her utterly delightful *Margie* (1946), directed by Henry King, was the most Pickford-like film in many years. Garbo, on the other hand, pointed toward the future through both the sexual

---

[51] See two books by Bosley Crowther, *The Lion's Share: The Story of an Entertainment Empire* (Dutton, 1957) and *Hollywood Rajah: The Life and Times of Louis B. Mayer* (Holt, 1960); also Penelope Huston, "Lion Rampant: The Record of M-G-M," *Sight and Sound*, Vol. XXIV (1954), 21–30.

freedom and the neuroticism of the films in which she appeared. She made her American sensation in 1927 with John Gilbert in *Flesh and the Devil,* but when the Great Lovers reappeared the same year in an adaptation of *Anna Karenina,* not oversubtly re-titled *Love,* and found themselves playing against Miss Gaynor and Charles Farrell in *Seventh Heaven,* there were many who thought that the youngsters had made the better love film of the two. It would be hard to say whether Janet Gaynor is better re-membered for her silent or her sound films, but her spirit was that of the silent years, and nobody could possibly have ended them more pleasantly.[52]

[52] See Chauncey L. Carr, "Janet Gaynor," *Films in Review,* Vol. X (1959), 470–78.

CHAPTER FIVE

"The Ladies ~ God Bless Them!"

M R S. W A R R E N'S profession may have been the first to which woman devoted herself and the earliest means she found to deliver herself from the tyranny of man, but that of the actress must certainly have been the second, and the theater is still probably the only arena in which the female of the species has equaled or surpassed her master's achievements. For all man's jealous clinging to his prerogatives, the worship of woman evidently fills a deep-seated need in his nature. We find it in the Court of Love romances of the Middle Ages and in the pure religious passion for the Mother of God, but on the ordinary human level certainly no institution encourages it more than the theater, and it is not for nothing that a distinguished female opera singer is called a "diva."

It would be difficult to think of any woman of the theater as inspiring and satisfying this impulse to worship more than Jenny Lind did more than one hundred years ago, or than Sarah Bernhardt did, in a very different way, in our fathers' and grandfathers' time and during the early years of our own lives. Compared to the motion-picture actress, however, all such stars suffered from a certain remoteness, yet the film star's position is curiously anomalous at this point.

When you went to see Julia Marlowe, the actual, living, woman was there before your eyes, and when you heard Melba, the silvery tones which caressed your ears moved upon them directly from the throat of a human being breathing the same air that you breathed. The film star, on the other hand, was only a shadow, and most of her devotees never encountered her in the flesh from one end of her career to the other. In a sense, then, you had much less contact with her than with the "legitimate" star, yet you always seemed to be having much more.

This illusion was due to two considerations: frequency of exposure and the almost embarrassing intimacy of the film star's medium. Even when we really had a theater in this country, and an established actress might safely count upon a forty-week season with a new play each year, most of her followers must still consider themselves fortunate if they were able to see her once each season; but the film actress came to you in a new film at least once a week in the early days and once a month for a considerable period even after the establishment of features. Moreover, with admission prices in the neighborhood theaters ranging from ten to twenty-five cents, you could afford to go to see her pictures as often as you were capable of finding enjoyment in them, and the real devotees of bygone days probably spent a larger proportion of their evenings each month with their chosen favorites than anyone would regard as reasonable or plausible now. The only approach to all this in the legitimate theater came with the old local neighborhood stock company, with its weekly change of bill, where leading women did, in a measure, anticipate the continued exposure and continued devotion which afterward appeared in connection with the film star. But even here the footlights imposed a barrier. We sit much farther from the stage in a motion-picture theater, but it is only when the lights go on at the end of the picture that we realize how far away we have been. Who ever "learned" the face of any actress of the "legitimate" as the movie fan learned the faces of his favorite stars, and familiarized himself with every nuance, every possible variation of expression?

The screen, then, has encouraged the development of a cult of glamour as it has never been encouraged by any other medium, and the list of stars who have embodied what the age at least considered an ideal, and consciously or unconsciously offered themselves as objects of adoration or imitation, is a very long one. This has often been deplored, and when we look at many of the specific habits and fashions in which one or another screen star has been aped, we certainly ought to be able to understand this judgment. Women who never saw him except on the screen are supposed to have committed suicide after Valentino's death, and there is an authenticated case of a young French girl who "identified" with Michele Morgan to such an extent as to go blind after seeing *La Symphonie Pastorale*.[1] Yet the difficulties and the weaknesses and the failures seem to me to have been caused mainly by an unwise choice of particular models and goddesses; I am not sure that the basic tendency toward hero worship is bad in itself. If there had been no movies, would the shopgirl who modeled herself on the latest flapper star have chosen one of the blessed saints instead? I doubt it very much. I think she might rather have modeled herself upon the neighborhood "tart." You can cut her off from "sheiks" by closing the local movie house, but that will not put the "drugstore cowboy" out of business, and the lure of sex has

[1] Edgar Morin, *The Stars*, translated from the French by Richard Howard (Grove Press, 1960), 173. This book is an incisive analysis of the whole phenomena of star-making and stellar worship. Paul Rotha, who attacks the star system with some violence in *The Film till Now*, injudiciously permits himself to complain that "American pictures are filled with people, for prominent among the movie beliefs of Hollywood is the misconception that the general public is more interested in people than things." The first part of this statement reminds me of the well-known cartoon of a roomful of baboons packing bonbons under the caption "Our Product Is Untouched by Human Hands." As for the last part, I can only hope it is true. Not to be more interested in people than in things is the best definition I know of damnation.

been known to operate quite as potently and devastatingly in a servant girl or a waitress as in a great courtesan. Is the beauty of women a menace to the spiritual lives of men? It may be so, but what then are we to make of the hosts of men we see all about us, hopelessly enslaved to women quite without beauty, without loveliness, without charm? Boys and girls cannot well be brought up in complete seclusion from each other, nor is it desirable that they should be; and I wonder whether the boy who has been exposed to Hollywood's glamour, cheap as it may be, as far back as he can remember, may not be better fortified to deal with the generally inferior variety he will meet on the street corner than his predecessor used to be.

I am not of course presenting the film star's appeal in exclusively sexual terms; this would be an unwarranted oversimplification. Men have found potential mothers and sisters and daughters as well as potential mistresses on the screen, and there have been women stars who have had far more enthusiastic admirers among women than among men. One distinguished scholar of advanced years was obviously a little anxious when he heard I was writing this book because he feared that Blanche Sweet might not be quite as important to me as she was to him. Another man made it perfectly clear that the movies had been important to him primarily because they had brought him the beauty of Madge Evans. And still another—a young man this time—assured me that my book would be worthless unless I heartily sang the praises of Bessie Love.

Well, I cannot love everybody, and I do not have the space to speak at length even of all the people I loved. In this book I have given a separate chapter to Mary Pickford and another to Lillian Gish, who also comes in for frequent consideration in the chapter about D. W. Griffith. Many other ladies must, I fear, content themselves with what I have been able to say of them in Chapters I and IV. I have been cold to some stars who have enjoyed huge followings, and I have been enthusiastic about some who have appealed to a much more limited group. In this closing chapter, I wish now to speak of a few who, for one reason or another, have been particular favorites.[2]

If I speak my piece about Lillian Gish elsewhere, I must speak of Dorothy here. Film historians in general have shown a deplorable tendency to consider the career of Dorothy Gish only as a footnote to Lillian's; this is both absurd and unjust, for Dorothy is a very gifted actress, and she would have had an important career even if she had stood quite alone. It has also frequently been declared, as if the statement were an axiom, that Mabel Normand was the screen's greatest comedienne. I too loved Mabel Normand, and I have no desire to detract from her glory, but that she was superior to Dorothy as a comedienne I am still waiting to be shown. I am sure that Dorothy would be more widely appreciated in this aspect if we could see again the long series of comedies which she made for Paramount after her success as the Little Disturber in *Hearts of the World*. Perhaps the best was that brilliant burlesque of Westerns, *Nugget Nell* (1919), which Mack Sennett admired and which caused so good a judge as Julian Johnson to label her a female Chaplin. She was fine too in *Remodeling Her Husband* (1920), which Lillian directed; who will ever forget the brilliant scene in which, having made a bet with a husband somewhat unmindful of her charms, that she could walk down a city block and attract the attention of every man she met, she collected by the simple expedient of sticking out her tongue, while the wonderstruck male, following close behind, was simply unable to understand why all the heads turned in her direction?[3] But I think the

[2] There is a much more extensive commentary on screen actresses than I shall attempt here in Theodore Huff, "40 Years of Feminine Glamour," *Films in Review*, Vol. IV (1953), 49–63.

[3] Other films in this series included *Boots, Battling Jane, The Hope Chest, Peppy Polly*, and *I'll Get Him Yet*. See Dorothy Gish, "And So I Am a Comedienne," *Ladies' Home Journal* (July, 1925); see also the companion articles by Lillian and Dorothy, "My Sister and I" and "My Sister Lillian," *Theatre Magazine* (Nov. and Dec., 1927).

climax of her brilliant career as a comedienne came with Marjorie Bowen's *Nell Gwyn* (1926), produced in England under the direction of Herbert Wilcox. I recently reviewed this film at George Eastman House in company with several film specialists, none of whom had seen it before. They literally shouted, whooped, and screamed their delight in Dorothy's performance clear through the screening.

I do not mean, of course, that Dorothy should be thought of entirely as a comedienne; even within recent years she has given many fine serious performances both on stage and screen. If we need a revival of her Paramount comedies, perhaps we need even more to review the wide variety of films she made for Mutual and Triangle between 1914 and 1917. During part of this period Lillian was absorbed by *The Birth of a Nation,* but Dorothy ground out film after film; when she "returned" to the screen after two months' absence in 1914, her employers thought it necessary to explain, in an advertisement in the trade journals, just what she had been doing and why she had been away so long! These films differed widely in character and no doubt in quality too. In his review of the year's achievements in *Photoplay* for September, 1916, Julian Johnson expressed his special enthusiasm for *Susan Rocks the Boat, Little Menie's Romance,* and *Betty of Greystone. The Mountain Rat* was a Western; in *The Little Yank* she was a border girl in love with a Southern officer but loyal to the Union; in *Old Heidelberg* she played the Kathy everybody has come to know since with music in *The Student Prince.*

When Mary Pickford was at the height of her vogue, during World War I and the years which followed, the screen was filled with young actresses who, however they might differ from her in personality and talent, all cultivated a distinct ingénue "line" and consciously or unconsciously exerted an appeal of youthful innocence. Among them were Marguerite Clark, Mary Miles Minter, Vivian Martin, June Caprice, Jewel Carmen, and Gladys Leslie. Among these it is safe to say that it was Miss Clark who gave

Miss Pickford most concern, especially during the days when both were with Famous Players.[4]

Marguerite Clark died in 1940, and so far as I know none of her films are now anywhere available for inspection. This creates a serious gap in screen history. Richard Griffith recently startled me by telling me he had never seen Marguerite Clark on the screen. To one of my generation this seems very much like saying you have never seen a silver birch or a daffodil.

Marguerite Clark was older than Mary Pickford, having been born in Avondale, a suburb of Cincinnati, on February 22, 1887; but she was less than five feet tall and weighed less than one hundred pounds, and she had no difficulty in looking like a child on the screen when she was well into her thirties. Her father was a businessman, and she had no theater in her family background. Both her parents died while she was a child, and her first dramatic work was done at her convent school. Financial necessity drove her to the stage; in her own judgment, her first "telling work" was in *Baby Mine,* during the run of which she was encouraged by Sarah Bernhardt. She played *Peter Pan* in the West; she appeared with John Barrymore in *Jim the Penman* and in a number of musicals with DeWolf Hopper. Under Winthrop Ames at the Little Theter she appeared in *The Affairs of Anatol, Snow White,* and *Prunella.* After he had seen her in the Barker-Housman play, Adolph Zukor brought her to the screen in 1914 by the simple expedient of offering her fifty times what she was earning on the stage.[5]

She won the heart of the movie public in such early Famous

[4] Miss Pickford won the *Motion Picture Magazine* popularity contest in 1918 with 158,199 votes; Miss Clark was the runner-up with 138,852. In *The Public Is Never Wrong*, Adolph Zukor describes the Pickford-Clark rivalry as enlisting Miss Pickford and her mother on the one hand and Cora Clark, who managed her sister's career, on the other. "Marguerite was not interested."

[5] See Miss Clark's own account of her career in a letter to Gladys Hall, *Motion Picture Magazine* (July, 1915), and two articles in the same periodi-

Picture 68 *(right)*, Betty Bronson as Peter Pan in Herbert Brenon's production of the Barrie play (1924); Picture 69 *(below)*, Wendy (Mary Brian) sews on Peter Pan's shadow.

MARJORIE DAW

*The delightful young ingenue who won prominence on the screen as Douglas Fairbanks'
leading woman, has been elevated to stardom. Under the Marshall Neilan banner she
appears in "The River's End"*

Marjorie Daw played in *Joan the Woman* with Geraldine
Farrar and was importantly encouraged by her. Later she
was leading woman to Douglas Fairbanks in a number of
films. When this example of elegant cheesecake by Alfred
Cheney Johnston was first published in 1920 it was considered shocking, and the writer of this book remembers men
queuing up to gape at it when it was posted before a Loop
theater in Chicago where one of Miss Daw's films was playing. Times have changed.

PICTURE 70

Marguerite Clark, with Jules Raucourt and others, in *Prunella* (1918). Directed by Maurice Tourneur; settings by Ben Carré.

May McAvoy

PICTURE 73

May McAvoy, with Richard
Barthelmess, in *The Enchanted
Cottage* (1924), before (Picture
74, *above*) and after (Picture 75,
right) the transformation.

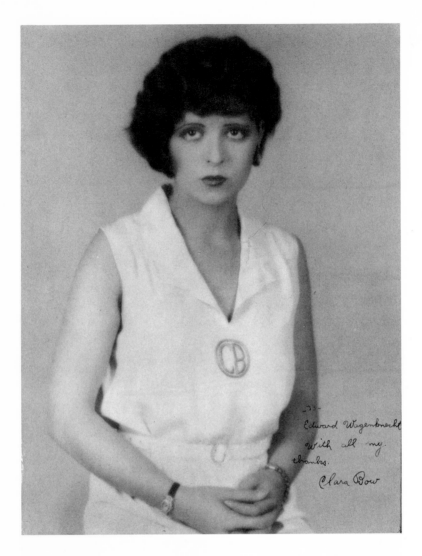

Clara Bow

PICTURE 76

Picture 77 *(right)*, Clara Bow in *Kid Boots* (1926); Picture 78 *(below)*, Clara Bow and Lawrence Grant in *It* (1927).

Mary Miles Minter

Players films as *Wildflower, The Crucible, Gretna Green, The Pretty Sister of José, Seven Sisters, Still Waters,* and *Molly Make-Believe;* later came *Uncle Tom's Cabin* (not, I think, one of her best films) in which she played both Topsy and Eva to Frank Losee's Uncle Tom, *Come Out of the Kitchen,* and *Mrs. Wiggs of the Cabbage Patch.* She left Paramount for First National in 1920, but by this time her heart was no longer in picture-making and her career was virtually over. She had married H. Palmerson Williams, Louisiana lumberman, sugar-plantation owner, sportsman, and aviation enthusiast, with whom she lived very happily in St. Mary's Parish, Louisiana, until 1936, when he was killed in a plane crash. The last three years of her life she was again in New York.

The Prince and the Pauper (1915), directed by Porter and Hugh Ford, was a charming film, somewhat out of her regular "line" though she had done it on the stage—she played both of Mark Twain's boys—but I think she is most fondly remembered for the two lovely fairy films she gave us for Christmas in 1916 and 1917; *Snow White* and *The Seven Swans.* The *Snow White* exteriors, filmed in Georgia, showed moss hanging from the trees, but the picture missed no element of Christmas appeal; at the beginning Santa Claus even came down the chimney. Her very finest film, however, was the screen version of *Prunella* which Maurice Tourneur directed for her in 1918. *Prunella* and Nazimova's *Salome* (1922) are the best examples of the "studio film" in America, and *Prunella* seemed to me much the finer of the two. Tourneur's unmatched pictorial sense did not function more effectively here than in *A Poor Little Rich Girl* or *The Blue Bird,* but the film was more of a piece. In *The Blue Bird* the occasional use of natural settings tended to be intrusive; here there was nothing which had not been

cal: "Filming Fairy Plays" (Feb., 1918), and "A Little of My Life" (July, 1918). For her life after her marriage and retirement see Beatrice Washburn, "Marguerite Clark Today," *Photoplay* (Apr., 1925).

made for the film or which did not exist wholly in terms of the film. I know of no motion picture at present unavailable to students of the cinema which it would be more important to recover.

Unlike most of her competitors, Marguerite Clark was not a blonde—she had light brown hair and hazel eyes—and though she was sweet, there was a cool, crisp quality in her personality which saved her from sentimentalism. The incomparable daintiness and refinement which enabled her to outdistance all other stars in whimsy and fairy splendor was at once her most precious endowment and the sign of her greatest limitation as a screen star. If she seemed at one time to menace Miss Pickford's supremacy, Mary long outlasted her, for she had a mischief and a vitality far greater than Marguerite's, and she appealed more directly to the emotions. "I have no desire to have my heart broken," Miss Clark once told an interviewer, "so I always take care not to leave it around or lose it." She disclaimed "views" on current problems and could not understand why, simply because she was an actress, she should be supposed to hold them. Nor was she afraid to state uncompromisingly that she was working "simply and solely" for her "bread and butter," and that she liked the stage better than the screen, though she knew she was not "supposed" to say so. I do not mean that she was coldhearted, and, despite all her precautions, her heart was broken in the end, for I have a very pathetic letter, written to a friend after her husband's death. But she was a lady; she did not "slop over"; she saw the elements of life in a reasonable relationship to each other; and she was never disposed to consider the business of play-acting as any more important than it really is. If she did not overestimate the films, she did not slight them either, and she learned, as those who come from the stage have not always been able to learn, that stage and screen are two different mediums. It was characteristic of her that though *Prunella* was her best film, she could still realize that "there is nothing in an indoor set that cannot be done as well or better on the stage. A photoplay is not handicapped by stage limitations. It has a field all its own and should exploit the field."

May McAvoy's refinement and idealism, to say nothing of her diminutive stature, have often caused her to be compared to Marguerite Clark, and it was suitable enough that she should have played her first small part as Asia in Miss Clark's production of *Mrs. Wiggs of the Cabbage Patch.* But she was a far greater artist, with a far greater imagination—one of the most sensitive actresses indeed that our screen has known—and I know no more convincing indication of our ineptitude than that we should have been able to make so little of her. She became famous at twenty, in 1921, when she played with Gareth Hughes and Mabel Taliaferro in John S. Robertson's fine production of *Sentimental Tommy,* another now lamentably unavailable film; and every critic in the land, including this one,[6] began, first, to sing her praises and then to berate the producers for not finding something else for her to do. It occurs to me now that we may have done more harm than good, for it is very difficult for a film mogul to grasp the idea that he may not be entirely perfect.

I fear it is quite useless to try to tell anybody who did not see *Sentimental Tommy* how good she was. I can only say that her

[6] Edward Wagenknecht, "The Neglected Genius of the Movies," *Vanity Fair* (Dec., 1924). In 1923, *Photoplay* was pleading in Miss McAvoy's behalf for *Peter Pan, L'Aiglon,* and *The Dawn of a Tomorrow.* She desperately wished to play Peter, and when Robertson seemed slated to direct it, she used to pray every night that it might be given to her. I did my share in the propaganda toward this end, and if Robertson had made the film, she probably would have appeared in it. The picture went instead to Herbert Brenon and to Betty Bronson, whose piquancy and lovely legs were relished by me as much as anybody. I should hate to have missed Betty in *Peter Pan,* or in *A Kiss for Cinderella,* which followed the next year, or even in such minor films as *The Cat's Pajamas* and *Everybody's Acting.* She was a breath of fresh air at a time when the screen badly needed one, but charming as she was, her talent was a small one compared to May McAvoy's.

Grizel was the most moving revelation of the gifts of a fresh and hitherto unknown young actress that I have ever encountered; perhaps Jean Simmons came closest to it, though with a totally different quality of personality, many years later, when she played her Ophelia to Olivier's Hamlet. Beauty and pity were the great elements in it, and all seemed to well up as it were spontaneously from the depths of an apparently inexhaustible sensibility. And if the touching perfection of a pure girl's limitless devotion was ever bared upon the screen in all its moving, vulnerable nakedness, it was in that performance and in that film.

May had her career; she became one of Zukor's Realart stars; she played prominently for Paramount and for Warners, and she did a good deal of free-lancing. She had the charm of the Irish, and it and her beauty illuminated all she did. Carl Sandburg once referred to her as a "star-eyed goddess," which was a tribute richly deserved, though the imagery was rather startling as coming from him. In the first part of *Morals* she inhabited a Turkish harem; once she was *A Homespun Vamp*. She played Esther in *Ben Hur;* she appeared with Jolson in *The Jazz Singer* and herself went on to *The Lion and the Mouse* and other talking films. But only once, in 1924, when she played with Richard Barthelmess in the film version of Pinero's *The Enchanted Cottage,* again under Robertson's direction, did she find a perfect vehicle. Here was a modern version of the age-old story of the ugly man or woman (Pinero doubled the situation and operated upon both) who is transformed by love. The fable has roots which run clear back to "The Frog Prince," "Beauty and the Beast," and "The Tale of the Wife of Bath," but it was never presented more movingly than by these two sensitive young players in a medium where, thanks to camera magic, we could actually see the transformation take place before our eyes.

Sometimes, though, Miss McAvoy found—or made—opportunities in unlikely places. You would not perhaps expect Willard Mack's play *Kick In* to offer much to Grizel, but as the girl-wife of a young thief, May had three scenes in the otherwise common-place film which was made of that work in 1923 which were un-forgettable. In one she told Gareth Hughes (without subtitles) that she was going to have a baby. I do not know quite what to say about that moment, but the pure gold of the cinema was in it; it was as fine in its kind as anything Chaplin ever did. (The effect was repeated, much less effectively, the following year, with Glenn Hunter, in *West of the Water Tower.*) In the second and greatest of the three scenes she came down a rickety staircase from the chamber in which she had looked upon the dead face of her young husband, laughing and chatting gaily to throw the police off the scent. Finally, in another vivid Dickensian flash, she threw herself into the night of the river.

I do not, I must hasten to add, mean to disparage *West of the Water Tower.* Because the film was a somewhat emasculated ver-sion of Homer Croy's novel, it was often condemned, yet it seemed to me that both May and Glenn Hunter were very successful in catching the sweet, bitter spirit of disillusioned, idealistic youth. She was very good also in at least one scene in *Tarnish,* where crushed over having just learned of the unworthiness of her lover, she was cornered on the street by a band of gay New Year's Eve revelers who would not let her go until she had said, "Happy new year."

Miss McAvoy was not exclusively a tragedienne, for she was never more delightful than in William C. deMille's production of *Only 38,* where she revealed a somewhat unexpected and wholly endearing sense of humor as the passionate young puritan who was shocked out of her life by her mother's (Lois Wilson's) desire to remarry. Lubitsch used her with Pauline Frederick and Marie Prevost in *Three Women* and again in *Lady Windermere's Fan,* but neither film seemed to me quite her material. In the list of her films which Miss McAvoy prepared for George Pratt of East-man House, she checked both *Ben Hur* and *The Jazz Singer* among the films she liked (she placed three check marks before only two titles—*Sentimental Tommy* and *The Enchanted Cottage*), but I did not think that either of these gave her much opportunity to do anything that any other attractive young actress might not have done almost as well. Yet this is ungrateful, I know, for when I recently saw *The Jazz Singer* again after many years, May's loveliness seemed to me quite to illuminate it, and the years rolled away, and I was a boy again.

May McAvoy was more fortunate on the screen than Mary Miles Minter, for if May's career was allowed to languish, Mary's was murdered. As a piece of motion-picture property, Miss Minter war far more valuable than Miss McAvoy, for she acquired an enormous following almost at the beginning of her film career and held it, through a succession of poor pictures, longer than anybody could have reasonably been expected to hold it. At her peak she earned $8,000 a week. As late as November, 1919, Julian Johnson wrote, "Mary Miles Minter is, I should say, a young person with a tremendous future if the enormous interest in everything she does is any indication."

Miss Minter was born in Shreveport, Louisiana, in 1902. Her real name was Juliet Reilly. As a child she appeared on the stage with Nat Goodwin in *Cameo Kirby,* with Robert Hilliard in *A Fool There Was,* and with Dustin and William Farnum in *The Littlest Rebel,* in which she acted so beautifully that even so hard-bitten a critic as Percy Hammond was still talking about it many years later. Her screen debut seems to have been with Powers in *The Nurse* in 1912, and in 1914 she appeared in her first feature, *The Fairy and the Waif,* directed by Mary Hubert Frohman and released through World. "Without doubt," declared the *Dramatic Mirror,* "Mary Miles Minter is the greatest child actress to be seen either on the stage or before the camera. She is exquisitely fascinating, sympathetically charming, and delightfully childlike and human."

Metro next presented her in *Always in the Way,* directed by J. Searle Dawley and released in June, 1915. On July 31, Metro took a full-page advertisement in *The Moving Picture World* to announce that "Little Mary Miles Minter has been given a Permanent Place in the home of Metro Stars by united request of all Metro Exhibitors and Exchanges." They added that "The career of a great star awaits her." On August 21 she was advertised as one of "The Biggest 4" among Metro stars—Francis X. Bushman, William Faversham, and Olga Petrova being the other three. The little girl was doing fairly well for herself.

For Metro, Miss Minter made *Emmy of Stork's Nest,* in which *The Moving Picture World* compared her to Mary Pickford, and *Barbara Frietchie,* in which she was supported by that fine veteran actress, Mrs. Thomas Whiffen. But her stay with Metro was brief. In May, 1916, it was announced that she had been signed with American, where she remained for three years, until Zukor beckoned her for Realart. Her first Realart film, *Anne of Green Gables* (1919), in which she was directed for the first time by William Desmond Taylor, was utterly delightful. Its successor, *Judy of Rogue's Harbor,* was announced in a four-page, two-color insert in *The Motion Picture News.* When she appeared in *Jenny Be Good,* her old admirers on the *Dramatic Mirror* declared, "Mary Miles Minter has a delightful personality, there can be no two opinions about that, and any picture that serves to bring out her charm and simplicity . . . is a good picture." After the Realart brand-name was discontinued in 1922, Miss Minter appeared in Paramount pictures until the expiration of her contract in February, 1923. Her last film, *The Trail of the Lonesome Pine,* appeared in the late spring of 1923.

How good an actress Mary Miles Minter was during her years of screen fame it would now be hard to say. The saccharine vehicles in which she was generally presented all too seldom afforded opportunties for acting.[7] She herself was not saccharine, however;

[7] Miss Minter was well aware of this, young as she was, and deeply distressed by it. See the excellent interview with her by Elizabeth Peltret, "The Golden Girl of the West," *Photoplay* (Feb., 1918).

she was a golden, peaches-and-cream kind of girl, in whom all the sweet, innocent charms of youth were embodied as irresistibly as in any human being this generation has seen, and those who did not like her might quite reasonably have gone on to declare that they did not like sunshine either. It is more difficult to describe Mary Miles Minter than it is to indicate the special quality of any of the other persons of whom I am writing in this chapter. She was not a dainty-fairy kind of person like Marguerite Clark; you could not tag her with the wistful spirituality of May McAvoy or the passionate vitality of Clara Bow. Her personality was too completely centered to be described in any such fashion. And though I certainly do not mean that she was colorless or lacking in individuiality, I may perhaps best express what I mean when I say that besides being a girl she was girlhood itself. In other words, she furnished a kind of norm by which others might be judged.

On February 1, 1922, William Desmond Taylor was murdered. His death is still one of the great unsolved mysteries of American crime, but one thing about it is quite clear: it finished not only his career but also those of Mabel Normand and Mary Miles Minter.[8] The case has now receded sufficiently from living memory so that I actually encounter people who are under the impression that one or the other of these actresses was suspected of having killed him. Though there were hardly any other limits to the asininity with which the case was handled, it is only fair to state that nobody was ever silly enough to suppose that. Miss Normand was involved because of her friendship with Taylor and because she was the last person known to have seen him alive; Miss Minter may be said to have knocked herself in the head by injudiciously proclaiming that she had loved Taylor and believed him to have loved her, and, as if this were not enough, she proceeded to violate another American taboo by engaging in an acrimonious public debate with her mother concerning finances.[9]

[8] See Erle Stanley Gardiner's account of the Taylor case in *True* (June, 1946); see Chapters 20–22 of *King of Comedy*, by Sennett and Shipp.

The author of this book wishes to make one point absolutely clear: He neither has nor assumes any special knowledge concerning the Taylor case nor anything connected with it. Like Will Rogers, he only knows what he read in the papers. But that is just the point. The American public only knew what they read in the papers. And it was upon that basis that Mary Miles Minter was thrown to the wolves.

Here is the inscription which Miss Minter wrote on the photograph of herself which was found in Taylor's house:

> For William Desmond Taylor, artist, gentleman, Man! Sincere good wishes, Mary Miles Minter, 1920.

And here is what she said about her attitude toward him:

> I never even called him "Bill" in my life. The man was too wonderful for that. I don't care what anybody says or what they prove against him. I know he was the finest thing in the world.
>
> I had always known that this was just an exquisite chapter in my life that must necessarily be a brief one. I couldn't bear to part with it. It was just a beautiful thing that seldom occurs in the world today as I see it, as it is forced upon me. It was simply a beautiful white flame. I had always been a reserved, very retiring young girl, and he was the first man and the only man who ever embodied all the glories of manhood in one private body. He represented that to me. He never, by look, or word, or by deed gave me any reason to doubt any of my ideals that were placed in him absolutely.

American yellow journalism has never in my experience behaved worse than it did in connection with the Taylor case. (Even the law seemed at times, as Gloria Swanson quite justly remarked, more interested in digging up something unsavory in Taylor's past than in apprehending his murderer.) Day after day Taylor and Miss Minter were kept on the front page through stories which

[9] California law at this time did not give people control over the money they had earned as minors. Later, after Jackie Coogan's controversy with his mother and her second husband, the law was amended.

235

affirmed nothing but insinuated everything. For years we were told at suitable intervals that a pink nightgown marked "MMM" was in the Taylor dossier, and it was not until Miss Minter finally got sufficiently tired of this so that she challenged the officials to produce the nightgown that it was at last stated authoritatively that no such article existed or ever had existed. One night two men stopped on the sidewalk before Miss Minter's house and had a fight. This had nothing to do with her and nothing to do with the Taylor case, but it was reported in every newspaper in America the following morning. One fool started a rumor to the effect that Miss Minter was not twenty-one years old, as was believed, but thirty years old, and this was solemnly passed on to the public with the implication that to be thirty years old was to be guilty of moral turpitude. Miss Minter merely replied that anybody who could prove her to be thirty years old would earn her undying gratitude, as this would enable her to command nine more years of the money she had earned.

It may be that I exaggerate the effect of the Taylor murder and its aftermath upon Miss Minter's career, but I do not exaggerate the responsibility of the newspapers. The quarrel with her mother did not really get under way until the summer of 1923, and by that time her Paramount contract had already expired. It may well be that the succession of poor pictures in which she had been presented had at last taken their toll, and that if she had been appearing in vehicles which still greatly interested the public, she could have ridden out the storm. I do not know about this. What I do know is that the whole industry behaved shamefully, though one would have thought that under the given circumstances even a fool must have known that an injury to one was an injury to all, and that if such an injustice could be perpetrated against any star, then no star was safe. It was, for example, stated as a fact, and not denied, that Paramount had been losing money on Miss Minter's films, yet Jesse Lasky himself stated, in a lecture at Harvard in 1927, that her pictures cost $100,000 each to produce and that each grossed $200,000. *Photoplay Magazine* sniped away at Miss Minter month after month; even the captions under her photographs were caustic.[10] And her own firm produced a film called *The World's Applause,* directed by William C. deMille and starring Bebe Daniels, about a public idol who was smashed through being innocently involved in a murder case! The only person besides the victim who emerged with any credit from this whole miserable mess was a fellow Southerner of Miss Minter's named D. W. Griffith, who, remembering the tradition of Southern chivalry toward ladies in distress, told the world that if Miss Minter wished to continue her career, there was a place in his company waiting for her.[11]

[10] *Photoplay* under James Quirk (not when Julian Johnson was in charge) was quite capable of such idiocy, and Louise Brooks has anticipated me by chronicling in minute and documented detail their war against Lillian Gish. See her "Gish and Garbo: The Executive War on Stars," *Sight and Sound* (Winter, 1958–59). When *Romola* appeared *Photoplay* reviewed it as: "A beautiful and expensive Florentine travelogue with little heart interest or human appeal. It cost nearly $2,000,000 and features the Gish sisters." Among the six best performances of the month they listed "Charles Lane in 'Romola.' " Their reviews of both *La Boheme* (May, 1926) and *The Scarlet Letter* (Oct., 1926) were disgraceful, nor did they capitulate until *The Wind* arrived and the end of Miss Gish's M-G-M contract with it. Jim Tully once called Quirk "the Mencken of the morons"; when he was in this mood "Mencken of the gutter" would have been more to the point. See Lawrence J. Quirk, "Quirk of 'Photoplay,' " *Films in Review*, Vol. VI (1955), 97–107.

[11] It seems strange that producers cannot remember either their own plays or players. In Jesse L. Lasky's autobiography, *I Blow My Own Horn,* he describes Mary Miles Minter as "a disciple of the brittle china-doll school of acting," more at home in a Rolls-Royce than a covered wagon. Since Miss Minter generally played "cotton stocking parts" one can only wonder whether he ever witnessed one of her films. Lasky could not remember *The Woman God Forgot* either, though it was one of the most elaborate and expensive productions of his early years. In both of the books about Zukor—Will Irwin's *The House That Shadows Built* and *The Public Is Never Wrong*— we are treated to what purport to be pictures of Mary Pickford in *A Poor*

Nearly forty years have passed since Mary Miles Minter made her last film. If it is of any interest to her to know that at least one of her fans still keeps the thought of her screen appearances among the precious memories of his life, let me now give her public assurance that such is the fact.

I was not allowed to speak up very loudly in behalf of Mary Miles Minter when she was passing through her ordeal—though I did finally get a letter into *Photoplay,* of all media—but I did much better some years later when Clara Bow was under attack, for I wrote an article which the Paramount publicity department sent out as a news release. It was headlined in the city where I then lived and created considerable consternation; I heard that I was responsible for the university where I taught promulgating a "rule" that henceforward members of the faculty must not issue public statements without first submitting them to the president's office. I paid no attention whatever to this, and so far as I know nobody else did either; had anything been said to me personally, it would have given me great pleasure to point out that the Bill of Rights does not guarantee freedom of speech to all Americans *except* college teachers.

I do not contend that Clara Bow never in the course of her Hollywood career did anything that might legitimately leave her open to criticism. But by the time the newspapers got hold of her in connection with the difficulties she was having with her secretary Daisy DeBoe and others, this was not quite the point. She was a human being, and she was being badgered. I do not believe

---

Little Rich Girl. Only, the picture in *The House That Shadows Built* is a still from *Pollyanna,* which Zukor did not produce at all, and the other is a scene from *Amarilly of Clothes-Line Alley. The Public Is Never Wrong* also contains what purports to be a picture of "Douglas Fairbanks and Mary Pickford with Adolphe Menjou in *The Taming of the Shrew* (1929)." Actually it is a studio shot, showing Fairbanks with the cast of *The Three Musketeers* (1921). Miss Pickford, who was producing *Little Lord Fauntleroy* at the same time, is sitting beside her husband in Fauntleroy costume.

that such campaigns are conducted by pure-minded idealists, and I do believe that when the writers of the scandal sheets arrive in hell, they are going to have to look up, not down, to find the most culpable of their victims, and this regardless of whether what they have printed about them is true or false.

I rise to a point of order [thus my article began].

We have a new indoor sport among us. Many enjoy it much more than miniature golf. It is a very easy game to play because there are no rules connected with it. The only requirement is that the player shall lack a certain sense of fairness and decency.

The game is played around a girl. She is a girl who has never done any of the players any harm, who has indeed given many of them a great deal of innocent pleasure. The object of the game is to disgrace her, to humiliate her, and ultimately to deprive her of her employment. To this end any tactics may be used. One may invent gossip and slander about her. One may repeat stories one has heard other people tell even though there is not a shred of evidence that they are true. One may watch her eagerly day in and day out and every time she makes a false step employ newspaper headlines to let the whole world know about it. One may use even her illnesses and misfortunes, even the wrongs she suffers at the hands of others, and twist them into a weapon to be directed against her. One may make a matter of public discussion out of intimate personal affairs which could not, by any stretch of the imagination, properly concern anybody but the girl herself. One may write open letters to her in which one pretends one has only her own interests at heart, but which, at the same time, one takes pains to fill with sly, covert, underhanded insinuations concerning her private life. One may make her a scapegoat for the sins of a whole community. One may quite tacitly assume that she is a person of no consideration whatever, that everything she thinks and says or does must necessarily be wrong, that not by any stretch of the imagination could anything about her possibly be right.

The game goes off rather more expeditiously if the girl has red hair. And there is one other little thing: her name should be Clara Bow.

I did not meet Miss Bow at the time, nor have I met her since, but I was very proud when she wrote me that my article had done more to encourage her to keep up her spirit than anything anybody else had done or said. "All I hope," she said, "is that someday I shall be able to do what you did for some other person who might be in a similar difficulty." And as late as 1947 she wrote me, "Yes—I remember the vultures and wish to thank you for defending me."

Whatever may be better or worse in American life today than it was in the 1920's, one thing is certain: newspapers no longer attempt to destroy people's reputations as they once did. That kind of thing is now left to the avowed scandal papers—which of course no decent person would touch with a pair of tongs.

Clara Bow was a Brooklyn girl who first appeared on the screen in Elmer Clifton's *Down to the Sea in Ships* in 1923, created a sensation as Alice Joyce's flapper daughter in *Dancing Mothers* in 1926, achieved stardom in Elinor Glyn's *It* in 1927, and remained thereafter one of Paramount's mainstays at the box office until the close of her career with them in 1931, after which she appeared briefly for Fox. It has often been stated that she was a failure in talking pictures, but this is not true; her rich, warm, though largely uncultivated, voice excellently suited her type of character, and at least one of her talkies, *Dangerous Curves,* a circus picture, was one of the very best things she ever did. A good many people who never saw her are under the impression that she was a "hard-boiled flapper." She was certainly a flapper, but she was far from being hard-boiled. She was warm, generous, and outgoing, completely incapable of calculation, and her natural tendency was to trust everybody. Sex was certainly a very important element of her stock in trade; how amusing is the scene at the close of *It,* where hanging to the anchor of a boat after having been thrown into the water, with her wet skirts clinging high about her naked thighs, she carefully pulls them down just far enough to make a modest gesture but not far enough to cover up anything that the audience might wish to see! Clara Bow's pictures were hardly photoplays in the ordinary sense; they were showcases for her body and personality, and the only reason we had to have a new one every few weeks was simply that we could not forever go on seeing her in the same vehicle. Cheap as many of them were, however, they were innocence itself compared to the fare with which we have been regaled since the "intelligentsia" got hold of the movies, and she seldom did anything really shocking on the screen. Generally she played good, though undeniably lively, girls, and when she did not, she was generally reformed in the course of the picture! The sex was there, but the *joie de vivre* of which she was one of the foremost exponents that the screen has known was quite as important. She stepped up the tempo of life for her millions of fans and made the air seem fresher and better worth drawing in. At the same time, paradoxically, there was something terribly vulnerable about her; brash as she seemed, you always wanted to shield her. Countless young women have tried to imitate her on the screen, yet there has never been anybody at all like her.

I am sometimes asked whether my interest in the screen actress has not at least survived the transition to sound, whatever I may believe about the respective merits and advantages of the sound and silent mediums. This poses a curious problem. For some reason which I do not pretend to understand, most of the "big" stars of recent years have been men, generally men in their fifties, sixties, sometimes even seventies. As George Arliss would say, I am a child in these matters, but I understand that on the distaff side the box offices and the magazine covers are greatly interested only in Elizabeth Taylor, Marilyn Monroe, and Brigitte Bardot.

I have no criticism of the way Miss Taylor's career has been managed, but both Bardot and Monroe have been exploited in a conscienceless, sometimes almost criminal, manner. I do not see how anybody who remembers Mlle Bardot in such early films as *Doctor at Sea* and René Clair's *The Grand Maneuver* can doubt that if she had been handled with sensitiveness and understanding, she must have become one of the best ingénues in screen history. There were flashes of this as late as *Mam'zelle Pigalle* and *The Night Heaven Fell*. But the powers that controlled her destiny preferred to sacrifice everything else to the thrill of waiting for Mlle Bardot to take off her clothes.

The death of Marilyn Monroe occurred on August 5, 1962, while this book was between galleys and page proofs. Though it was at first reported a suicide, there is no reason to suppose this, for a person who used "tranquilizers" and sleeping pills as freely as Marilyn did must have lived close enough to the danger line so that an accident could have occurred at almost any time. Disregarding those who could not resist an opportunity for cheap moralizing (though the dead girl's private life had given no occasion for it), or who used her poor corpse as a stick to beat Hollywood with, there was a world-wide reaction of grief and pity which proved that human beings can still be profoundly moved by a purely personal sorrow and that a motion-picture actress can still be important to the world. It would have pleased Marilyn, for she was tired of being, as she expressed it, "a thing," but it would not have surprised her too much, for though she was a little afraid of "the public," she trusted people.[12]

It is true, of course, that she had been one of the great sex symbols of our time, but her curious innocence and naïveté robbed her sexuality of the vulgarity it might otherwise have had and generally did have in her imitators. If you must dehumanize her, then she was also a symbol of sweetness and tenderness, and though it may seem absurd to say it, her popular image being what it was,

[12] See her last interview, in *Life,* August 3, 1962, which, incidentally, shows her in a completely normal state of mind. Contrary to newspaper reports, she did *not* say in this interview that sometimes she felt as if it would be a comfort to be done with her life. What she did say was that sometimes she felt it would be a relief to be done with her *fame* and get on with more vital things. The fullest account of her career is in Maurice Zolotow, *Marilyn Monroe* (Harcourt, 1960).

she was one of the few stars of the fifties who would have been quite at home on the screen in the age of innocence, when she would have been handled in a very different manner and one, I think, more calculated to make her happy. (And, oddly enough, though in many aspects her personality is very different, this can also be said, as I have already suggested, of Brigitte Bardot.) Actually Marilyn was not a symbol at all. She was Marilyn, "a living, breathing work of God," a complicated, gentle, oversensitive, and highly developed human being, who died in the making, and after she was gone a good many people who had thought of her as a kind of surrogate for lust must have been astonished to find that what they had felt for her all along was something much closer to love. In place of the circuses that many Hollywood funerals have been in the past, all her well-wishers owe Joe DiMaggio thanks for having given her a simple, dignified ceremony which harmonized with what she was rather than what some persons erroneously supposed her to be. May Eternal Light shine upon her.

We are not without interesting young actresses during these later days; one can only wonder why so little is made of them. The series of sensitive portraits of young girls which Jean Simmons limned for us during a number of years after her triumph as Ophelia is certainly to be remembered with gratitude. Miss Simmons is still recognized as a fine actress; critics praise her; she gets excellent parts in important pictures; yet she never receives any kind of award, and nothing sensational happens at the box office when she appears. Grace Kelly's career, so suddenly cut off by her marriage, was also definitely on the credit side of the ledger, though one got a little tired of hearing people say they liked her because she was a lady, as if no motion-picture actress had ever been a lady before. In the early days of the talkies, Evelyn Venable was certainly a lady—and probably a finer actress—but because she had a mind of her own she was soon cast aside, and nobody seems to remember her now. Taking her stage and television and recording activities into consideration, Claire Bloom can point to the richest achievement of any young actress of her time; nobody else still in her twenties has such a record. Her beautiful voice and impeccable diction, her intelligence and sure sense of character—the screen has known these as well as the stage, but where is there any evidence that the screen cares anything about them?

There is no gratitude in Hollywood, of course, and nobody remembers anything overnight. For that matter, there is no longer, in the old sense, a Hollywood.[13] Only a few years ago, Margaret O'Brien was Box Office in capital letters all over the world. Yet the movies not only did nothing to help her bridge the always difficult gap between girlhood and young womanhood; they will not even give her a chance now that the gulf has been crossed. In 1951, when she was fourteen, I saw her give an unforgettable performance in Boston in Clare Boothe's inept play about the martyrdom of St. Maria Goretti, *Child of the Morning*. In the spring of 1958 I witnessed an amazing expression of her talent on television. On Friday afternoon, May 7, she appeared in a virtuoso-bravura kind of role in Benn W. Levy's fine play *Mrs. Moonlight,* in which she brought out every trick in the book and exercised every kind of appeal of which a female is capable. Just ten days later, on the night of May 17, with James MacArthur in a piece called *Tongues of Fire,* she did an utterly different kind of acting— simple, naturalistic, profoundly restrained, and overwhelming in its effect. In a healthy theater she would have had half a dozen playwrights busy writing plays for her.

Some years ago, when Dickens still seemed to have some vogue in Hollywood, I suggested to Lionel Barrymore, who, I knew, loved Margaret as much as I did, that he try to get M-G-M to do *Little Dorrit* for her, with himself as William Dorrit. Barrymore thought well of the idea in both aspects and went nobly to work but got nowhere. As he wrote me, you can't tell what "those people" are thinking even when they seem to be agreeing with you.

It may be, then, that the screen actress has now fallen upon

[13] See Beth Day, *This Was Hollywood* (Doubleday, 1960).

evil days. Certainly the screen itself has fallen upon evil days. She— and it—may experience a revival. A few years ago many people thought that by now television would have made an end of the age of celluloid. Fortunately this has not happened; instead, television has got so unbelievably bad that many people have been driven back to the theaters in sheer self-defense. Yet we of this generation may still be grateful for the particular joys our screen favorites brought us, whatever they were called, and I think we may be sure too that woman's glamour will always find its outlet in some medium, whatever it may be.

Lillian Gish: An Interpretation

$\left(\mathrm{T}\right.$ H E following essay was first published in the spring of 1927 as Number 7 in the "University of Washington Chapbooks" series [Seattle, University of Washington Book Store], edited by Glenn Hughes. *Lillian Gish: An Interpretation* was the author's first publication between covers, and it attracted a reasonable amount of attention. From time to time I receive indications that interest in it has not yet quite died out, and since it has long been out of print it has seemed well to me to reproduce it here. Both because of its definitely 1927 outlook [it necessarily ignores all Miss Gish's later years], and because the youthful, definitely lyrical quality of its prose could hardly be blended with that of this book as a whole, it was obviously impossible to take it up into my text; I have therefore created an Appendix for it. I have also made a few cuts—sometimes of topical references now badly dated, and sometimes of passages whose expression no longer pleases me.)

Just what it is that makes a fine artist in the theater is a subject on which probably no final decision will ever be reached, but at least it is now clear that the popular impression of the great actor as a chameleon-like creature who wholly sinks his own individuality in the role that he plays, who nightly reduces himself to putty and then proceeds to construct a new and alien character from its foundations, is an excellent definition of what such an artist is not. Without great personality, great art simply cannot exist, and this truth has long been recognized in connection with the other arts. The individuality of the great painter is evident in all his canvasses: a Corot cannot be mistaken for a Millet or a Van Dyck for a Frans Hals. In literature too it is only the second- and third-rate stuff that might have been written by anybody: Chaucer or Fielding or Conrad are "there," visibly and incontrovertibly "there," in every line that they wrote. It is so also in the theater, for the creative process is essentially one in all the arts. An actor may, according as his experience of life has been wide or narrow, according as he himself is simple or complex, single- or many-sided, work in a wide field or he may specialize within a comparatively narrow range. What is worth remembering, however, of a really versatile player like David Garrick, as against the limited portrayer of a type, is not that Garrick has submerged his personality, but rather that, through sympathetic comprehension and intelligence, he has enlarged it to embrace a much wider segment of life. Zola conceived of art as a corner of nature seen through a personality. If acting is in any sense among the arts, why should we not grant to the actor this same privilege—to re-character his material in terms of his own personality—which we impose upon the poet as a duty? We may grant it or not as we choose; we may even justify our obtuseness by the cant that acting is not "creative" but merely "interpretative." Still the actor will continue to do it, as he has always done it, because it creates the only condition under which acting can exist at all.

I admit that this is dangerous doctrine, but I do not happen to know any true doctrine that is not dangerous. I am not trying to absolve the actor from "faithfulness" to the author whose plays he presents; I am simply suggesting that in acting itself there is a larger creative element than is commonly supposed. The plain truth of the matter is that unless a play is purely a "closet-drama"— and therefore devoid of all essential dramatic quality—it is not finished at the time it is printed: it does not really come alive until some man or woman of genius makes it live upon the stage. The very great plays—*Hamlet,* for example—are never completed. *Hamlet* is no longer Shakespeare's exclusively but the world's, and it will not be really finished until the last great actor has presented his conception of it.

In short, I believe that the actor, like the poet, cannot possibly create anything greater than his own soul. It is precisely this experiencial quality that marks the difference between mere vulgar impersonation—which is of no significance—and genuine portrayal of character—which is of value because it assists in the understanding of life. That which the actor does not understand, and which has not been passed through his own alembic, may indeed startle for the moment through technical brilliance; but in the long run it is ineffective, like the famous legendary sermon which the devil once delivered with great energy against all the hosts of darkness, and which won no converts, simply because the preacher himself did not believe in it.

The bearing of all this upon my subject is, I trust, fairly obvious. Miss Gish is not, in the usual sense, a versatile actress. Her temperament is not naturally and obviously "dramatic," and she always claims the right to make her roles over to suit Lillian Gish. Yet she has come to be accepted as the outstanding serious artist of the screen, the authentic, incomparable interpreter of the drama of the shadows. As far back as 1920, John Barrymore called her an American artist worthy to rank with Duse and Bernhardt, an American girl who had equaled if not surpassed the finest traditions of the theater.

I hope I may not be misunderstood. I am not saying what the unenlightened so often say: that "Lillian Gish is always the same." Each of her portraits is an individual achievement: he who feels or who pretends to feel that her Mimi and her Hester Prynne are the same person, or that her Angela Chiaromonte is not an essentially different girl from her Henriette Girard, is surely completely blind to other than very elementary and wholly obvious distinctions: fine shadings in art are not for him. Versatility, in the usual sense, is comparatively easy for the character actor: he presents, one after another, wholly different *types,* and he has all the resources of make-up to sustain the illusion. But Miss Gish is not a character actress. She has played only sensitive young women, most of them about the same age, many of them facing not wholly dissimilar problems. The business of differentiation for such a player is ten thousand times more difficult than it is for the character actor; I think hardly any careful student of acting will deny that she has triumphantly met the test.

But what is more to the point for my argument is that in and through all her carefully differentiated characterizations, she has expressed also her own point of view, a distinctive something which is Lillian Gish and nobody else on earth. Her Hester Prynne is not precisely Hawthorne's Hester: she is Lillian's Hester. This point has sometimes been cited against her; as a matter of fact, it is the highest praise that could be given. Hawthorne's Hester Prynne *exists* in Hawthorne's pages: why should Lillian Gish seek to create her over again? Is it not better to begin under Hawthorne's spell but to go on from there independently to work out her own conception as he did his?—a conception which, precisely because it does represent the reaction of another individuality, will help us better to understand not only Hawthorne but the life experience which both artists, and which all artists, seek to interpret?

This, I believe, is the essentially "poetic" note in the work of Lillian Gish—a thing to which so many have referred but which hardly anybody has understood. The girl's work seems "poetic" because she is a poet, that is because she is a creator. She is like the poets in that there is something distinctive in the way she apprehends life, and she uses her roles as the poet uses words and the musician tones—not to reproduce what somebody else has done but to express directly her own authentic impression. Hence also the marvelous sense of completeness, of perfection that she gives you. The part and the actress are one: there is nothing extraneous. In a very deep and very true sense, she is the profoundest kind of actress: that is to say she does not "act" at all; she *is*.

This is not of course what most people mean when they refer to Lillian as "poetic." Usually, I am afraid, they mean that she is pretty. Sometimes—God forgive them!—they are even trying to say that she is weak. The novelist Joseph Hergesheimer was one of Lillian's most ardent admirers, yet he would seem to have been blind to some of her most important qualities. Hergesheimer objected strenuously to *The White Sister,* for example, which he claimed he never went to see. "I had no wish to see Lillian's pale charm against the rigid whiteness of a nun's headdress." But it was precisely the qualities which repelled Hergesheimer in *The White Sister* that attracted Lillian: she wanted to do the story, as she once told me, most of all for the privilege of filming the assumption of the veil, a ritual which she considered one of the most beautiful things in modern civilization.

I do not, however, wish to convey the impression that I am in any sense unmoved by Lillian's beauty. She is completely a being of lyric loveliness, even to her very name. The affinity between her given name and her spirit is a commonplace; if there were only one thing in the world by which to symbolize her, one would instinctively choose the lily. To most persons I suppose her surname means nothing, but this is their misfortune. It should mean romance, the pathos of distance and of faraway perfect things; it should carry them back to buried Babylon, to the Gilgamesh epic and the marvelous adventures of Gish.

Lillian's physical frailness—her Dresden china quality—connects here, and it is this which is commonly regarded as her most serious limitation. Actually it is nothing of the kind. It is true that it bars her from playing coarse types—which make up the most of life—and that it limits her capacity for heroic expression. It is hardly conceivable that any other producer than D. W. Griffith could have discerned her gifts at the time she entered pictures: to anyone else,

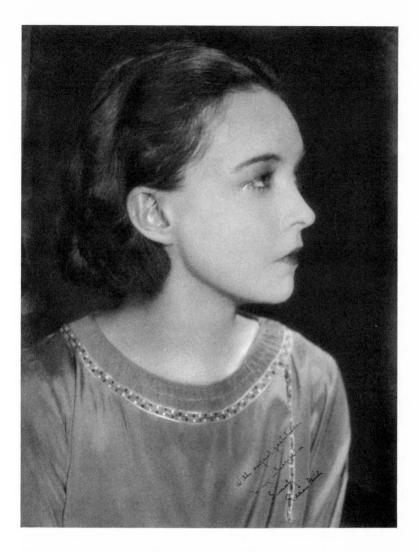

After he had published *Lillian Gish, An Interpretation* in 1927, Miss Gish sent Mr. Wagenknecht this photograph by Ruth Harriet Louise, inscribed "With deepest gratitude to my interpreter."

Lillian Gish in *The White Sister* (1923), directed by Henry King.

Lillian Gish as Mimi in *La Boheme* (1926), directed by King Vidor.

Lillian Gish as Hester Prynne in *The Scarlet Letter* (1926), directed by
Victor Sjöström.

Lillian Gish, with Lars Hanson, in *The Wind* (1927), directed by Victor Sjöström.

These early, very romantic photographs of Lillian (Picture 85, *left*) and Dorothy (Picture 86, *below*) Gish go back to Mutual or Triangle days.

Lillian Gish as Romola (Picture 87, *above left*) and Dorothy Gish as Tessa (Picture 88, *above right*) in Henry King's production of George Eliot's novel *Romola* (1925).

Dorothy Gish in *Nell Gwyn* (1926), directed by Herbert Wilcox.

PICTURES 89, 90, 91

the pale child she was then must have seemed, as a dramatic actress, the world's worst bet. Griffith, with his passion for delicacy and his uncanny knowledge of his craft, perceived at once that what might have handicapped her on the stage was precisely what would make her on the screen. In a large auditorium, physical coarseness of feature is no handicap; it may even be an advantage. But the merciless camera, with its magnified features and its enormous close-ups, brings the actor almost on top of his audience, registering every movement, showing up inevitably the most trifling defect. Except Mary Pickford, there is nobody whose contour quite suits the camera, quite stands the test, as does Lillian's. And it would be difficult to find two actresses who appear in more radically different lights. Mary photographs always with cameo-like precision: she stands out against her backgrounds with crystal clarity, like Lucrezia Bori at the opera. Lillian's outlines, on the other hand, are dreamlike, subdued; she seems to float on the screen like a remembered vision of Botticelli's women.

This lyrical coloring in Lillian seems immensely precious: doubly so because she lives in an age when most girls have definitely outlawed overtones, when everything must be frank and open, everything ruthlessly displayed, no matter how ugly it may be. Something of the lyrical goes into whatever she does, glorifies it with the interpenetrating quality of the imagination, makes it impossible for her to be drably realistic, no matter what her role. Frequently she plays what are called in the movies "cotton stocking" parts. But what she gives you of poverty in these instances is never its drabness and hardness but only its singleness and sweet humility. The star example is the scene in *Way Down East* in which Anna Moore, her mind oppressed by the dread dogma of infant damnation, herself baptized her dying child. Miss Gish played the scene with utter realism—her walk, her expressions, the very arrangement of her clothes all suggesting the strain of recent childbirth. Many an actress could have done that, but I do not know who could have followed her in the next step she took, who could have lifted the whole scene, as she did, away from squalor, beyond the physical, who could so beautifully have suggested the age-old miracle of the girl become mother.

But Lillian's lyricism could never have served to win her present place for her had it not been coupled with a dramatic intensity all the more striking because the body through which she expresses it seems so frail. The effect is virtually to blot out the flesh: when she really lets herself go, she is like nothing so much as a pure white flame. Though she has done finer things since, her closet scene in *Broken Blossoms,* the helpless child's pitiful terror of the brutal father who was hammering against the door, trying to get in and kill her, will remain in the memory of all her audiences as the best single expression of her wonderful capacity for utter surrender to emotion. It was hysterics photographed, yet it was fine art; hysterics are not naturally beautiful.

I have already touched on the exaltation, the profound mysticism of Miss Gish's playing. Even her beauty is not a thing in itself: you never think of her as a "beauty" in the sense in which you think thus of many women of the theater. She is essentially the Puritan in art: there are many phases of experience that she does not care to touch. It is indeed because of her own sensitiveness, because through all these years in the theater she has, in a sense, kept herself in a world apart, that she has become so incomparable an interpreter of the experience of sensitive women. In the ordinary, vulgar sense of the term, there is no more sex in her screen manifestations than there was for Dante in the Beatrice of the *Commedia.*

Miss Gish's work on the screen is pure emotion: there is no suggestion of mind in it, and here, as always, she is profoundly right, for the visible presence of intellect in acting can only rob it of spontaneity, make it labored and self-conscious. But all who have watched Lillian's development know that the mind is there notwithstanding: nothing could be farther from the truth than to imagine that the lovely things she has created came into being

spontaneously, as mere emanations of herself. And she is still growing, for each appearance marks, in some respect, an advance. Twelve
years ago, in *The Birth of a Nation,* I did not indeed find her ex-
traordinarily effective; of all her more important characterizations,
this of Elsie Stoneman seems to me the least. But as Annie Lee in
Enoch Arden, released that same year, she did immensely fine work,
running the whole gamut from youth to age, and doing it with
splendid sincerity and with poignant, touching sweetness. As the
French girl Marie in *Hearts of the World* she went even deeper,
and after I saw her in *Broken Blossoms* in 1919, I told her, out of
my ignorance, that I did not see how she could ever equal the performance she had given here. Yet Lillian has gone far, far beyond
what then seemed unutterable perfection.

In four of her recent pictures, Miss Gish has been engaged in
a profound and beautiful study—the study of woman's attitude
toward her love. In *La Boheme* it was the love which gives blindly,
eagerly, in answer to desire. In *Romola* it was the austere love
which, precisely because it loves, will accept nothing from the beloved except the best. In *The White Sister* love and God were in
conflict, and God won. And in *The Scarlet Letter* the love was
tainted with sin and worked its way out, through suffering, to salvation.

Of these four characterizations, it is difficult to make a choice,
but I think the one which moved me most was precisely the one
which has been the least popular—*Romola.* This film surely did
not earn very much money for its sponsors, for it was enormously
expensive, and it wholly lacked the melodramatic appeal which a
great costume film must have if it is to capture the movie public.
Lillian's own role, too, was not essentially dramatic, there was no
furniture broken, and the general public could not do other than remain comparatively indifferent to her quiet, gently incisive baring
of a woman's soul. Lillian herself—the artist's divine dissatisfaction
upon her—did not quite share my enthusiasm for this picture. "I

hope you will like *Romola* when you see it," she had written me. "It caused me so much trouble and there are so many things in it that I would have different from what they are that I can never think of it now without a great feeling of sadness for what we might have done with that beautiful story." Nevertheless, it is here that she has given us a characterization worthy, in its perfection, to rank with Mary Garden's portrait of Mélisande in Debussy's ultimate opera. For the first time, as I watched *Romola,* I felt that I was really beginning to understand what supreme devotion, what never-failing effort it must have cost Lillian Gish to develop her art to the point to which she had brought it here. The old-time violence, the occasionally hysteric quality that was the hangover from her Griffith days, was gone, but the dramatic intenseness that had accompanied it and saved it and made it beautiful remained—repressed, quivering with life. A twitch of her expressive mouth, a shift of expression in her eyes, and she had accomplished what in the old days it took all the resources of her body to achieve less perfectly. The finest example of all this in *Romola* comes at that moment in the house of Tessa when Romola first realizes that Tito has been unfaithful to her. Actually Lillian did nothing in that moment save look at Tito and then back at Tessa's baby which she was holding in her arms. Slowly the realization dawned that her husband was the father of this child, and the tears welled up in her eyes, but they did not overflow. Amazement, incredulous wonder, wounded pride, and the pure woman's instinctive recoil from an unchaste man—they were all there in that look; yet beneath and above them all were love and pity—for Tito, and for Tessa, and for the child.

In *Romola,* Lillian appeared to be turning inward—more self-contained than she used to be—an entity complete. In a measure this may have been due to the accident of material. But in a deeper sense I do not believe it was, for Lillian is growing daily, broadening, developing, shifting the stream of her life to deeper channels.

If this tendency continues she will in the future be less of an "actress" than now; she will be rather a symbolist, an "essentialist"—if there is such a word—and her screen images will be not so much characterizations as projections, pictures, embodiments (I know not how to name them) of the varied aspects of the spiritual life. One shudders to think what effect such a process might have upon Lillian's box-office popularity, but what a sense of wonder she could bring to our souls, what deepening and beautifying of this amazing mystery we call life. And Lillian could do it if her managers would give her the chance, could leave behind her "pictures of the floating world" which might well live as long in the imaginations of men as Homer's portrait of Nausicaä.

Indeed, I believe Miss Gish to be capable of much greater roles than any she has yet played. She has etched a precious number of lyrical and dramatic moments, but frequently the stuff from which she has wrought has been the veriest melodrama. Imagine what she might be in *Lancelot and Elaine* or as Mélisande or Francesca da Rimini. Imagine what she might do with Ophelia or with any of the later spiritualized heroines of Shakespeare—with Miranda or Perdita, for example. She is not easy to fit with roles that shall be at once adaptable to the screen and suited to her genius: for the mere clash of earthly passion—the quality most frequently and most picturesquely exploited by "emotional" actresses—is simply not for her.

Sometimes I am inclined to be a little impatient about these things: I suppose everybody, now and then, feels that the careers of his favorite artists are being less intelligently managed than he himself could manage them. Yet the last time I saw Lillian, one night in Chicago, when she and her delightful mother left for California, it came over me suddenly that all such fretting was futile. What difference does it make what Lillian plays so long as she is Lillian? That at least no casting director can ever take away from us. Here is the source of the impression she makes, for she herself is among the poets. She may bring us art and literature from the treasure houses of Europe, or she may float on an ice cake down some river of her native land. Whatever she does, she will always be beauty — emotionalized beauty, through which one catches sudden, radiant glimmerings of the wonder of life.

Index of Names

Index of Titles